BEAR ATTACK IN THE SMOKIES

MEMOIRS OF A NATIONAL PARK RANGER

JERRY GRUBB

RIVER PRESS

Published by

French Broad River Press

French RIVER PRESS Broad

An imprint of Writing & Photographic Services, LLC

Cover Design by
Jason Grubb

ISBN: 978-1-7347536-1-5

Dedicated to Glenda Bradley

FOREWARD

"Don't worry about the mule going blind, just load the wagon."
~ Park Ranger Mike Farley, circa 1978

The following stories and events are my personal memories. They are true and factual and represent what is was like for me to be a National Park Ranger.

A Park Ranger's job is unique and allows for extraordinary and very diverse duties. The envy of a Park Ranger has been the catalyst that draws people to the Park Service. The visions of a Ranger riding a horse, hiking the mountains, being in the wild outdoors is diminished by the reality that the National Parks attract a lot of people and with the people comes a lot of crime. To handle the escalating crime, the Park Ranger's primary role is being a cop, and most Rangers see the National Parks through the windshield of a patrol car. Law enforcement is the primary job of a Park Ranger. At any given time, a Ranger may be arresting a serious felon or investigating a motor vehicle fatality or writing a speeding ticket. But within moments he may have to change roles to fight a raging wildfire, perform technical rescues, provide emergency medical response, or deal with wildlife situations. National Park Rangers now face more personal dangers due to the soaring criminal elements prevalent in the National Parks. I was a Ranger for 26 years and loved every day of it. It was dangerously exciting, and making a difference in people's lives was fulfilling and rewarding. I would not have wanted it any other way.

I was eventually forcibly removed from a job where I had so much passion and enthusiasm. Being a National Park Ranger, like I had envisioned it as a young boy, had been diminished. I tried in vain, like so many other Rangers, to maintain a positive and professional image, and do my part to uphold the National Park Ranger legacy.

My story was inspired by a couple of life events that identified a hidden message or a divine intervention that occurred as my life's journey came full circle, and the dreams I had were identified 60 years later. I hope my story gives those who read it, a ray of hope for achieving their own impossible dreams.

Most Park Rangers transfer around to many different parks during their careers. I was not motivated to pick up the family and move every couple of years. I enjoyed working at both Gulf Islands National Seashore and the Great Smoky Mountains National Park. I had no desire to become a Park Manager, which would mean sitting in an office rather than being in the field. To be a manager, one has to keep on the move. I also did not possess the education requirements sought by the National Park Service to become a Park Manager. Having the college education didn't outweigh the common sense that is required of a National Park Ranger, as I experienced in my years of service. College could not teach nor replace experience and training of a National Park Ranger.

I worked at the Gulf Islands National Seashore for about 13 years and transferred to the Great Smoky Mountains National Park for another 13 years. I had many law enforcement details to other Park areas, from the Grand Canyon, to the historical forts in San Juan, Puerto Rico, Civil War Battlefields, Everglades National Park, Alaska, Independence, and other places. I also experienced many wildland forest fire details throughout the country.

In my early days, I was excited to be a National Park Ranger. The pay was lousy, there were no benefits, and working conditions weren't too great many times. But it didn't matter; I was just lucky and happy to be where I was. As the years passed, it became more difficult to maintain the enthusiasm and drive as the National Park Service quickly became a bureaucratic nightmare. As you read to the last chapter of this book, you may think I was a disgruntled government employee but that is far from the truth. I still cherished the job of a National Park Ranger. I was honored to be one, but the ongoing harassment that a lot of other Rangers and I endured took its toll. At the end of this story, the bear attack that killed Glenda Bradley generated myths and folklore and haunted me for almost 20 years. This book includes the true story of the bear attack and the reason a wild bear in the Great Smoky Mountains National Park chased down Glenda Bradley. She became the first recorded person ever killed by a black bear in the park and in the southeastern United States.

My story shares a different perspective of what National Park Rangers really do. It identifies how a complicit government agency manifested the intrigue and vagueness that puts the visitors and Park Rangers unknowingly in jeopardy, and wastes valuable money and resources for the personal relevance of the top bureaucrats.

This story will, I hope, lead to the closure I am looking for and complete the journey I embarked on long ago to become a National Park Ranger. I hope this will bring closure to you, the reader, as well, since it includes facts previously omitted from all official reports of this story.

1

Coast Guard Days

I grew up in the tobacco fields in the small community of Welcome, in the Piedmont area of North Carolina. I had little hope of ever getting away from the tobacco fields or factories where a lot of my fellow school mates began their working careers.

During my early school years, when I was probably 11 or 12 years old, we would go to the old Welcome School library, where we would check out books or read the magazines. I always got the *Boys' Life* and other outdoor magazines. I was fascinated by the stories where young boys would camp, hike, fish, and were a part of the outdoors. I was always drawn to the back of the magazine, to the advertisements to go to school to become a taxidermist or go to The Northwestern School of Conservation to become a wildlife officer or conservation officer. I would fantasize and imagine having a job as a taxidermist or go to college to become a Park Ranger. But I just accepted that it was too expensive for me to ever attain a job like that. I continued reading those same ads every time I was able to get an outdoor magazine.

Sixty years later, I realized these simple ads in the magazines had a hidden message that identified my purpose in life and that's when I realized my life's dream had been fulfilled.

When I was younger, I was an avid hunter and fisherman, but the tobacco fields consumed much of my time and most of my early years were spent around Davidson County, North Carolina. My involvement with the outdoors was limited to fishing in my neighbor's fish pond, running my beagles to chase rabbits, and squirrel hunting. Once a year, after the tobacco was harvested, my brother, some neighbors, my dad, and I would travel to the North Carolina coast to fish. It was a big event with a lot of planning, getting equipment ready, and marking a route on a folding road map. There were few interstates, and the roads were only two lanes of traffic. The trip was a four-hour drive, but as a small boy, it seemed an eternity as we drove to the beach in the old, packed Chevrolet station wagon.

The ocean seemed so massive compared to the small community of Welcome, that I could not comprehend it. I really liked the ocean and had visions of living on the coast where I could fish every day. As it turned out, I was called to leave Welcome, and I lived much of my adult life on the coast as a U.S. Coast Guardsman, and later, as a National Park Ranger.

I graduated from North Davidson High School in 1968 in Welcome, North Carolina. I knew my next step, when I graduated, was to get a job. College was not an option and even if it had been, I knew when I got out of high school, I was done with institutional instruction. I just wanted to get a job, and not work in the tobacco fields. At this point, I didn't have any idea what a "destiny" was. (It was 30 years later, when I watched "Forrest Gump" for like the twentieth time, and saw Lieutenant Dan explain to Forrest that everybody had a destiny.)

After I graduated from high school, I immediately got an invitation to attend a real 'prestigious' gathering in Charlotte, North Carolina. It was at the Selective Service, Army Induction Center. Yep, I was fixing to get drafted and head on over to Vietnam. I met about a thousand men at the induction center, but we didn't have much to talk about. They were mostly boys walking around in their underwear, standing in a big, long line, being pricked and prodded, and examined very closely for any defects that might interfere with them getting shot. I just remember the needles, shots and prodding, and the examiners looking up everybody's rear. I have a very vivid and clear recollection of the hot milk and bologna on stale white bread for lunch. I couldn't, at the time, figure out why we were getting such shitty food, but several years later I figured it out. Nobody there was worried about eating anything. The Army knew that, so they didn't spend a lot of money on food, knowing they were going to use the money saved to buy us bullets. I was just focused on cheating these bastards out of passing the Army physical, get some clothes back on and get as far from Charlotte as fast as I could. The only good thing about this place was it tested your sexual orientation. Seeing a thousand naked boys and men for about eight hours can help you identify your sexual preferences. I was pretty sure I would not pass the physical, since I only weighed about 100 pounds, stood about five feet and looked like someone's 12-year-old child, who was in this line with his daddy. When the physical was over, we all lined up to get our results, and boy, was I surprised. 1A! Passed that sucker, and the examiner who was looking up everybody's rear gave me a 'special wink.'

They shuffled us out of there, and we loaded on the buses and started the long ride back home. I was about as sick and depressed as I ever remembered. I didn't know much about Vietnam, because we didn't have much of a television, and I was like the kids nowadays who couldn't care less about the news. I just knew when I watched the news, Walter Cronkite would be hiding in a fox hole or behind a bunker and telling us how many soldiers were being killed, with a lot of shooting and Huey helicopters flying around. This had really turned out to be a bad day. I had never been out of Welcome, North Carolina, and now some crazy bastards were shipping me off to Vietnam. I didn't even know where the place was, only that it was somewhere on the other side of the ocean, but I didn't even know which ocean. We didn't have a Britannica and back then, I couldn't Google it and find where it was.

When I got home in the late afternoon, I was really depressed and confused. I had just graduated from high school and this was my reward. I picked up the Winston-Salem News Journal newspaper. I vividly remember looking at the paper and on the front page, there was a column called "Ask SAM, The Sentinel Answer Man." If you had a question, you could write to the paper and the answer man would give an answer. The first question was, "Where is the nearest Coast Guard recruiter?" I was mesmerized with what I had just read. The only problem was, I didn't know what the Coast Guard was or where it was. I figured it had something to do with the coast and I had been to the coast with my dad, fishing. Since I liked the coast, it had to be better than Vietnam.

Next morning, Boom! I'm off to Greensboro, where the nearest Coast Guard Recruiter was. Unlike the Army Induction Center, the Coast Guard was very personable. The recruiters were helpful getting me through the process to enlist in the Coast Guard. Unlike the Army, there was a written test to be completed and passed, to be accepted in the Coast Guard. The physical examination was done by a private doctor. I guess the Army knew you were probably going to get your ass shot and they didn't have to test you for any academic achievements. Instead of hot milk, stale bread, and bologna, we went to a restaurant where the Coast Guard picked up the tab for a good lunch. Now, I am liking this. They told me I didn't have to crawl in the mud, I'm eating like royalty, and I would probably not get my ass shot; I was ready to sign up. The only problem in the way was the stupid Army. The Coast Guard had a waiting list and I was going to be at the bottom of it, and at any time I could still be drafted. I also had to consider the Army was only a two-year commitment and the Coast Guard was a four-year commitment. I still envisioned Walter Cronkite on TV talking about all the soldiers who were being killed and the noisy Huey helicopters, so the extra two years wasn't a factor.

Hopefully, I would be joined in the Coast Guard in about two months. I was somewhat relieved, stimulated, and thrilled I wouldn't be going to Vietnam as a grunt crawling in tiny holes in the ground and swimming in the muck. The Coast Guard had an active role in the Vietnam war, but operated quite differently.

I received a letter from the Coast Guard after about two months. I was excited to get it and find out when I was going to leave for my basic training. I ripped the envelope apart, got the letter unfolded and began reading it. My emotions were drained. I was stunned and in shock as I read the letter. The Coast Guard had notified me I was not physically qualified for the Coast Guard, and I had been turned down to enlist in the Coast Guard. I began a rollercoaster of emotions from anger to a state of confusion. How on earth could they possibly turn down an 18-year-old who, according to the Army, was as fit as Rambo? Vietnam was now becoming a reality. I hurried over to the Coast Guard Center where I learned the reason I had failed the physical. I was 18 years old. I was pretty darn smart. When I was examined at the Army Center, I had taken the advice of some other very smart 18-year-olds, and they told me 'just tell the Army you have a bad back,' and I would get a 4F classification and not qualify for the Army. So, on my Army Induction form, I checked I had a bad back. Apparently, this was the number one answer on the Army physical application, and you automatically were accepted after a few formalities while you stand in line all day and watch all these guys walking around in their underwear.

I was informed by the Coast Guard they found my physical condition to be great, but they had reviewed my Army Induction physical and found a discrepancy about my back. I tried to digest my response to this and was very apprehensive to tell the Coast Guard that I had LIED on the Army physical. I was sure when I tried to give a foolish and sophomoric response, I was just going to complicate things even more. So, I did the honorable thing, and trying not to cry big boohoo tears, I told them I had not been truthful, and I had actually lied and then started begging and apologizing for being so stupid. I told them I had the best back in the world, and I would do anything to get in the Coast Guard. Now, years later, I have come to realize that on that day, I had exhibited true qualities for becoming a government employee, because lying is a pre-requisite for government employment.

The Coast Guard officials allowed me to get a private doctor's examination and certify my back was good, and with no other physical defects, I immediately got a doctor's endorsement and the Coast Guard accepted it. Unfortunately, this set me back for about three months and I was again on a waiting vacancy to be accepted in the Coast Guard. This meant I was hanging out there and the Army could still draft me. I almost immediately began envisioning Walter Cronkite again. The next three months were nerve-racking, watching more violent newscasts on TV about Vietnam. The Viet Cong had just started the TET OFFENSIVE and our army was needing to boost its forces to provide more targets for the Viet Cong. There were pictures of thousands of coffins of young soldiers killed because a president, living a lie, sacrificed these guys for his own personal agenda. I had pretty much accepted the fact that I was going to be drafted and I was going to Vietnam.

At the very moment I was accepting this, I was notified that I had been accepted in the U.S. Coast Guard. Goodbye Army! Although I chickened out for the Vietnam party, I look back and realize my good fortune. So many other young men who went to Vietnam for their senior trip ended up being sacrificed at the sake of a bunch of politicians with the ruse of protecting our country. I haven't figured out, to this day, how sacrificing 53,000 young men, wading around in the rice fields of some jungle in the middle of nowhere, threatened our democracy. If they would have been Viet Cong in the tobacco fields in Welcome, I could see the threat, but these poor bastards couldn't even get across a river, much less an ocean. Besides, if they had worked in them tobacco fields, they would have taken their happy asses back to Vietnam PDQ!

I went to boot camp in Cape May, New Jersey, in January of 1970. I had never seen so much snow and wrote back home to tell everyone it snowed on the beach. I was excited to get to the Training Center until I got off the bus. Apparently all the nice guys in the Coast Guard were in Greensboro, because when that bus pulled up and stopped, some of the most vile and nasty men I had ever seen started yelling and screaming at us, calling us names, talking about our mommas and throwing tantrums that scared the hell out of me. I considered these guys were just having a bad day, but as it turned out, they had bad days for 13 weeks. I had never seen so many outraged men kicking and throwing 30-gallon galvanized garbage cans (later called shit cans) around every day and I was hoping I didn't get one of these jobs.

The day after I graduated from boot camp, these same guys transformed overnight into some of the nicest guys you would want to be around. As it turned out, the Coast Guard was a great outfit. My new adventure was about to begin. I was assigned to my first duty station on board a 255-foot Coast Guard Cutter named the *Sebago* in Pensacola, Florida. I arrived at the ship late at night and I was surprised at what I saw. I didn't know the Coast Guard had boats this big. We were taught in boot camp, when we arrived at our ship and approached the quarterdeck, that would be kind of like walking up on the front porch, and we were to salute the rear ensign or flag. We then saluted the quartermaster and requested to come aboard.

Sebago

Since it was late, I got a cab at the bus station to take me to the ship. I was very nervous and didn't know what to expect. My cab driver was an old Navy veteran and he coached me as we drove on how to salute the quartermaster and the flag. The ship had just gotten back from Vietnam and the guys on the ship were worn out from their luxury cruise. Coast Guard ceremonies and routines didn't much matter, as the old guys just wanted to get off the ship. There were a few guys sitting around the quarterdeck talking with the duty quartermaster. I walked up on the gangplank, turned sharply, executed a precise salute and turned, sharply saluting the quarter-master and requested permission to come aboard. I expected the quartermaster to tell me permission was granted to come aboard, just like I had learned in boot camp. Instead, the quartermaster and all the guys there began laughing. They weren't just laughing, laughing, but were rolling around screaming with laughter, trying to get their breath. They were calling for more people to come to see the new kid who looked like a 12-year-old with a shaved head and Dumbo ears holding up a Coast Guard Donald Duck hat on his head.

Jerry

I stood there, without a clue as to what I was supposed to do, and finally the guys were able to regain their composure, and I went onboard and began my adventure with the U.S. Coast Guard.

I had very little life experience other than working in tobacco fields and on the farm. I quickly learned the ship routine and got pranked and harassed regularly by the old "salts" of the ship. Those old guys could really give a rat's ass about a kid who just graduated from high school and didn't know shit from Shineola, but I was quickly accepted by the crew. It was up to me to prove I was worthy of their company and I went on to have lead positions while I was aboard the ship.

Unknowing at the time, my shipmates proved to be a new, lifelong family. These guys were like dads, uncles, teachers, professional boozers, brothers, and there were just a couple of them who were kind of like my sister. After a year and a half aboard the ship, I transferred to a land-based Search and Rescue, small boat station on Pensacola Beach, Florida. The Coast Guard Station, Santa Rosa was on a barrier island and located inside Fort Pickens, a gated State Park. This assignment was too good to be true. I arrived at the Coast Guard Station as an E-3 Seaman and left 4 ½ years later as an E-6, 1st class Boatswain Mate.

40 ft rescue boat

I worked as a boat coxswain, operating rescue boats in search and rescue operations in the Gulf of Mexico and surrounding bays. I watched the newscasts that still included images of young men being killed by the thousands in Vietnam, while I was living the life, where I woke every morning on a quiet, pristine, Florida beach. I was 21 years old and in charge of my own rescue boat, working in a dangerously exciting environment!

2
_____

Lighthouse Keeper

$\mathcal{I}$ was given the honor of being one of the many Lighthouse Keepers who maintained the Pensacola Lighthouse. I was assigned as the Aids to Navigation coordinator and was charged with keeping the navigation lights lit in the Pensacola area and Intracoastal waterway and this included being a Lighthouse Keeper. The lighthouse was built around 1815 and still served as a primary Aids to Navigation marker. If it went out, it had to be fixed immediately. It was a main beacon for incoming ships and other vessels coming into the main channel. The lighthouse was next to the Pensacola Naval Air Station runway and had a red aircraft warning light that marked the location of the lighthouse for the pilots to see. If the light went out, regardless of the time or weather conditions, I had to go and fix it.

The lighthouse sat off the roadway in a grove of live oak and pine trees with Spanish bayonets scattered around the myrtle bushes. There was a secluded, sandy shell road that led to the back of the lighthouse. There was always an eerie, quiet, and haunting atmosphere at the lighthouse, even in the daytime. With no one around, and only the noise of an occasional aircraft landing on the runway of the Naval Air Station, you could almost sense eyes watching you, or feel someone close to you as you walked around the lighthouse and the old buildings.

There was a lot of history associated with the old lighthouse, including its survival during the Civil War, when it sustained many cannonball rounds that have been patched over. The lens of the lighthouse was lowered to save it from cannonball fire. The hand cut, Fresnel lens was about the size of a large dump truck and was almost impossible to reproduce or replace. The lens was supposedly taken to Alabama and buried until the Civil War was over. After the war, it was brought back and replaced.

As you entered the lighthouse, there was an emergency generator inside the door. The lighthouse was powered by commercial electricity, but the generator automatically started when the commercial power was off or interrupted. There were 177 spiraling, wrought iron steps that took you to the top of the lighthouse. The acoustics were phenomenal, and a heartbeat could be heard as it echoed throughout the lighthouse. Alone, and at nighttime in the lighthouse, was just plain spooky. I didn't ever see a ghost, but I heard them several times and I know they were walking with me up those 177 steps. One afternoon I walked around the front porch of the house. There was no wind or breeze blowing at all. There were three rocking chairs on the porch and as I came up on the steps, one of the rocking chairs was rocking by itself. As I stepped up on the porch, the rocking stopped. I could feel the hair on the back of my neck standing up and I backed down the steps, hoping the boogers weren't surrounding me. There was no explanation for it and I suspect it was one of the old lighthouse keepers that was still helping look after the place, taking an afternoon break, rocking in the chair overlooking the Gulf of Mexico. It was a pretty unsettling experience, and I quickly left for the day to regain my nerves.

I visited the lighthouse a time or two a week and performed maintenance on the generator or went up on the walkway at the top of the lighthouse and had lunch or sunbathed, listening to the radio to help drown out the sound of any haunts. I polished the lens of the lighthouse with small lens cloths and kept the light in good shape so I wouldn't have to come over in the middle of the night. My beagle, Mitsy, went everywhere with me, riding on the boats, on search and rescue missions, including going to the lighthouse with me. Mitsy seemed to get along fine with the spooks around the lighthouse and never became alarmed. As just a young'un at 22 years old, I could run up and down the lighthouse stairs with Mitsy and never stop or breathe hard. Mitsy seemed to calm my anxieties of encountering any boogers there.

One night, there was a massive thunderstorm in the area. There were high winds, lightning bolts shooting across the skies, and heavy seas pounding the surf on the beach. The power went out on the lighthouse and it was dark, with no aircraft warning light visible. The emergency generator was supposed to kick in and supply emergency power to the lighthouse until the commercial power came back on, but it was out also. It was late at night around 11 or 12. The Coast Guard Station, where I stayed, was about an hour from the lighthouse, but still visible across the bay from the Coast Guard Station. Mitsy and I got in our old van and went to the lighthouse to get the lights back on. The storm was unnerving, and as I got on the shell road, there were large tree limbs down, blocking the road. The rain pelted down. I was able to clear a trail and get to the lighthouse and it was almost like a horror movie as the lightning crashed all around. The huge bolts lit up the outside of the lighthouse. I ran up to the doorway in the pouring rain with Mitsy right behind me. I had an old flashlight, but in order to see if the flashlight was on, I had to light a match and check it. It barely lit the room where the generator was. I got the generator fired up and the lights came on and everything seemed to work fine. The lights were dim, but were bright enough to light the inside. I lay my flashlight down by the generator and Mitsy and I started to climb the stairway to get to the top, where the aircraft warning light was.

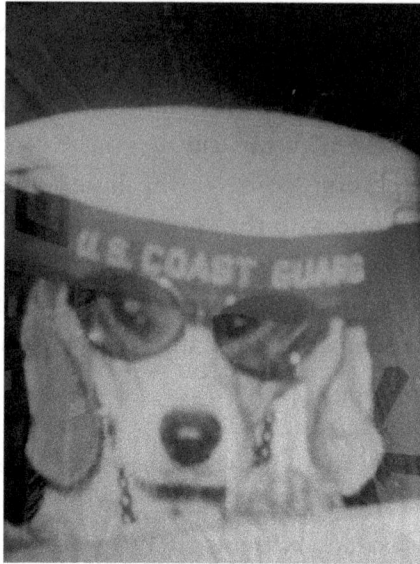

Mitsy

The storm was still intense, and you could hear the rain and wind blowing against the outside of the lighthouse, and I could feel the building shudder from the roaring thunder. There was a window about halfway up the tower, where the light shown through whenever the lightning flashed. It was a very spooky and unnerving experience, but we continued up the stairs to the top. As Mitsy and I got about forty or fifty steps up, the generator stopped and all the lights went out. It was as dark as if you had your eyes closed, with the exception of the occasional lightning flashes that would light up the place through the small window. The place resembled an Alfred Hitchcock movie. I had left my flashlight lying by the generator and had no light at all. I could walk back down the steps holding the handrail but couldn't see the steps. I stood there a moment, collecting my thoughts, when Mitsy began barking as if she saw something. I could feel her by my feet and screamed as she barked. I got hold of her while she barked without stopping. I nervously worked my way down the steps, knowing that any second, a booger was going to grab me. I finally got to the generator, where I located my dim flashlight.

Mitsy and I ran out the door and back to the van, where I radioed the Coast Guard station for someone to come and help me get the light fixed. I really didn't need anybody to fix the light, just somebody to watch for boogers, but I didn't tell them that. There was no one available and it was up to me. Mitsy had enough and she wouldn't get out of the van. I had to drag her back into the lighthouse. I got the generator fired up again and took my flashlight and started back up the stairs, with Mitsy following. I got to the top unscathed but scared shitless.

I got the light working and it burned brightly. It cast a brilliant glow into the rain and darkness over the Gulf of Mexico. The aircraft warning light was still out, and I had to get it back on. There was a heavy, metal door that was secured by a bolt at the top that had to be removed to get outside on the first level catwalk. I took the bolt loose and the wind blew the door open. Hollywood could not capture the moment, as the heavy rain blew in, with high winds and lightning flashing through the sky. I had to go out onto the catwalk,

Aircraft warning light

climb up a ladder to the next level catwalk, then climb almost vertically up an iron ladder, to get to the aircraft warning light. The light was designed to flip another light bulb in position should one burn out, but the bulb had become stuck somehow. Rain poured in the open light with 120 volts of electricity powering it. Miraculously, nothing shorted and I didn't get electrocuted. I fixed the light and got everything working. I was drenched and Mitsy was scared to death. I had to carry her back down the 177 steps. When I got to the bottom, I ran back to the van with Mitsy and watched the lighthouse for a moment. Everything seemed to be working and we got out of there.

The next day, I had to go back and make sure everything was okay. The storm cleared with blue skies and peaceful, quiet surroundings, just opposite from the night before. From the top of the lighthouse, you could see for miles into the Gulf of Mexico, now resembling a swimming pool with a gentle lapping surf, much different than the massive swells and crashing waves the night before. Mitsy and I spent most of the day tidying up around the lighthouse, napping and sunbathing on the catwalk and having lunch on top of the lighthouse.

Unfortunately, I was only assigned to the Aids to Navigation unit for about six months and had to go back to operating the search and rescue boats. The Aids to Navigation unit was easy duty compared to the intense and daily operations in search and rescue.

As a National Park Ranger, I went one day to visit the lighthouse before it was made a museum. I didn't stay very long, but I had to go to the front porch to see if that rocking chair was moving. I walked up onto the porch and felt a chill as I looked at the rocking chairs, but they never moved. I backed down the steps and left.

The lighthouse is now a museum, still operating as an aid to navigation and serviced by the U. S. Coast Guard. I have visited the lighthouse many times and recently visited the museum as a tourist, forty years after I was the lighthouse keeper. It wasn't the same, being there with a crowd, following along, reading the displays and listening to the interpreters telling everyone the history of the lighthouse. As I walked onto the catwalk at the top of the lighthouse, I envisioned my days with Mitsy, sunbathing alone and without the presence of the many visitors who climbed around the place. While I ambled along with everyone, I could not help but reflect on my days working there as the keeper, and the night I was almost kidnapped by the haunts.

Pensacola Lighthouse

The National Park Service declined to accept the lighthouse as part of the Gulf Islands National Seashore, even though it is surrounded by many historical forts with a culture dating back to when this area was one of the first and oldest settlements of America. After years of mismanagement by the National Park Service, the lighthouse is much better off. Instead, it is operated by donations and private funding, along with the State of Florida, and is in very good condition allowing for public visitation, giving visitors an experience they cannot get from walking around looking up at the towering lighthouse. If it had gone to the National Park Service, it would be neglected and locked down, prohibiting visitor use like much of the National Seashore today. Being a part of the history of the lighthouse, at the time I was the keeper, was nothing special. I viewed it as a job. Now, 47 years later, I look back and reflect on just how special that time in my life really was.

3

The Old Coast Guard Station

*A*bout six months after I arrived at the Coast Guard Station Santa Rosa, The Fort Pickens State Park was changed to Gulf Islands National Seashore. I had been on leave and away from the area for a couple of weeks. When I returned, there was a big sign erected, replacing the Fort Pickens State Park sign with a new "Gulf Islands National Seashore" sign. Unbeknownst to me, the National Seashore was in the makings for several years, and was in transition, as I arrived for duty at the Coast Guard Station on Santa Rosa Island.

Gulf Islands Sign

Mr. J. Earl Bowden, a prominent citizen of Pensacola and the Northwest Florida panhandle, was known as the "Father" of Gulf Islands National Seashore. There were long stretches of undeveloped seashore in Northwest Florida and commercial development was imminent. Mr. Bowden began a campaign, assisted by Congressman Bob Sikes, who introduced a bill to preserve the seashores of Northwest Florida. As a result, over 140,000 acres were preserved. This included many historical, cultural and other natural areas as the Naval Live Oaks preserve. Gulf Islands National Seashore also included the preservation of the barrier islands of Horn, Ship, and Petit Bois Islands in Mississippi. The Seashore was created in five years, a record, because getting a National Park established could take upwards of twenty years. The enabling legislation of the 1916 Organic act required the National Park Service to promote and regulate the use of the National Parks for the purpose of conserving the scenery, natural and historic areas, wildlife, and to "provide for the enjoyment in the same manner and by such means as will leave them unimpaired for the next generations." "Providing for the enjoyment" would take on a new interpretation in the coming years as the seashore was closed, with locked gates, and controlled by a government bureaucracy that tightly regulated the enjoyment of the National Seashore.

I had no idea what the National Seashore was. I knew very little about the Park Service except for "Yogi Bear" and "Ranger Rick." As goofy as the cartoon was, it secretly appealed to me and I could envision myself being a "Ranger Rick." I occasionally watched it Saturday morning as a child if I didn't have to work in the tobacco fields. I knew a little about the Blue Ridge Parkway that was close to my home in North Carolina. I never got to visit the Parkway, but relatives and neighbors shared their stories where they "drove up to the mountains" in the fall and got some mountain apples and drove on the Blue Ridge Parkway.

I didn't see any activity associated with the National Seashore and there was nobody around the place for several days after the signs were replaced. I learned from others at the Coast Guard Station, the National Seashore was replacing the State Park. I really wasn't excited or impressed and didn't know what or why anything was changed. I was just 20 years old, carefree and careless, and was excited to be a part of the Coast Guard Search and Rescue Station.

At the same time the National Seashore was taking over the State Park, the Coast Guard was going to upgrade and build housing facilities next to the Coast Guard Station. We were excited to get the new facilities and all the plans had been approved and construction was to begin. This is when I learned a little more of what the Seashore was about. The National Park Service was concerned about the historical Coast Guard station that was over a hundred years old and the Park Service was also concerned about building living quarters where the area would have to be excavated to build the facility.

The newly formed National Seashore quickly identified their authority and relevance. The news media began reporting the Coast Guard's plan to build their facility was being halted by the newly formed National Seashore authority. Headlines proclaimed that "bulldozers were poised to destroy the seashore," which led to the Coast Guard halting their plans to improve the Coast Guard Station, showing authority and relevance where there was a "new boss in town." A few months later, the Coast Guard Station was getting a new roof. The old roof was cedar shake shingles, painted with Tile Red paint that was visible for miles into the Gulf of Mexico and assisted in mariner navigation. Because of the cost, the Coast Guard elected to replace the shingles with red asphalt shingles instead. When the National Park Service management found out the cedar shake shingles were being replaced with asphalt shingles, the Coast Guard plans were again halted and the old cedar shake shingles were replaced by new cedar shake shingles. The National Park Service was adamant that the Coast Guard Station was an historical building and had to be maintained and preserved. This would prove only to be a power play by the National Park Service, using its authority to continue to prove its relevance as the new boss in town. The Coast Guard Station quickly became a derelict after the National Park Service became full proprietor and owner of it.

The National Park Service did not have to pay for the costly shingles. The Coast Guard was operating on a thin budget to begin with. As a result, the cost to install the cedar shake shingles had to be mitigated. Contractors were hired to nail the expensive shake shingles on the roof, but it was left up to us at the Coast Guard Station to paint the singles. This was a complicated job. The roof was very steep, and impossible to climb on. Only a couple of us could get on the roof, much less do any painting. We mixed 50-gallon barrels with Tile Red paint and drew it up to the roof in small buckets. We tied ourselves off with ropes anchored to the lower porch post or vehicles. Using old swab mops, we swabbed the lead paint on the wooden shingles. We wrote a new chapter in the OSHA manual, utilizing safety precautions and chemical hazard awareness. I had so much paint on me, I could lie on the roof and be camouflaged where no one could see me. I must have ingested a gallon of it, and it stuck to my skin, giving me a red complexion for days.

But to conform with the National Park Service instructions and preserve a historic structure in its original condition, we went beyond our call of duty and were proud of what we achieved in the end.

The old surf boats used to be kept inside the Coast Guard station and were rolled out on rails over and through the dunes where they would be used for rescues in the Gulf of Mexico. The Park Service diminished any signs the Coast Guard station was ever a Coast Guard Station. There are no signs or historical interpretations or pictures concerning the Coast Guard. It is now a campground registration office and the old heart pine columns, covered by office petitions. The historic significance has been disregarded and one of the oldest structures and a part of the history of Santa Rosa Island has been left to fend for itself. For a structure to receive historic status, it is supposed to be 50 years old with historic significance. The Coast Guard Station is 150 years old and has weathered decades of destruction but was repaired and kept in pristine condition with minimum resources and the hard work of the Coasties.

U.S. Coast Guard Station prior to hurricane of 1979

The National Park Service was now in charge and mandated to protect these historic structures. Through transgression and misfeasance, the laws and rules to protect this historic structure were disregarded by the management of the National Park Service. There were other historic buildings in the park dating to the early 1800s that were also remodeled to include modern building materials and turned into offices and living quarters. Some of these living quarters were used exclusively for employee housing and some free of charge by government V.I.P.'s for temporary vacation quarters, courtesy of the taxpayers. I knew all of this when I was with the Coast Guard.

First Coast Guard Station on Santa Rosa Island

The National Seashore had been established. I had been back to the Coast Guard Station for a couple of days and I hadn't seen any park service people around and was beginning to think they were going to just put up a sign and leave. The gate to the park was still locked. When it was a state park, the gate was locked at night and opened in the daytime. All of us at the Coast Guard Station had keys to get in at night. I had a small motorcycle I rode around the beach, and at night when the gates were locked, instead of getting off the motorcycle and opening the gate, I just squeezed between two gate posts. It was easier to do this than get off and fumble with a key in the dark. (I probably left it in my car anyway.) Late one night, I came back to the Coast Guard Station, and when I got to the gate, I just zipped around the posts and into the park. The park entrance station was a couple hundred feet inside the gate. As I drove by the station, I observed a car backed in alongside the entrance station building. When I went by, the driver of the car honked his horn at me. I politely beeped my little motorcycle horn back at him and continued into the park. The Coast Guard Station was about four or five miles away. The road was desolate with nothing between me and the Coast Guard station. Santa Rosa Island is a barrier island with nothing but a roadway between the dunes for about seven miles and dead ends at the old Fort Pickens. The dunes along the roadway were massive, reaching over 40 feet high until Hurricane Frederick, in 1979, leveled the islands to below sea level, connecting the Pensacola bay and the Gulf of Mexico in several places.

I had gone about a mile or so and I could see a vehicle coming up behind me. The vehicle closed in on me and began blinking its headlights and blowing the horn. I was concerned that I must have pissed somebody off when I beeped my little motorcycle horn, and now this bastard wanted to kick my ass. The top speed of my motorcycle was only about 50 miles per hour, and I was maxed out. This crazy bastard was now blowing his horn at me, blinking his lights and pulling up alongside me. I had the motorcycle wide open, but it was evident this sucker meant for me to stop. I had to consider my options. I could stop and take a chance I could fight this crazy bastard, talk to him and apologize for pissing him off, or let him run me over. I was about a mile or so from the Coast Guard Station, and I considered taking off across the dunes on the motorcycle. I began slowing and considered my options and came to a stop. The vehicle pulled up behind me. I could see two people getting out of the car in my mirrors and I got ready to gun it and hope I could make the next mile before they could get in their car, catch me and kill me. As I was about to drop the clutch, I saw, over my shoulder, this guy with a big ole hat on. I looked over my other shoulder and there was another guy with another big ole hat. When they approached me, I could see they wore uniforms. I don't remember if they identified themselves or not. I just remember the one guy gave me holy hell because I drove around the posts. I then realized these guys were National Park Rangers. I guess I must have shown a driver's license and told them I was with the Coast Guard. I was let go for committing this heinous crime. After many years I have come to appreciate these two guys for steering me in the right direction. I have not driven around any gate post since then.

Over the next couple of weeks, I became acquainted with the park staff, including the superintendent and the Southeast Regional Park Service officials. At the onset, I really didn't get to know the one Ranger, Jim Kerns, who chewed me out for violating the law. I did, however, get to be friends with Ranger Dick Kegley, who was with Ranger Kerns the night I encountered my first National Park Rangers. After a couple of weeks, the park staff got situated and I visited with most of them almost daily, except Ranger Kerns. I never knew where he hung out and what he really did. He was always driving around in a gray Ambassador with "Government Service" on the side. I later found out that was his patrol vehicle.

One day, I had been fishing off the Fort Pickens Fishing Pier that was on the end of the island, about two miles from the Coast Guard Station. I left the pier and when I arrived back to the Coast Guard Station, I realized I had left my tackle box on the pier. Rather than take my car back to the pier, I jumped on my motorcycle and headed back. About a half mile from the Coast Guard Station, there is Ft. Pickens Campground and a campground store. I don't think I drove too fast, but I probably drove like a bat out of hell, trying to get back to get my tackle box. Just a couple of yards from the pier there were some housing units, and Ranger Kegley stayed in one of them with his girlfriend, Pat. As I approached the pier, I saw Dick and Pat sitting on the porch. When I got closer, Dick walked out to the road and I stopped to greet him. He had his portable radio with him, which at the time I remember, it was the size of a traveling suitcase with a telephone attached to it. As I greeted Dick, he replied to me, "Well, you've done it again."

I was perplexed at his response and he then pointed behind me. Ranger Jim was exiting his Ambassador, putting his Ranger hat on and started towards me. Dick was more scared than I was, of what was about to happen. He left me there, alone, as Ranger Jim approached and again wanted to make sure I had a driver's license. Ranger Jim had looked at my driver's license more than I had. He looked at it pretty close to make sure he hadn't missed anything when he checked it a couple of weeks before. He then proceeded to inform me of all the statutes of law I had violated, and how many jails I was fixing to visit after he was through towing my motorcycle. Then, he was going to call my momma. He upset Ranger Dick so bad, he went in the house. Now, I wasn't 'skeered,' but I was really concerned, this guy may have the contacts to get me committed. The hat was intimidating enough, but the guy under it was pretty intent in getting a message to me to STOP VIOLATING THE LAW. I humbly apologized over and over and assured Ranger Jim I was straightening up and he wouldn't have to check my driver's license again. He let me off this time, and I didn't do anything to get Ranger Jim on my ass again. One thing I did learn that day, I finally found out where Ranger Jim hung out. Not exactly sure, but it was somewhere around that campground store.

As the park began to get more staff and more Rangers, I became friends with about all of them. Ranger Jim and I became good friends and have remained so throughout the years. I just thank the Good Lord for Ranger Jim, because without him I was destined to become an inmate with an expired driver's license.

I remember the first field Ranger I met named Ranger Dave. Dave had transferred on a temporary duty assignment to Gulf Islands National Seashore to assist while the permanent staff was being assigned. Dave was from Everglades National Park. Dave shared with me many of his experiences in the Everglades that included drug interdiction at its earliest stages. Dave loved to catch them drug runners and collect all that marijuana. More than that, he also liked to smoke it.

I didn't identify with it at the time, but Dave was my first encounter with a dishonest and rogue Park Ranger, even before I became a National Park Ranger. Seems Ranger Dave liked marijuana so much he started his own marijuana business. I don't think it lasted too long before he was apprehended, incarcerated, and fired from being a Park Ranger. Seemed like a nice guy, though.

Throughout the rest of my tour with the Coast Guard, I interacted with the Park Rangers and Park managers from the Atlanta Southeast Regional office of the National Park Service. The park managers were more friendly and personable, very much unlike the Park Service Management today. These guys would hang out with everyone in the park, and it didn't matter what your rank was. At the end of my career, you would be lucky to talk with the superintendent and had to make an appointment just to see the Chief Ranger. For some reason, these guys from the Atlanta Regional Office were always at Gulf Islands National Seashore, taking care of business. I would get invited to card games, dinners, alcohol testing seminars and I just generally hung out with them. They were intent on making Gulf Islands National Seashore a vacation destination. I finally realized Gulf Islands National Seashore was a nicer place to hang out rather than the regional office in downtown Atlanta. There was always unfinished business at the Seashore. Unbeknownst to me at that moment, this time in my life would lead to a new job down the road.

I became very close friends with Ranger Len who came to the seashore as one of the first Rangers assigned there. Ranger Len was my kind of people. He was a Park Ranger and a TAXIDERMIST. I had never known a taxidermist and now I got one as a best friend. He worked with an old, local taxidermist, Carl Anderson, on his days off from the park. I used to go to the taxidermy shop, visit, and watch them stuff animals I didn't know could be stuffed. I was amazed by it, but really didn't consider I could do taxidermy work. I didn't know the secrets of how you could hang a dead animal or fish on the wall, without it stinking. As the years went by, I learned more about taxidermy watching Len and ole Carl Anderson. Little did I know I would soon be a taxidermist, something I aspired to be as a young boy, reading about it in the *Boys' Life* magazine.

Ranger Len and I loved to hunt and fish. We would duck hunt and fish every chance we got. I envied Ranger Len as a Park Ranger and was able to learn more about the National Park Service because of my relationship with him. I had never considered becoming a Park Ranger, even as I associated with the people in the park on a daily basis. It would be tough to get a Park Ranger position so I never considered I could come close to qualify.

I ended my Coast Guard career six years after entering with the rate of 1st class Boatswains Mate. I was halfway to having a very comfortable career with the Coast Guard. I knew I would be transferring from the Coast Guard station soon and I considered Pensacola Beach as home, so I decided not to re-enlist. There were a couple of things I hadn't considered when I resigned. During my time with the Coast Guard I was well taken care of. I would wake up every day with a quiet, private view of the beach. There was free room and board, lots of groceries with our own personal cook and open galley where we could prepare anything any time. Fishing was extraordinary. Life around the Coast Guard Station was very simple. I had trained and established a great deal of knowledge and experience, but the main thing was I had a JOB. After resigning, it didn't take long to realize I was going to have to take care of myself. I became a lame beach bum, growing my hair long and spending my saved-up money trying to figure out a new identity.

I hadn't ever considered a career in any kind of law enforcement, but a friend I had made with the Florida Marine Patrol advised me they were hiring, but I would have to have a law enforcement commission to work with them. Now, this seemed right down my alley, driving boats. I had some law enforcement experience boarding and inspecting vessels, but the Coast Guard did not require a law enforcement commission. It seemed like an opportunity and I thought back about the *Boys' Life* magazine where I had aspired to become a conservation officer. This seemed like the big chance. I applied for a school loan under the GI bill and attended the Police Officers Standards Training Academy at the local Pensacola Junior College. The training was basic police training and there were a lot of people there aspiring to become police officers. There were a lot of people there who were already police officers but did not have a certified law enforcement commission and were attending to get it. You could tell all the new guys because we were all skinny and reserved and all the "cops" were sort of large and loud.

In all, it was a great class, and in about three months I was certified to be a Florida Law Enforcement Officer. Now the hard part was pursuing that Marine Patrol job. Everything sounded exciting and easy when my friend suggested it to me prior to attending the law enforcement training. However, in the real world, it was becoming clear that politics and friends was the only way to get a job as a Marine Patrol Officer. I scratched that idea and decided to try something else. I had the GI bill that would provide me the schooling of my choice, but I just didn't like the idea of more institutional, organizational training. I had spent the last seven years training and I thought I needed to just get a working man's job. I bummed around for another couple of months, hanging out at the beach, visiting with my friends at the Seashore and hanging around the taxidermy shop.

I was at the taxidermy shop one day and Carl Anderson told me about the first taxidermy school offered with college credits. Carl was on the advisory board of the school, but the school was in Roxboro, North Carolina, a small rural area where there were lots of tobacco farms. This was only about an hour from Welcome, where I had grown up, raising tobacco. I could attend it under the GI bill and get college credits. I was close to attaining one of my earliest desires by becoming a conservation officer with the Marine Patrol and now I was going to learn how to become a taxidermist. I wasn't sure how the taxidermy thing was going to turn out, but I needed a job and I had to be trained. Besides, if taxidermy didn't work out, I had made a full circle back to where tobacco fields were plentiful.

As it turned out, there just weren't that many secrets about stuffing and hanging dead animals on the wall where they didn't stink. I found out taxidermy was an art. Things were cooking along well, finally setting my sights on something I was going to enjoy and having a job. I enrolled at the school for the first three months, learning the basics of taxidermy and mostly mounting deer heads. I also learned you didn't use the term "stuffing." Everything was "mounted." I would find every kind of animal or bird I could and spent all my time learning to mount them. I also studied human relations, business and a few more boring subjects that were required because of the curriculum guaranteeing college credits.

After the first three months of taxidermy school, I was contacted by my friend Ranger Len at Gulf Islands National Seashore, back in Pensacola, Florida. Len was transferring from the seashore to another park and Gulf Islands was needing law enforcement Rangers. The General Authorities bill, in 1976, required law enforcement Rangers to have a law enforcement commission and most all the Rangers did not have a commission. A lot of them didn't want one. This sent the Park Service scurrying to find qualified Rangers with a law enforcement commission. Because I had completed the basic law enforcement training and was a military veteran, I was eligible to work for the National Park Service. Ranger Len helped me get on board just before he left for his new assignment. Without my relationship with Ranger Len, I could never have achieved my early dreams. I owe Ranger Len everything for his guidance and friendship that allowed me to become a National Park Ranger.

As it turned out, my dream of being a taxidermist and a Conservation Officer became a reality, at precisely the same time and the same day in March of 1977.

Since Ranger Len was transferring to another National Park, Carl needed help to replace Len. My childhood dream had come true, although it would be many years after I had worked a full career when I realized my destiny inspired me to write my memoirs. I had been guided through life by divine intervention that could only be explained when I found two small faded pieces of paper tucked in the pages of a bible I had as a child.

After my mother died, my sister went through Mother's collections of pictures and memorabilia. My mother kept a white Gideon Bible stored that I had received when I was a small boy. The bible was still in its original box and I placed it in a drawer at my home when I got it. I opened the bible recently and found the two faded pieces of paper I had saved years ago. These were the ads I had torn out of the *Boys' Life* and outdoor magazines in the Welcome school library years ago, where I had

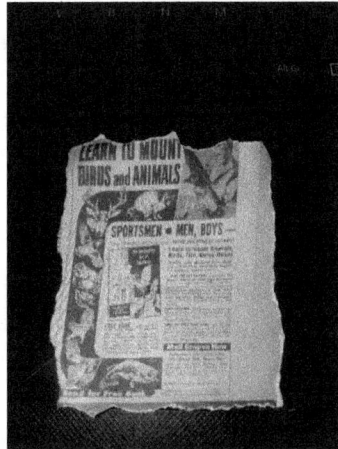

Taxidermy School Ad

imagined as a young boy being a taxidermist and a Conservation Officer. It was shocking to find and a chill came over me as I recalled the days when I would eagerly get these magazines and become fixated with these simple ads. Although I don't remember tearing them out, the presence of mind I had at the time must have been a guiding factor for a career I would cherish for many years. It was at this time I remembered Forest Gump, when Lieutenant Dan told Forest, "Every man has a destiny."

Park Ranger Ad

At the time I was hired, the National Park Service was undergoing major changes. My position was called a Park Technician rather than a Park Ranger. I was informed at the onset I would never be a Park Ranger. I started as a "Seasonal," working only nine months a year. Park Rangers were considered educated with a college degree and assumed leadership positions as park managers. The Park Technicians were a lower class of Park Rangers, gaining their status through work experience. The Park Technicians patrolled and did basically the same job as a Park Ranger. The work series and grade were different, and it provided the Park Service the needed personnel for pennies on the dollar. The seasonal Park Technicians were not paid any benefits, retirement, nor guaranteed any enhanced career status. The Park Technicians could be hired in a different GS grade series, usually a GS-3 or GS-4, with very lousy pay. The Park Rangers were expected to fill the supervisory and other management positions. They relied on their college education to guide, plan and supervise, but received very little enhanced training or required any further continuing education. They gained experience on the job just like Park Technicians but received enhanced pay as Park Rangers. The seasonal technicians would not be required to move but could move around, on their own, to different parks, to gain experience in hopes of landing a real Park Ranger position. It didn't matter to me at the time what they called me. I was just excited to be employed by the National Park Service and work on the National Seashore and they could call me whatever, as I would have worked for free.

I had worked as a Ranger a few years before Hurricane Frederick devastated the National Seashore in 1979. I was called by the superintendent's office to pick up the superintendent for a tour of Fort Pickens, to assess the damages. The superintendent, back in that day, was very different than the big shots of today, where the Rangers must have an appointment to talk to them. I was only a lowly seasonal Ranger then, but he wanted me to tour him around the seashore. I picked him up at Pensacola Beach in an old 4-wheel-drive CJ7 jeep. I drove him around like Miss Daisy and we talked about a lot of stuff. As we came around the point of Fort Pickens, there was a flooded area with standing water. I was sure we could not get around it, and if we drove through it, we would surely get stuck. The superintendent told me we could make it and keep going. I knew this was not going to end well and the superintendent chided me while he laughed. I took off and hit the water and the jeep sank to the frame and became stuck. The superintendent laughed while I tried to figure out what to do next. The jeep had a winch, but there was nothing to anchor to, to pull the jeep out. My supervisors called on the radio. The radios did not work very well, but I could hear them tell me I had to get the superintendent back because he had the news media wanting to talk with him. The superintendent then told me to "turn that damn radio off." We walked back to the Coast Guard Station to see if anyone was there. It was about a three-quarter mile hike back along the beach. I was pretty sure no one was there because I had already visited it earlier. I had turned my radio down low, but I could still hear my supervisors calling, over and over. The superintendent didn't want to be bothered and enjoyed the hike along the desolate beach. He enjoyed smoking cigarettes and he had plenty of them, so there was not much of an emergency.

When we got to the Coast Guard Station, there was no one around. The superintendent and I were the only people for miles on the desolate beach. As we walked up to the entrance walls, going into the Coast Guard station, I spotted the antique anchors on the wall. I told the superintendent if we could find an anchor around the Coast Guard station, we could use it and winch the Jeep out. He asked me if one of those antique anchors would work. They weren't very heavy, but they would get the jeep out. The only thing was, these anchors were antiques and used as decorations for the Coast

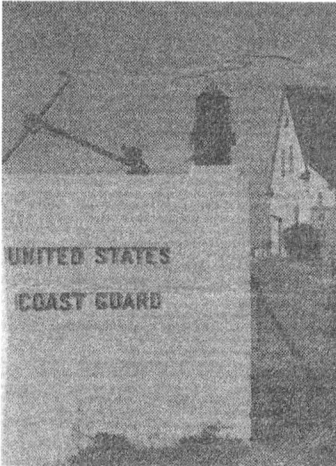

Anchor

Guard Station. I had painted them myself and knew they were valuable antiques. I told him they would work, and he climbed up the wall and took one down.

We hiked back to the jeep. I thought it would be easier to call someone on the radio to come rescue us, but the superintendent was adamant we were going to rescue ourselves and told me to stay off that "damned" radio.

We got back to the jeep. With his cigarette hanging out of the corner of his

mouth, he waded through the water with me and we buried the anchor in the sand, hooked the winch cable to it and within a few seconds we were out of the water hole. We headed back to the Coast Guard Station and put the anchor back on the wall. We saw a couple of vehicles heading toward us. The hurricane had leveled the island and you could see for miles as these vehicles quickly approached. It was some of my

supervisors, coming to locate the superintendent. One of them got out of the vehicle and immediately started shouting at me for not answering my radio. The superintendent intervened right away and said, "I told him to turn that damn radio off and what the hell do you want?" I was a little uncomfortable with their exchange, and I happened to remember I needed to crawl under the jeep and find something to fix. The supervisors, and a couple other park employees, figured out they needed to check more of the park. So, I brought the superintendent back to his vehicle at Pensacola Beach.

4

Law Enforcement & Fitting In

*A*s the years passed, I somehow became a real Park Ranger. It was difficult to get a position with the National Park Service and most Rangers had to start as seasonal or part time, doing their time, only getting paid a minimal wage with no benefits. There are many types of National Park Service Rangers as everyone is called a Park Ranger, including maintenance personnel. Everyone had the same uniform and wore the same gold "Buffalo" badge. It was and still is confusing trying to identify who is a Park Ranger. While the uniforms are the same, the job descriptions were quite different. The traditional Park Ranger was known as the authority in the park with law enforcement duties included with other Ranger activities, while other "Rangers" provided Interpretation, giving tours and education programs, or specialized in science-related fields in Wildlife, Archaeology, Natural History and other activities, but were still identified as Park Rangers.

Law enforcement Rangers had to have formal law enforcement training. In 1976 the General Authorities Bill was enacted, requiring the National Park Service to require the formal training in Law

Enforcement, and Rangers to be Commissioned; that allowed Rangers to carry firearms, make arrests, and investigate crimes within the National Parks. Up until this point there was no law enforcement training required, and all Rangers were given a ticket book and a firearm. Crime in the National Parks was escalating. The General Authorities Bill left the National Park Service without qualified law enforcement Rangers. Most of the personnel did not want to be law enforcement officers and the Park Service scrambled to fill positions with people having law enforcement training.

The Federal Law Enforcement Training Center (FLETC) in Glynco, Georgia, was not set up for NPS law enforcement training. Only a few Rangers were selected to other law enforcement training programs with other agencies at FLETC. Waivers were given for the National Park Service to hire personnel that had formal State training and other law enforcement training and certifications. I had just completed the Florida Standards for a Police Commission and I was hired under this waiver because of my formal law enforcement training. Eventually, there was a training program set up to include law enforcement for the Land Management Agencies including the National Park Service, U. S. Forest Service, Fish and Wildlife Service, and Bureau of Land Management.

The General Authorities Bill required the Rangers to be commissioned but was mitigated and open to interpretation by management of the parks. The superintendents of the National Parks had little or no law enforcement training, emergency, or firefighting experience, but dictated the law enforcement program of their National Park. Law enforcement and visitor protection within the National Parks was considered by the management of the NPS to be a low priority. Rangers who were authorized to carry firearms were restricted from wearing them in the open and were required to leave the weapons either in a briefcase, under the seat, stored in the glove box, or locked in the trunk and kept out of sight of the public. The firearm became lost when we tried to find it somewhere in the vehicle, forgetting where we hid it. The firearms could be worn if there "may" be a law enforcement encounter that would require you to protect yourself or a visitor. This meant evaluating each situation and determining if you had to shoot somebody, and then go to your vehicle, find where you hid your gun, along with finding your handcuffs that you could not wear either. You could wear the weapon at night while on active patrol because you were alone, and the park management and other divisions were at home and less likely to be offended by the sight of a firearm. If a Ranger was armed, and went into a visitor center, bathroom, restaurant, or administrative building, they had to leave the firearm contained out of sight.

Criminal activity and Law enforcement activities in the National Park Service were escalating very quickly. The mandatory guidelines of the law enforcement program required qualifying with the firearm twice annually and attending a 40-hour law enforcement refresher course yearly. The management of the National Park Service was apprehensive in allowing for active law enforcement and only allowed the Rangers to be 'barely trained' and only provided with the minimal equipment to perform law enforcement activities. This dangerous policy came to haunt the National Park Service quickly as will be discussed further in the book.

5
———

This Is How You Do It

*A*t the time I was hired as a Park Technician, it was one of my duties to man the entrance station, collect entrance fees, while being a primary response to law enforcement problems. If there was a problem, I would have to close the station, lock up the money and go find my firearm and handcuffs and put them on my trousers belt. I was given a trusty .38 caliber revolver that held six qualifying rounds called "wad cutters." These are the type of bullet that we shoot at paper targets. I was issued probably a half dozen extra rounds that had been reloaded by the District supervisor in his garage and carried either in a briefcase or glove box of the vehicle, along with a pair of handcuffs. Crime was recognized by our superintendent at the seashore when I began to work as a Park Technician. Although he supported the law enforcement program, it was considered by his management staff to be nonexistent and the seashore law enforcement program was managed as a required aggravation rather than a necessity, to protect the visitors and resources. Criminal activity in the National Parks has always been downplayed for the many years I was a Ranger, to keep the visitors immune from the real

39

world. Programs were established to educate the visitors of the natural and cultural resources of the park that resulted in visitors of the parks thinking they are in La-La Land or Jellystone Park and immune from all the bad guys. The Park Service management has always tried to mitigate the fact real criminals do not visit the National Parks and criminals will not cross over the imaginary line that separates the Park Boundary from reality.

Park Service jurisdictions include Proprietary, Concurrent, and Exclusive jurisdictions within the National Park boundaries. Gulf Islands National Seashore, at the time I was there, included a Proprietary jurisdiction, meaning we could only enforce rules under Title 36 of the Federal Codes. Jurisdictions have since changed over the years to allow for most parks to assume Concurrent status, which allows Rangers to assimilate and enforce State laws as well as Federal laws in the National Parks. There are some exceptions that allow only Exclusive jurisdiction, such as the Great Smoky Mountains National Park, which allows only Federal enforcement authority. These Proprietary rules at Gulf Islands National Seashore primarily related to picking flowers, dogs off leash, and a list of other minor problems, with the focus of protecting the National Seashore facilities and resources. All the major crimes against persons such as assault, larceny, theft, rape and murder had to be handled by the local Sheriff department, unless it was serious enough that the FBI would intervene (that was never). The problem was, we would be dispatched to these serious crimes with no back-up, guns locked away, with minimal dispatch, no jurisdiction for arrest, and acting only as a witness to a serious crime. We had minimal authority to hold a subject for the local jurisdictions, or appearing as a witness to a serious crime. The National Park Service dispatch usually consisted of someone listening to the radio either at a desk or the entrance station, while they did some other activity. The radios were frequently monitored by Rangers' wives at their homes, who made calls for assistance and back-up.

Regardless, I was proud to be there and carried on, responding to major crimes including rapes, murders, suicides, larcenies and assaults. The Escambia County Sheriff Beach deputies provided me with back-up, even though they were 10 miles away, if they were available. I owe my professional career to being associated with these many deputies, as they taught me street etiquette, law enforcement techniques, and the mental awareness of being a law enforcement officer. They would constantly come to my rescue and saved my ass many times.

I was on the job for about two days, and at the entrance station one afternoon, when I got a complaint there were drunken sailors staying in one of the campsites at the campground. The Pensacola Naval Air Station was located across the bay in Pensacola and it wasn't uncommon to have a group of sailors having a good time. This was my first real law enforcement situation. I had never made an arrest and never really responded to a serious complaint. I found my trusty .38 caliber pistol under the seat. It was loaded with bullets with the capability to shoot rats. I threaded my gun holster onto my trouser belt. I found my handcuffs and put them in my pants pocket and I was ready to 'git me some action.' Barney Fife would have been envious as I set out to answer the complaint. As luck would have it, Deputy Gary Montee, with the Escambia County Sheriff Dept., came by the entrance station and he went with me to the campsite.

When we arrived, there were two sailors at the campsite, quite inebriated. They had a campfire built on the ground, which was a serious violation according to Park Service regulations. I was driving a plain, government vehicle that looked like it came from a used car lot. Deputy Montee had his fully marked police cruiser. I walked up to the drunken sailors who sat on the picnic table, while deputy Montee watched. I explained the campground rules and that they were creating a disturbance, and asked them to be quiet. They both laughed and one of them got off the table and came up to me. He was right in my face and then took his finger and poked me several times in my Buffalo badge that said U.S. Park Ranger. I was pretty sure he was not supposed to be assaulting a Federal Park Ranger and I was trying to process my next plan of action. Suddenly, BOOM! Deputy Montee reached across in front of me and grabbed the sailor, throwing him to the ground, and dragged him through the campfire, handcuffing him in the ashes and throwing his ass in his cruiser.

I figured out this was the proper way of making an arrest and dealing with drunks, and at the same instant I grabbed the second sailor who immediately submitted to being arrested and didn't give me the opportunity to drag him through the fire. I was proud I had subdued the second sailor and had him cuffed and figured Deputy Montee would have been impressed. After both of them were secured in his cruiser, Deputy Montee then began screaming at me, telling me, and I quote, "If you ever let me see you have someone lay their hands on you again, I'm taking your ass to jail!" Deputy Montee was really pissed I had let this guy poke me, and from that day on, no one ever laid hands on me again. I have a very vivid recollection of this event, and with this one experience, I had a different and better perspective of law enforcement. Without the guidance and 'ass chewings' from the deputies, I could not have obtained the necessary experience to survive 26 years of law enforcement in the National Park Service. Some of these deputies bitched about having to back me up and having to drive 10 to 15 miles and usually finding nothing. But the truth is, they really enjoyed driving their police cruisers 100+ mph and hoping I was getting my ass kicked when they got to me.

6

Airplane Crash

I had worked with Gulf Islands National Seashore for about a year and began my second season as a Park Technician. On May 8, 1978, National Airlines Flight 193 crashed in the Escambia Bay while approaching the Pensacola Regional Airport. The aircraft was a Boeing 727, and had been given the name Donna, and was on its final stop for the day after the flight originated in Miami, Florida.

As the aircraft approached the runway in Pensacola, it encountered a thick fog. Because of pilot error, the aircraft missed the runway, as the pilot put the aircraft down in the Escambia Bay, miles from the airport runway. According to reports at the time, the pilot mistakenly thought he saw runway lights from a barge operation that occurred in the bay. It was supposed to be a routine landing. There with no warnings and this was not an emergency landing. The plane impacted the water, and water began rushing into the cabin of the aircraft as it quickly settled half submerged in the shallow water of Escambia Bay.

There were 52 passengers and six crew members aboard. Three people tragically drowned, with many more seriously injured. The mother of a two-year-old boy handed off her son to rescuers, and he was the first person rescued from the aircraft. The mother was reportedly a skilled and professional swimmer and after she handed off her son, she went back to rescue passengers. Two victims who had drowned were immediately recovered, but the mother disappeared and could not be located.

The passengers were panicked and strewn over the bay waters after being separated from the aircraft, using the plane's seat cushions and other floating devices as they exited the plane. The seat cushions were not flotation devices, and life preservers were not provided on the aircraft. The passengers struggled to remain afloat until they were rescued. A tugboat and a barge operating in the area quickly responded in the thick fog, rescuing many passengers. Emergency calls went out to anyone and everyone with a boat to assist in the rescue.

Frank Pridemore was the Superintendent of Gulf Islands at the time and contacted Ranger Mike Farley and me, asking us to respond and assist in the rescue. The crash site was several miles from where our boat was docked and because of the thick fog, it was slow and difficult reaching the crash site. Visibility was less than 50 feet at times, as we navigated to the downed plane. The Superintendent launched his personal boat and immediately responded. He was one of the first to arrive and rescued several of the victims and assisted in the search and recovery of the floating debris.

I had just completed six years of Coast Guard duty and was still an active Coast Guardsman reservist. I had navigated the waters in and around Pensacola, Destin, Fort Walton, and Orange Beach for at least four-and-a-half years performing many search and rescues in the area. This crash was right down my alley. When we arrived at the site, all the victims had been rescued or accounted for except the young mother. There was debris floating all over Escambia Bay and rescuers searched for the mother. Leaking jet fuel covered the water and burned the eyes, making rescue efforts more difficult. I don't remember who the incident commander was or who oversaw the rescue.

Ranger Farley and I were assigned to get divers and bring them to the scene. The divers were located a couple of miles further away from the site and the water was too shallow for the Coast Guard boats and bigger watercraft to get to them. Our 18-foot Boston Whaler was equipped with an outboard engine and could navigate the shallow water.

Back in those days, there was no GPS or other electronics to navigate, like we have now. I had navigated for years with nothing more than a magnetic compass and a navigational chart around the area bays and Gulf of Mexico. On that night, we navigated by instinct and experience, as we tried to find the boat ramp located at the end of the Interstate 10 Bridge. It was a miracle we found the boat ramp in the dense fog, but it was a given we were going to run into the bridge in one location or another.

We quickly overloaded the Boston Whaler with several divers and dive gear. The biggest chore now was finding the downed aircraft several miles away. There was a slight breeze and only the tidal currents that affected the compass course that I used to get to the boat ramp. Even with a compass course, there were a lot of calculations that prevented us from ending up precisely where we wanted to be. We could easily miss the downed aircraft with zero visibility due to the fog. We proceeded with idle speed due to the fog and a seriously overloaded boat.

After about an hour, I became concerned we could not locate the aircraft and would be wandering around in circles. The divers were excited when they learned I was an ex-Coastie, and I would surely find the aircraft. After all, I found the boat ramp. (I was going to find it anyway when I ran aground and could see the bridge lights and billboard signs)

It was more difficult on the way back because the incoming tide drifted toward me and with the slight breeze, brought the heavy jet fuel fumes toward me as well. I quietly (and cleverly) navigated the boat in and out of the jet fuel fumes coming directly from the aircraft.

I didn't let the divers know my navigation technique, and within a few minutes, we located the aircraft.

The divers were amazed I was able to find the plane and praised my navigation skills. Of course, I didn't tell them it was pretty much dumb luck we found it and I couldn't bullshit Ranger Farley, as he hid his smirk, while my ego was getting stroked. We off-loaded the divers and they searched around the plane trying to locate the young mother. Within a few minutes, the divers found her, lodged in the mud under the wing of the plane. I never heard an explanation of how a professional and expert swimmer could become trapped in the manner she was found.

After the victims had been accounted for, Ranger Farley and I continued back to the Ranger Station, in the dense fog once again. It was now into the early morning and the fog did not lift. We made our way somewhere out in the middle of Pensacola Bay. I had no clue where we were, but occasionally, I found a buoy that gave me a new reference point and an opportunity to get a new compass reading. A that time, Vietnamese immigrants had settled in the area after the Vietnam war. There were many of them with shrimp boats in the water. When we came across one of these boats with several occupants, I tried to communicate with them to confirm my location, but none of them could speak English. We conversed back and forth, intently trying to comprehend each other, but I might as well speak pig Latin, while they spoke Vietnamese. They only laughed and pointed at the fog. I thanked them and headed back into the fog.

After a while, I figured I was close to something and radioed District Ranger Art Johnson, who stood at the Ranger Station with the headlights of his patrol car on and blue lights flashing and siren going. The acoustics of the fog made it easy to hear the location of the patrol car, and within a few minutes, we could see the lights shining through the fog.

The next day, after the fog lifted, you could see the massive aircraft from the Pensacola Bay Bridge as it rested in the shallow water. There had been hundreds of volunteers and professional responders involved in rescuing the survivors, locating victims, working in blinding conditions because of the dense fog. Even though our contributions were small, Ranger Farley and I were proud to have been one of these responders.

As I mentioned before, when Hurricane Frederick leveled Santa Rosa Island in 1979, it reduced the 40-foot sand dunes to below sea level. I remember the day after the storm as a Park Ranger. There was no one on the entire island. The peace and quiet was overwhelming, with the Gulf of Mexico only gently lashing at the shoreline with clear blue skies. Hours before, the Gulf of Mexico was violently churning with 40-foot waves, overtaking the huge dunes that yielded a surplus of golden sea oats. Now, they were no more. Santa Rosa Island was leveled, and all that was left was the sugar white sand.

The Coast Guard Station was built at the highest elevation on the island and survived the storm, but the infrastructure, including the docks and buildings, were taken out. The Coast Guard station was over a hundred years old at this point and it was quickly decided the Coast Guard would build a new station across the bay on the Pensacola Naval Air Station.

Inside the abandoned Coast Guard Station, there was no power. It was dark with the only lighting coming from the early morning sunshine through the windows of the old station. There was an eerie and quiet atmosphere that echoed throughout the old building as I walked around. I began to reflect on my personal experience, having lived and worked at the Coast Guard Station for four-and-a-half years, and envisioned all the other Coasties who had been fortunate enough to be a part of the old station that had been here for so long. The Coast Guard station was always kept in pristine condition by the Coast Guard. It was always painted and groomed daily. Now that Frederick left its mark, the station appeared old and weathered. It would go on to be a neglected historical treasure, abused by the management of the National Park Service. The National Seashore had no permanent facilities for a Ranger Station and the Coast Guard Station was now being inherited by the NPS.

The National Park Service took full possession of the Historic Coast Guard Station, Santa Rosa. The National Park Service, which was once concerned about the old Coast Guard Station, now had its chance to preserve a historic treasure.

The station had been lying in neglect and the surrounding buildings had deteriorated from the rot and mildew. The roof that had been proudly restored by us Coasties had to be replaced from the damage of the hurricane. Now that the National Park Service had complete possession, the rules were changed regarding the historic rehabilitation and use of the Coast Guard Station. The roof was replaced with ASPHALT SHINGLES! The inside of the station was remodeled and the beaded pine boards on the walls were replaced by dry wall, ceilings were rehung with modern materials and offices created all through the station. A large cell tower was also erected in the yard. The brick entrance walls where "Coast Guard" was engraved were covered over. The antique and ornamental U.S. Lighthouse navigation lights were removed, along with the antique boat anchors that decorated the entrance to the Coast Guard Station. These walls were intact after Hurricane Frederick because I had to borrow one of the antique anchors from the wall.

I moved back into my old home that has now become the Ranger Station, where I had a permanent office space along with the other Rangers.

As the years passed, crime in the National Park Service escalated. Serious incidents occurred more frequently with more major crimes committed. The Park Service management was still apprehensive about implementing an aggressive law enforcement program. I worked mainly the night shift, alone, and I encountered more serious incidents. Luckily for me at the time, the superintendent of Gulf Islands was a personal ally. I had known him before I became a Ranger, when I was in the Coast Guard. I had a conversation with him about how it was a pain in the ass to have to find my gun under the seat or in the trunk before I could confront a violator, and how dangerous it was. I could wear my gun on my pants belt at night but did not have a real duty belt to carry my gun, handcuffs, mace, and flashlight holder. We were still issued the old night stick, but most carried a large Kell Light, which was used in place of the night stick.

The Kell Light was effective and convenient because it was always in your hand. But because too many heads were being used in arrest techniques, it was quickly prohibited by all law enforcement agencies as a use of force weapon.

After a couple of days, the Superintendent came out one night and gave me a duty belt with a holster and told me to wear it when I was working at night. The holster and belt were black, and nothing close to the Sam Browne belts that was later issued by the NPS. The holsters in the day resembled the cowboy quick draw holsters, but did not secure the weapon very well, and allowed a suspect to take your gun away from you. But it was better than having it on your trousers belt. I was told to just not say anything and at that point on, I wore the belt, careful not to wear it at any functions, visitor centers or headquarters. Although I was more equipped, I was still apprehensive about causing a confrontation with other employees who shunned the sight of a gun in front of them and park visitors.

A lot of the law enforcement responses at the Seashore were due to Disorderly Conduct, because of Intoxication. If there was an Intoxication call, it always included Disorderly Conduct. Because Pensacola Beach was next door, alcohol was prevalent. It was allowed in the Seashore, and openly consumed, as long no one was a danger to themselves or others. People enjoyed the new National Seashore with Gulf Islands becoming one of the most visited National Parks. With more visitors coming to the park, it was a given there was going to be more criminal activity. One of the biggest criminal violations were "car clouts" as we called them, or burglary from a vehicle. These criminals were usually harmless, capitalizing on victims who had no clue the car burglars would be lurking around trying to steal everything they had while they enjoyed the beach, oblivious to their surroundings. The burglars knew all their valuables were left in their vehicles and usually purses left under the seat. While a lookout was posted on the dunes of the beach, another thug would smash the window or use a jimmy tool, sometimes called a Slim Jim, to unlock the vehicle, grab the valuables and be gone.

These people usually worked in groups. One day, Ranger John

Bradberry caught them in the act. Ranger Bradberry called me for back-up and he followed them when they went to a local Tom Thumb convenience store. As they exited the store, we arrested them but had to call for the County Sheriff department and turn them over to them to be charged and tried in state courts while we appeared as witnesses. Turns out, these guys were hard core criminals, with all of them having serious criminal records and incarcerations. They were booked in the jail by the Sheriff's department and released on bond.

Ranger Bradberry had a girlfriend at the time and unbeknownst to John, she was an acquaintance of one of these thugs' girlfriend. She learned the thugs were trying to get a contract to have Ranger Bradberry killed. She became a confidential witness, and the FBI intervened and began investigating the threat because Ranger Bradberry was a Federal Officer. The local authorities were also alerted. As far as I knew, I wasn't named in the contract, but it was very concerning I may get collateral damage as a result of being with Ranger Bradberry when these thugs were arrested. Several months passed while we were on edge. One day, one of the thugs, Buddy Ray Travis was being watched by an Escambia County deputy as he went into an old beer joint. He was alone and his partner in crime was not with him. The deputy saw him from across the street carrying something wrapped in a towel as the thug entered the beer joint. Travis spotted the deputy and threw the towel up onto the porch roof of the beer joint. The deputy went and found the towel that had a sawed-off shotgun wrapped in it. Travis was immediately arrested and due to his criminal record that included a charge of murder, Travis was sentenced as a habitual offender, and ordered held without parole. Travis' partner, William Lockhart, laid low and nothing else was heard from any of these thugs until about four years later.

One day, four years later, William Lockhart, whom we had arrested along with Buddy Ray Travis, came with another thug to the park. One of the girls at the entrance station, for whatever reason, immediately identified Lockhart as being the other accomplice in the car burglaries Ranger Bradberry had caught four years earlier. They entered the park, and Ranger Art Johnson was notified. He responded in his private vehicle to try to observe them. He came upon them in a parking lot parked next to a vehicle with their trunk open on their vehicle while he observed them burglarizing the vehicle next to them. Ranger Johnson exited his vehicle with his weapon drawn, holding the thugs at gun point. I responded to back up Ranger Johnson who held the thugs with their hands up. Lockhart was standing right next to the open trunk of his vehicle with his hands up. As I held the suspects at gun point, Ranger Johnson went up to handcuff the suspects and on looking in the trunk; there was a loaded revolver within hand reach of the thug. Ranger Johnson backed off and drew his weapon. We kept them at gunpoint and ordered them away from the vehicle and to the ground. I remember Lockhart kept looking down and he was apparently focused on trying to get the gun that laid next to him. I guess they considered their options by lying on the hot asphalt instead of being shot with rat shot from our trusty .38 caliber guns. This was number two of the thugs who was also given habitual offender status and removed from the roles of criminal activity in the National Seashore. As a rookie, it was now becoming apparent to me that there were actual criminals within the National Park Service who would kill you if they had the chance.

7

Rogue Ranger

$\mathcal{A}$fter a few years on the job, I was confident and comfortable as a law enforcement officer in the National Park Service. Things were usually pretty quiet during the day unless there was a car burglary, which happened regularly. Stakeouts were set up to try to catch the thieves, but most of the time, it was just happenstance to catch them. During one of the summers, we had a long string of car burglaries along the seashore road. Thousands of dollars were stolen along with a lot of personal property and vehicles damaged from smashed windows. We organized a stakeout and set up to catch the thief. The burglaries occurred daily, but we were unable to identify anyone, and we discontinued the stakeout. As soon as the stakeout or surveillance was discontinued, the same pattern occurred, hitting in the same location and the same approximate time. We got very frustrated until one day, we finally got a break.

Who would believe a National Park Ranger would commit these burglaries? It was true.

Seems one of our own Rangers supplemented his paycheck by breaking into these cars. After totaling up the amount of money taken throughout the summer months, there was an average of four hundred dollars a day for a long period of time, not to mention the damages. The Ranger was seen weeks earlier breaking into a vehicle by some visitors. They reported it to the Naval Air Station by letter, identifying what they had observed. The visitors who saw it identified the vehicle as lime-green and they were not familiar with the National Park Service vehicles and assumed, because of the presence of the Naval Air Station, it was one of their vehicles. The Naval Air Station police forwarded the letter to the Chief Ranger of Gulf Islands, who placed it in his desk drawer, not disclosing any of the information to anyone. The thefts kept occurring, while this letter was in the desk drawer of the Chief Ranger. This employee was an Affirmative Action hire, and the Chief Ranger did not want to confront the complications regarding the Ranger's minority status, and hoped he would just quit breaking into cars. A couple of weeks later, some more visitors saw the Ranger again breaking into a vehicle, and they came to the dispatch office and reported it to the dispatcher and wanted to report it to an officer. The dispatcher tried to convince the visitors he would report it to the proper people, but the visitors weren't convinced this would happen, and went and filed a complaint with the Escambia County Sheriff Department, who in turn, let the cat out of the bag. The Chief Ranger office was in headquarters of the park, right next to the Superintendent's office. When the Superintendent found out all this occurred, he was livid and to the point of exploding. Headquarters quickly became known as "Hindquarters" because it seemed most decisions that affected the quality of visitor protection came from the south end of a northbound mule.

A surveillance was set up to catch this guy. We knew his schedule, knew where he was hitting these vehicles and knew he liked stealing money and camera equipment. Two supervisors and I were briefed about the surveillance. It was like being in a Colombo movie, setting up the takedown. We had a new fee collector girl arrive the same day we were going to make the bust and no one knew her car. She was convinced we needed to borrow her car the next morning. We also flew in a Law Enforcement Ranger from the Natchez Trace Parkway. The plan was working well. We used the Natchez Trace Law Enforcement Ranger to lie on the beach with the fee collector, of course to protect her from any danger, and the car was parked along the road, baited with marked money and camera equipment. This was a real law enforcement situation and we found our guns and ammo and strapped them on, preparing to arrest this rogue Park Ranger.

The Chief Ranger was stationed across the road, hidden in the dunes, with a high-powered camera. It was about 9 a.m. and the rogue Ranger, who was armed and with a radio, was going to work in his little VW bug. The two supervisors and I were at his duty station office. The plan was to arrest him at the station when he came to work, if he burglarized the vehicle. If not, then we slipped off in the opposite direction, and he wouldn't see us. The other part of the plan was the signal to use if he broke into the vehicle. Being this was going to be put on the radio, and he had a radio, there had to be some sort of generic signal. That signal would be from the Chief Ranger who hid in the dunes, where he would say, "I'm heading east on Ft. Pickens Road," if he broke into the vehicle, but if he continued on and didn't stop, the signal would be, "I'm heading west on Ft. Pickens Road." The plan was in motion, just like they do it in the movies. The supervisors and I waited in the office, discussing how we would position ourselves in the office to keep from being in a crossfire, if a shooting occurred. This Ranger had been trained and served in the U.S Army for 20 years and we were afraid his actions could lead to a shooting. During the discussion, we refreshed ourselves on what the signal was. It was at this point we had forgotten which direction the signal was supposed to indicate whether he broke into the vehicle or not. While we tried to figure out the signal, the radio went off and the Chief Ranger alerted us that he was at the vehicle, but we didn't know whether we were to get out of there or arrest him. The rogue Ranger was now heading to us. The decision was made for him to come on to the office at which time he would be put on administrative leave by his supervisor, to make sure we didn't make a bad arrest to prosecute him. He would be relieved of his law enforcement duties, and be fired, regardless.

The rogue Ranger was now at the station and came up the steps, whistling, and unlocked the door. When he opened the door, he immediately spotted the supervisors and turned and looked at me behind the door. His eyes were about to pop out of his head in disbelief as we were there, fixing to arrest him. As luck would have it, when he entered the room, he stepped inside and his gun was inside the door with his hand on the outside on the doorknob. I pinned him with the door and relieved him of his weapon and then he was handcuffed. I guess that's the part of being placed on administrative leave I didn't know about by handcuffing him before he was informed he was on administrative leave. But as it turned out, all was good. The chief Ranger had snapped a box full of 8x10 glosses as he broke into the bait car, taking all the money and camera equipment. He was charged with only one count of breaking and entering as we could not, or more than likely, would not prove all the other burglaries. He pleaded guilty and received a six-month sentence in the Federal Penitentiary. This was the end to this string of burglaries and, sadly, the National Park Service lost a valuable Affirmative Action employee.

8

Activities on the Beach

*A*ctivities at the seashore weren't very hectic until nighttime. That's when all the supervisors, managers, and other seashore employees would go home. The seashore became quiet after all the bureaucratic activities, with the nightfall bringing out the usual thugs. I worked mostly nights, alone, and encountered more law enforcement events. There was no back-up and only sparse dispatch coverage. If there was a serious encounter, dispatch would then relay through the telephone to the closest police department or Sheriff department to get back-up. Back-up was usually at least 20 to 30 minutes, depending on how close the officers were. Twenty minutes may not seem like a lot, but when you are getting your ass kicked, it was an eternity. The seashore was in three primary counties, relying on three different Sheriff departments and three city police departments for back-up. I owe these guys a lot for bailing me out in some serious situations and especially the Escambia County Sheriff department. These departments provided me with more situational training than any training the NPS gave me. I really credit my survival to these deputies who responded time after time to provide me with assistance and back-up.

Unlike other law enforcement agencies, as Rangers, we had the responsibility to protect all the Seashore's natural, cultural, and historical resources. This would include daily violations of minor offenses of picking sea oats, driving on the dunes, defacing and destroying historic structures, and so forth. Because the park was a seashore and had miles of beaches, it was common to answer complaints of people being nude on the beach, sunbathing or "other things." Homosexual activity was increasing, and visitors complained of their lewd and lascivious activities. There would be many of these guys who would gang up in the bushes and trees, opposite the Gulf beaches on the sound. Trash, trampled paths through the vegetation and dunes, resulted in the natural area being overused. It would not be uncommon to find many of these guys in a pile engaged in lewd and lascivious acts. Rangers would patrol and go undercover to catch them, arrest them, and cite them into Federal magistrate's court, that would result in a significant fine. The activities decreased but were still prevalent.

One afternoon, I learned a valuable lesson in law enforcement tactics. There was a large magnolia tree atop a large sand dune that overlooked the dunes and the roadway next to the Gulf of Mexico. This tree would soon be infamous, and we would call it the "Yum-Yum Tree." There had been a transvestite bar in Pensacola years prior called the Yum-Yum Tree. I guess there may have been some correlation somehow and the magnolia tree was so named. This magnolia tree, atop a large dune, was a favorite meeting place where these guys would parade around, trying to hook up with each other. I was undercover one afternoon and went to the magnolia tree where I encountered an individual who walked around the trails. When he saw me, he began following me and I went up the trail to the magnolia tree. I watched the guy as he followed me under the tree. I stood, leaning on the tree as the guy watched me. Neither of us said anything, as I had to be careful so as not to entrap him into committing a crime. After a couple of minutes, I spotted a pair of expensive sunglasses in the sand and pointed to them and the guy picked them up. He then approached me and reached up to the tree limb I stood under. Only a foot over my head was a big, sweaty black guy in a bikini "root suit." He reached down and got the sunglasses, while I took off. I couldn't believe this guy stood on the limb, only a foot over my head. I was shaken and walked out onto the open dune to regain my composure.

The other guy walked out and stood beside me. We still weren't communicating, and again, I turned and walked back to the tree. When I got back to the tree, the guy in the tree was butt ass naked and had stripped off his "root suit". He held onto one of the tree limbs and masturbated profusely. The other guy walked under the tree, stripped off his "root suit," and joined the guy in mutual mastur-bation, watching each other. I could now arrest these guys, but I didn't want to touch them. I had carried a bag that had my badge, gun and handcuffs in it. I opened the bag to get my badge and handcuffs and my gun fell out. As I told them they were under arrest, the guy in the tree, saw my gun, put both of his hands in the air while balancing on the tree limb, and told me not to shoot as he yelled "I love life." The other guy raised his hands. They were both naked and looked like Brahma bulls. I ordered the guy in the tree to the ground and he jumped off the limb onto the sand. I only had one pair of handcuffs and I gave them the handcuffs and ordered them to handcuff their opposite arms together and crossed with the one pair of handcuffs.

I had called for a back-up and another Ranger arrived. I had to walk them across the dunes to a patrol car with them still butt ass naked. I took them to jail where they got their jail suits, and booked them to appear in court. The back seat of the patrol car was flushed with water and bleach. There would be many more of these arrests, but it was impossible to stop the activity. I began to wonder if I was being drawn into this culture and was fixing to be arrested myself. The lifestyles of these guys were pitiful and disgusting.

One of those I encountered, was a priest I knew from the local Catholic Church, where he taught kids in Sunday school. I found Father Rodger before he could commit an act to be arrested. I had a one-sided conversation with him, and he decided to leave quickly and never return again. I met with the head priest and reported Rodger's conduct and within a couple of weeks he was transferred to another church.

One of the more comical instances was when we received a complaint of two nude females on the beach, engaged in a lewd act, next to a family with small kids. Ranger Andy Adkins went to the call and walked up to the two females who were totally engaged in their activity and failed to see the Ranger standing over them. He cited them both into Federal Court for Disorderly Conduct.

On the court date, there was a female U.S. Magistrate presiding over the court, and there was a female prosecutor representing the government. The two female defendants' case was called, and the magistrate ordered all the witnesses to the bench. This was odd as the magistrate and the prosecutor, along with the two female defendants, discussed the case being tried before the bench. Ranger Andy stood away from the bench and could not hear any of the conversation being whispered. After a while, the magistrate then asked Andy if the information, that he could not hear, was correct and Ranger Andy confusingly said "Yes." The magistrate then found the defendants guilty to pay a fine.

After the court was over, we approached our prosecutor to find out why the proceedings had been secretly handled this way. Usually, when a defendant is found guilty, a statement of facts for the record would be read out in court. None of this occurred in this case. The defendants, prosecutor, and magistrate were of the female persuasion, and Ranger Andy stood alone as the only male in the hearing. There were several defendants in the courtroom and the magistrate deemed this case to be embarrassing in the courtroom but okay out in the open on the beaches in front of families and children and poor Ranger Andy to witness. The magistrate quietly and discreetly conducted the proceedings with no one knowing what was occurring. The females wanted to get this over with, pay a fine and get out of there. They had an excuse for their actions and related it to the magistrate to mitigate their fines. It was good that the magistrate had not let us hear the defendant's excuse, that would have most certainly caused the courtroom to be disrupted. The defendants had not told Ranger Andy of their dilemma on the beach that day, and it could have been handled by a trained first responder like Ranger Andy, and avoided the citations for the lewd activity they were engaged in. Seems they had a small emergency, and when they came to court, to mitigate their punishment by the magistrate, they told the magistrate they were looking for an "ingrown hair." Had Ranger Andy known this, he could have simply gotten his first aid kit and assisted with the emergency, instead of making a Federal Case.

9

Colville Fire

We were also responsible for wildland firefighting at the seashore. We had very little equipment and none of us were properly trained. We had a fire truck with a pumper unit, but we mostly just kept it cranked and running. The only wooded area was where there were large Naval Live Oak trees that were hundreds of years old. They had been preserved by the U.S. Navy, which had used them to build vessels when sailing ships were made of wood. As newer types of vessels came along, there was no need for these trees, and they were set aside and eventually included in the National Seashore for their protection.

One afternoon, I got a call of a woods fire in Naval Live Oaks. The City of Gulf Breeze adjoined the Naval Live Oaks area and they responded. There were no seashore employees working and I took the fire truck and went to Live Oaks where I met the Gulf Breeze fire department. They had a lot of equipment, but like me, they knew very little about wildland firefighting. I had trained in structural fire-fighting and had fought several vessel fires from my rescue boat while

I was with the U.S. Coast Guard. Wildland firefighting was different and required different knowledge and skills. I was still a Park Technician and not a Park Ranger, so I didn't have the status, knowledge, and training as a real park Ranger, as to what needed to be done at the fire. I found out at this fire; the real Park Rangers were not real Park Rangers either.

Between my fire truck and Gulf Breeze's trucks, we were able to get enough hose to the fire and put water on it. The fire did very little damage, and we extinguished it fast. Feeling proud I had saved Naval Live Oaks from extinction, I returned and traded my fire truck for my patrol car. Late the next day and just before dark, I got another call that Naval Live Oaks was again on fire. This time the fire was intense and further into the woods where we could not get a fire hose to it. It required more fire fighters. We did not have any trained wildland firefighters and Gulf Breeze's firefighters didn't fight fires where the water hoses didn't reach. We did have employees who weren't trained but were kind of required to respond and help put out the fire.

I remember it well when the fiasco started. I again worked alone. We had seasonal part time employees who were fee collectors, interpreters, and maintenance, who lived in seashore housing at the end of Ft. Pickens. Dispatch already called supervisors and other Rangers at their homes. When I went to the park housing to find some help, there was no one around, although there were probably a half dozen seasonal employees who lived there. The dispatcher also had trouble locating any other employees and supervisors who might help with the fire. I arrived at the Ranger station to get the fire truck and met the superintendent, who came to the park and got a park jeep and headed to the fire. He had his wife and small son in the jeep and came to me and yelled at me that I was going to put this fire out tonight. When I got to the fire, it was burning pretty good, but wasn't a serious fire yet. It was the same as the night before, with Gulf Breeze fire department in the parking lot with hoses trying to get to the fire that was too far away. I had no clue as to building a fire line to stop the fire and had no equipment, personnel, or knowledge. I was focused on getting our fire truck close enough to the fire to get water on it and put it out.

One of my educated supervisor/Park Rangers arrived and he did not have any wildland fire training either. He also had a couple of afternoon toddies under his belt. He drove the fire truck through the woods to the fire, running over big trees and brush, tearing the hell out of the fire truck, and pulled it up to the fire that was running toward us quickly. Within just a short time, the fire truck was emptied of water and the fire gained intensity, heading for the fire truck. When I tried to move the truck, it would not go into gear. The fire was probably less than 100 feet away, creeping toward the truck. The heat was very intense as I tried to get the truck going. I was able to crawl in the brush, under the truck, and I found a large stick between the gear shifting levers. I got the stick loose and was able to get the truck out as the fire crept within just a few feet of the fire truck.

While this occurred, I saw shadows emerging from the smoke and darkness. To my surprise, there were probably a dozen figures coming out of the smoke, in the middle of the woods. I remember the images looked like a scene out of the movie *The Walking Dead*. Most of them were park employees, but some of them were regular civilians. Some of them were in flip flops, shorts and casual dress, smoking cigarettes, carrying beer and mixed drinks, armed with shovels and other fire tools. Seems my dispatcher had found all the employees I had been looking for. They were all at the local Mai Kai bar on Pensacola Beach. As the employees left the bar to come to the fire, some of the bar patrons followed them with the intent of helping save Naval Live Oaks. I can't describe the circus atmosphere at the time, but they were digging and chopping trying to slow the fire, going through motions not included in the wildland firefighting training. I then drove the fire truck back through the woods, again tearing the hell out of it, and got back to the parking area to refill the tank with water from the Gulf Breeze fire tanker. I was barely able to function from exhaustion, and the medics would not allow me to go back to the fire. I told them I didn't want to go back to the fire, but I really wanted to finish seeing the circus that the fire had created. Gulf Breeze fire department eventually got the fire out for the night.

As it turned out the next day, the fire was not really that big and intense as it seemed the night before and did not threaten much of the area. The fire the day before was the same fire that had been left smoldering under the peat and roots and fired up the next day. In fire procedures, the fire should have been patrolled for a few days, and a dirt fire line dug around the fire. This removed any fuels that could ignite if the fire started up again and smoldering and smoking fuels extinguished. Without the fire training and experience of wildland fire fighting, I had no clue. My supervisors, who were "real" Park Rangers, didn't know either, or weren't certified in Wildland Firefighting. In probably less than a week, wildland fire training was conducted at the park, and a few others and I were red-carded or certified as basic wildland firefighters. I went to a few big fires as a firefighter and gained a lot of experience in wildland fire fighting. I also attended the Federal Law Enforcement Training Center (FLETC) and trained and certified as a Wildland Fire Arson Investigator.

I figured out early, wildland firefighting was hard, dirty work, requiring strenuous hours in all types of terrain, traveling to all parts of the country, sleeping on the ground, in tool sheds, or any other place one could lie down. I recall loading on a bus leaving one fire and going to another that was close by. We were exhausted, so anywhere we could lie down to get a couple of minutes sleep was welcomed. We arrived at a large open field next to a resort, and the fire bosses decided we would sleep through the night and be fresh and ready for the fire the next day. It was dark and fire will usually go to sleep at dark also. There were probably a hundred firefighters on the buses. We relied on the expertise and knowledge of our fire bosses to keep us safe and we were supposed to trust their judgement. They had located this nice open flat field and pulled the buses over and we scrambled out onto the field to get a spot to sleep. We threw out our sleeping bags and had been asleep for only a short time, when 50 automatic water sprinklers came on and began drenching us. Before we could exit the field, it was as if we had been in a rainstorm. Seems our fire bosses we were supposed to trust had bedded us down on a golf course where the irrigation system was timed to come on in the middle of the night. The rest of the night was spent trying to get dried out while napping when we could. The next morning, we were treated to a great breakfast at a local restaurant, courtesy of the U.S. Government, in attempts to mitigate the disaster the night before. This made things better and we were refreshed and ready to get back on the fire.

As a young action junky, I jumped at the chance to go to the fires even knowing it was going to be hard work. The biggest fire I experienced was in Kettle Falls, Washington, in the Colville National Forest. This was in 1988 when the Yellowstone fires occurred. I hoped to be part of the Yellowstone fires, but drew the wrong cards, and I ended up at the National Forest. Even though I was a National Park Ranger, I was part of the federal inter-agency fire program. This included all the federal land management agencies. We were mixed with fire-fighters from Bureau of Land Management, Fish and Wildlife Service and U.S. Forest service and our assignments did not necessarily mean you would get to fight fires in your park or forest.

Jerry at Kettle Falls

The Kettle Falls fire was very difficult and routine. It was here I learned, action or not, I really didn't like going on 10-mile death hikes to get to the fire, working on a fire line all day in 120-degree temperatures and freezing my ass off at night, patrolling a smoldering fire. Because the fire camp was situated by a large creek, the temperature at night was naturally a lot colder. The fire camp was huge, with thousands of fire fighters coming and going. There were portable restaurants with hot food, and showers with hot water, but very few covered tents for sleeping. That meant sleeping out in the open in the freezing temperature. We had been camped along the creek for over a week and a sleeping tent came available for our crew. We were excited to move into a shelter. Our crew boss, who was an idiot, looking to put a feather in his hat, declined the tent and it was passed on to the next crew. Our crew boss tried to impress his supervisors that he had a "tough unit" and we could handle sleeping on the ground, out in the open, freezing temperatures. This guy had to have been chosen later and included in the NPS management team somewhere to assist in helping screw up the NPS, literally.

We stayed for another week or so and the temperatures on the fire line reached 120 degrees in the middle of the day, to freezing at night. Sleeping bags were distributed in the camp, and they came in large boxes. When I found out there were big boxes, I went and found me one and used it to sleep in. There were several big boxes throughout the camp, and it sort of looked like a homeless camp with people sleeping in them, but it did provide some shelter, keeping the morning dew from falling directly on you. When I arrived at the fire, it was only about 300 acres, but when I left, three weeks later, the fire was 300,000 acres and still growing as more, fresh fire crews rotated in. It was unbelievable the size of this fire and the money being spent on fighting these fires. During this fire, I remember three D-9 bulldozers used to build fire lines, burning up as fire overran them while the crew escaped.

To manage a fire this size, there was a lot of confusion as one could expect, trying to organize the resources needed to fight it. What didn't help was having an idiot, like our crew boss, who had very little experience, but was saddled with the responsibility to manage and supervise a fire crew. A fire crew was 18 to 20 firefighters, led by a crew boss. In the fire crew there were squad bosses, supervised by the crew boss, and they supervised from two or more firefighters. The fire crews were usually equipped with hand tools that were used to dig a fire line. The fire line was dug about three feet wide and into the mineral soil, removing all the fuel that could be ignited and catching rolling embers from inside the fire line. Once the fire line was completed, and depending on fire conditions, a backfire would be set to burn the fuel in the direction of the fire. The fires would come together, and the fuel would be reduced, and the fire could be managed better. Miles of these fire lines would be built, but due to the wind, terrain, and fuels, there would be a spark blown over the line and ignite a new fire. In mountainous terrain, the fire would most likely gain intensity because the fires would burn upslope and a raging fire could develop quickly. These direct attacks on these fires were very dangerous and many fire crews have been lost and killed that have been trapped in a wildfire. It was imperative the leadership in these fires were experienced and knowledgeable with experienced crew leaders.

Each crewman wore a yellow shirt and green pants that were Nomex or fire-retarded clothing with a helmet, goggles and a head lamp. Fire packs contained plenty of water and first aid supplies and each person had a fire shelter. The fire shelter was worn on the belt. If you had to deploy the shelter, it would unfold into a large aluminum tent and you would lie under it if you were trapped in a fire. It was called your "Shake and Bake" as you resembled a baked potato wrapped in aluminum foil, and it allowed the fire to burn over you, giving you a better chance of survival.

Each crew member was issued a hand tool, either a shovel or Pulaski. A Pulaski is a tool that has an axe head on one side and chopping hoe on the other. It's a lot heavier than a shovel, but more functional. It is very sharp, and the user is susceptible to serious injury from the sharp axe and hoe heads. The shovel, on the other hand, is very light and my choice for carrying for miles. Each person has a partner and the shovel and Pulaski would be traded out periodically and partners were to watch out for each other. There was one guy on the crew who loved using the Pulaski and didn't want to trade it out for a shovel. This was the guy I picked for my partner because I didn't want to have anything to do with the Pulaski. Me and this guy remained partners throughout the fire and he was very aggressive and carried more of the weight as we fought the fire.

One late night, we had been working a fire line where the fire had burned over an area. The fire had jumped the fire line and continued burning. Most of the fuel had been burned and all that was left was burned trees or snags that hadn't fallen. It was dark, dusty and sooty and we walked the burned fire line. You could hear trees falling all through the woods, but you didn't know where they were falling. The crew listened and looked for any sounds of a tree that may fall and if someone yelled tree, you would try to take cover. It was very unnerving as we walked through the area. My partner and I were the last two in line, when we heard a tree falling very close. Everyone scrambled to find cover and a large tree fell within feet between me and my partner. I had run forward to get away from the tree and I couldn't see my partner. We called for him and couldn't see anything from the ashes that the tree had spewed off the ground when it fell. I thought he had been crushed by the tree, but within a few minutes, he appeared. When the tree began falling, he ran the opposite way from the rest of the crew. We quickly assembled and finally got out of the area.

We arrived at a staging location one night to relieve a fire crew. My partner and I were assigned to take a five-gallon gas can to a portable pump somewhere out into the darkness. There were fire hoses laid out in all directions that went into the fire. We were to find the pump by following a fire hose that was several hundred yards into the fire. We walked the fire hose and found a maze of fire hoses, strewn all through the woods and they all looked the same. We continued searching for the pump carrying the five gallons of gasoline, hanging from a shovel handle we used to carry it with. We eventually came to the end of the fire hose and no pump. Somewhere further back, we had gotten on the wrong fire hose. We felt we were in the area of the pump .Carrying the 40 pounds of gasoline now felt like a 100 pounds, as we walked around trying to find the pump, in the dark, using only our headlamps for light. As we searched, I noticed we were in the middle of the fire that had burned out with smoldering snags and logs and we walked on an old logging road. It was obvious we were lost, and not only lost, but lost in an active forest fire that surrounded us, carrying five gallons of gasoline. My partner insisted we continue through the burning woods, and I insisted we were lost, and somebody would come to look for us. My partner decided he would keep going on the road, while I found a place to cuddle up and get some sleep, waiting on daylight, or someone to rescue me. We had ditched the gas can. I could see the dim light of my partner's headlamp fading away as he walked into the darkness. I sat for quite a while in the darkness, watching the fire embers across the hills and mountains. The fire had already burned over the area and there was no fuel left for a major fire to erupt and I was safe, up against an embankment.

It was eerily quiet with no sounds of any kind. The fire had lain down to sleep for the night, and the stars were shining brightly above the lingering smoke. The fire had cleared the area of all wildlife, so I wasn't going to be dinner for any bears, cougars or sasquatches. They were more interested in getting away from the fire than getting lunch. It was apparent I wasn't going to be rescued any time soon, and I settled in, looking into the darkness and the stillness of the night. I fell asleep, waking up at the crack of dawn. As the sun climbed over the mountains, I could see for miles, a burned forest with a lot of smoke and some burning snags and trees inside the fire area. Even though the fire had devastated the area, it was peaceful and quiet. The fire had kept the night warm and I had rested throughout the night. I decided to walk, trying to get back to my fire crew, and I headed back to where I thought I would find the fire hoses. I saw a vehicle way across the fire, heading in my direction. It was probably a couple of miles away from me and it disappeared as it went up and down the mountain, but it still headed toward me. I waited, and it finally topped a hill coming to me. My partner was in it and the driver was a division leader who was part of the overhead crew of the Incident Command. The Incident Command was the headquarters of the fire planning, and this guy was a division chief and part of the tactical planning. My partner had walked for miles and found this guy and they came back and rescued me and we went back and joined our fire crew. Ordinarily, you would think someone would have been concerned of our disappearance and how we got lost and where the hell was that gas can. I expected headlines in the paper that two fire-fighters were lost in the massive fire and search crews were exhausted looking for them. Come to find out, no one even knew we were gone for many hours. There was so much confusion, we just slipped back into our fire crew and carried on to the next debacle that would occur the next day.

We arrived early the next morning, by bus, to where we were let off to assemble and go back on the fire line. The fire had begun firing back up and crews tried to get around it and build more fire lines. Our idiot crew boss had instructions to go to a certain point and begin building a fire line. We marched off in single file down the hill, over a mountain, and back over the hill, and down the mountain, while our crew boss tried to comprehend and read the map he was given, to get to the location he was directed to. There was fire every-where and all around us, but he couldn't locate the position we were to be, so we just kept marching and looking, and trying to stay out of the fire's path. We must have marched 10 miles over several hours when we finally found the location we were directed to, to build a fire line. It turned out, we were within eyesight of the roadway where bus had let us off, and only a short distance away where we were to build the fire line. It took us so long to get there, the fire line was no longer needed in this location, so we marched back to the roadway and joined up with local fire tankers and firefighters, hanging around, doing nothing. We didn't get any more assignments that day. I don't know if it was because there was nothing planned, or the Incident Command decided they wouldn't take a chance of getting a fire crew led by an idiot be killed. After that, we didn't get any more direct attack assignments, and went into areas where mop ups occurred. Mop ups were boring, as the crew walked up and down the fire line looking for smoldering or smoking snags, logs, or other burning fuels that may escape the burned-out areas. It didn't take much expertise to walk around a given area that had been burned over, and definitive fire lines were already in, so even an idiot crew boss could supervise.

I remember vividly the day the Forest Service burned up a pickup truck that was used by a fire scout. The night before, my crew patrolled a burned-out area as mop up, looking for any signs of smoke or heat. Even though the temperatures were 120 degrees during the day, at night it was cold as hell, and we mostly just sat around the fire line, doing nothing, as the fire was extinguished. Our Strike Team Leader looked out for the crews. He brought a big coffee pot and built a big fire at the end of a cul-de-sac and made coffee for the crew. We took turns as squads, sitting around, having hot coffee during the night. Come daylight, we left and went back to the fire camp.

The Strike Team leader also left. Then comes the fire scout, early in the morning, to clear the area by scouting around the fire line, double checking for fire. When he returned to his vehicle, it was burned to the ground. Seems he parked his vehicle, with the tires on the hot coals from the night before, where the coffee fire had been burning. When everyone left, there was just dirt thrown on it, and the fire and coals were not visible. I often wonder if someone got their ass chewed out for anything, but in these fires, the vehicle was just like losing a shovel.

Colville Fire

After three weeks, I returned to the Gulf Islands National Seashore, with ample experience to use when Naval Live Oaks burned again.

10

Grave Diggers

*G*ulf Islands National Seashore was rich in cultural and historic resources. Pensacola was one of the earliest settlements, inhabited by the Spanish. There was also a large settlement of Native Americans that inhabited the Naval Live Oaks area. The large trees gave them shelter and the area was rich in seafood. There were numerous Indian Mounds or shell middens in the Naval Live Oaks. These middens were basically a dump site where waste and trash were piled up by the Native American settlements. These sites included pottery shards, lots of oyster shells, animal bones, and other debris. By the time the Seashore was established, most of these sites were destroyed as poachers dug up the sites and got whatever they could find. Most of the damage to the sites had occurred before the Seashore was established, and when the poachers realized the penalties for digging up these artifacts, the activities subsided.

The famous Indian, Geronimo, was also a resident of the National Seashore. Geronimo was brought to Ft. Pickens where he was supposedly held as a prisoner in one of the fort rooms. Apparently, he was not a prisoner, but was free to roam about the fort and sunbathe on the beaches. He was an ambassador of the area at the time. People liked getting their picture taken with Geronimo and collected a souvenir from Fort Pickens.

According to the State Park Rangers who administered Ft. Pickens prior to the National Seashore, they had a large brick pile they had to move. Rather than picking up the bricks and hauling them off, they made a sign that stated "Geronimo was held captive in the fort" where the bricks were piled. Tourists would steal a brick, thinking it was from Geronimo's cell, thus moving the brick pile for the State Park. I don't think this is archived in the history of the fort, but I am sure it did occur as I spoke with the original State Park employees regularly while I was with the Coast Guard. I am sure they would not have moved a brick unless it was necessary.

Gulf Islands National Seashore had a rich history of Civil War activities. There were two graves at the Naval Live Oaks area, where a Union soldier and a Confederate soldier were supposed to be buried. Somehow, some kids from the local City of Gulf Breeze found the graves and dug up one of them, stealing the artifacts in the grave. I was told by one of our historians, the soldiers may have been buried with their rifles. The graves were not marked and had been overtaken by vegetation.

When I got to the area, all I found was a hole about two feet deep in the sand, where there had been recent digging. I found pieces of pewter handles that had been on a casket, a button from a Civil War uniform, and pieces of charcoal in the hole. It seems, the soldiers buried at that time were burned in the caskets due to yellow fever. There were no more artifacts I could find, and I didn't perform an archeological survey or dig any further. I didn't find any bones or any indications there may have been a body there, so I left, unable to find any evidence that would lead to the people who dug the hole.

There was nothing to go on, and after a couple of days it was pretty much forgotten. Apparently, this grave digging was the talk of the community. I was in Hardees restaurant in Gulf Breeze, and an individual sitting behind me asked if I had found the persons who dug up the grave in Naval Live Oaks. When I turned around, the person had a newspaper, holding it up, covering his face, like a gangster movie informant, trying to hide his identity. He proceeded to tell me where I could find the persons responsible, but gave me minimal information, and didn't describe any certain treasures that were taken. He did give me an address that was in Gulf Breeze on Dolphin Street. It was a pretty strange encounter, and I was apprehensive any of the information was credible. I went to the address where I located a middle-aged husband and wife in an affluent neighborhood. When they came to the door, I identified myself as Park Ranger. (I was still a Park Technician, but they didn't know any better.) I asked them if they knew anything about the grave digging at Naval Live Oaks, as a witness had given me their address, implicating their involvement. They were perplexed by my question and replied they knew nothing. They had a son about 15 years old, and they called him to the door.

The father sternly asked the son if he knew anything about the grave digging and the son replied he and some of his friends had dug up the grave. The kids responsible were all juveniles and there was no litigation that would be brought against them. I told them all I was interested in was getting back any artifacts they had taken and figured they may have the rifle. The father instructed the kid to get the artifacts and the son went into the house and returned with a large paper sack. I was sure they had gotten a mother lode of artifacts by the size of the big Delchamps grocery bag. He handed me the sack. It was a shocking find when I opened it. The mother and father watched me as I pulled out the artifact, and it was none other than the well-preserved Confederate or Union soldier's skull. The mother shrieked, the father grabbed her, and I was shocked myself. There was nothing else in the sack and the kid said they did not find anything else in the grave. They had located the grave by using a metal detector and I assumed that detected the pewter, nails and metal buttons. They had no knowledge of any rifles buried with the soldier, and it was happenstance they found the grave to begin with. There was no indication any rifles or any other artifacts were in the grave without further excavation. We didn't have anyone interested or experienced to do an archaeological dig. Archeologists wanted to be paid when they were called to dig up something and there was no funding for it, so no further evaluation and excavation of the site was done.

This was a pretty shocking discovery. I took the skull back to the Ranger Station where I did some research and determined it was possible it was the Confederate soldier's skull because of the button I had found in the grave confirming it was from a Confederate soldier's uniform. If this discovery was made today, it would be massive national news coverage. Every archaeologist in the country would descend on the Seashore putting out little yellow flags, closing the schools and highways and arming themselves with a toothbrush and a teaspoon, anxious to start digging. There was no news coverage and only a quiet conversation concerning the find with a few park employees. I sort of became attached to the soldier, riding him in my patrol car while I did the investigation. I found myself having a conversation with him and I gave him a name that I can't recall.

It was late at night and I was alone in the old Coast Guard Ranger station with the soldier, while I finished my report. I had the soldier sitting on my desk as I prepared the report. It was very quiet in the old 100-year Coast Guard station (which was eerie with its own resident boogers). I tried to type and have a conversation with the soldier, but the quietness and solitude overwhelmed me, and I couldn't focus on the report. I remember looking around and the soldier's skull, which sat on my desk behind me, stared at me while I typed. I can remember getting a chill and I turned the guy around, facing the wall, so I could finish my report. We didn't have any more conversations after that, and when I finished my report, I put the soldier's head in his big Delchamps grocery bag and set it beside my desk and left.

The next day, I came to work and found the soldier in his bag, sitting next to my desk where I had left him. There was no indication he had left through the night. There were no more conversations and no ceremonies, and the case was closed. I didn't have time to bury the soldier that day and I asked one of our maintenance guys, Abe, to come to the Ranger Station. Abe worked at the seashore for many years as the garbage collector in the maintenance department. He had also seen many of the haunts around Ft. Pickens and was no stranger to the boogers that frequented Ft. Pickens, including the woman wearing a long white dress, riding a big white horse around the Fort at night.

He had no idea about the soldier. I was going to ask him to take the soldier back to his grave and bury him. When I pulled the soldier's skull from the bag, Abe freaked out. After he calmed down, he agreed to take the soldier back to his grave. Abe placed the soldier's skull back into the shallow grave and covered it back up. It's been 40-plus years since this occurred. For many years, when I was on patrol, I went to the grave site and reflected on the activities that occurred in the area at the time the soldier was buried there. To my knowledge, no one knows where the grave site is, as it is unmarked. If any archeologist ever digs up the grave, they are going to be perplexed wondering if this soldier tried to escape the grave with his skull buried upright and very shallow. I often wonder if the Union soldier is there as well. I can still find the grave after all these years and I sometimes think just how cool it was to be this close and personal to a real Confederate soldier.

***

Abe worked in maintenance and oversaw the restrooms in the campground. The restrooms were divided with an open partition in the center where the plumbing pipes were. At the end of the restrooms was a doorway leading into the access area. The restrooms were old and there were holes in the walls where the plumbing fixtures protruded. If you looked in the holes, all you would see would be the dark plumbing pipes. That is, unless Abe was behind the walls looking into the showers and restrooms. We had a couple of campers arrive in the campground with a small baby. They were destitute and indigent. Soon after these campers arrived, they decided to take a shower. This was in the middle of the morning. The male camper was in the shower and noticed the holes in the plumbing. He looked through holes and thought he would see his wife in the women's shower. Instead, he saw two eyes staring back at him. He ran out of the shower and Abe ran out of the restroom, but the visitor saw him. The visitor gave pursuit as Abe left the campground. He chased Abe to the Ranger Station, where Abe locked himself inside. The visitor pointed an old single barrel shotgun at the Ranger Station. Abe screamed on the radio for me. "112, 112, I need some help." I was on the beach in a jeep and it was slow for me to respond as Abe screamed on the radio. I got to the Ranger Station and observed the visitor with the shotgun. I had no clue what had happened except this person was not supposed to have a shotgun. I jumped out of the jeep using the jeep for cover, drawing my trusty .38 caliber Ruger, and screamed at the subject to put the gun down. The subject yelled back, telling me he was going to kill the SOB. After a few minutes I was able to convince the subject to put the gun down and I arrested him.

***

This incident began an episode that only the National Park Service management could concoct. The park management covered up this incident like they did with the Ranger breaking into vehicles at the seashore. It was a fact Abe peeked in the restrooms and was caught. After investigating the visitor's complaint and Abe's admission, it was clear Abe was a peeping tom. The management of the Park did not want to have the incident exposed and tried to protect Abe, even though he had committed a major violation. Because of the visitor's indigent and destitute status, it was decided by the management to offer the visitor a deal. In exchange for free camping, there would be no charges or complaint filed against Abe. The park would allow them to stay in the campground without paying any fees, to give them the opportunity to find a job and a place to stay. This idiotic plan was soon to backfire.

***

After several days, there were complaints in the campground that the infant was lying on a blanket, on the ground, with no shelter, and had ants crawling on it. It was very hot and humid. The only shelter was their small, two-seat sports car, where the child would sleep at night. The couple had no food for the infant and solicited money and food from the other campers, who in turn complained of the couple's destitute status. The only asset the couple had, besides the car, was the old, single barrel shotgun, which I had confiscated, and part of the "deal" was to return it to him when he left the park. He made a deal with the campground store concessionaire to trade the shotgun to him in exchange for food for them and their infant. The old shotgun was worth about two bags of potato chips, but the concessionaire felt sorry for them and traded quite a bit of food and supplies in exchange for the shotgun.

This deal was unbelievable. Had I not been there and witnessed all of this, I would not believe the story to be true. Being in possession of the shotgun in the park was a violation of the law to start with. Threatening a federal employee at gun point was definitely prohibited. Because the visitor had the park over a barrel by not pursuing charges of criminal actions against an employee, the visitor pretty much called the shots. And he was not leaving any time soon.

After the deal by the concessionaire, I became a principal to the crime of possessing a firearm in the National park, by facilitating the exchange of the gun to the concessionaire, for the groceries. You just can't make this stuff up.

***

For several days we agonized over the presence of the two visitors and the infant, knowing we were hostage. Complaints from other campers were reported because of the infant's care. As much as I hated to, I went and checked on the infant one day. The infant was lying on a blanket and it had numerous insect bites from the ants and other bugs. It was clear this had to stop. I contacted the Florida Child Services and reported this to them, and a counselor came to the campground and observed the condition of the child. The counselor went back to get a protective court order to seize the child, and returned a short time later.

I was to meet the counselor at the entrance of the park and go with him to the campground, where he would take custody of the child. As we approached the campground the subjects headed out of the park. We turned around and caught up to the subjects and I stopped them in the roadway. I had no back-up except the counselor, and when he presented them with the court order to take the child, all hell broke loose.

The counselor tried to take the child and the subjects began fighting with the counselor. I fought the male subject in the road, while the counselor tried to get the baby away from the mother. A motorist stopped in the road and tried to assist me in controlling the situation. I eventually got the subject handcuffed, while he and the mother and the baby screamed. It was a very intense and emotional time. The counselor took the infant, while I had to handle the parents. After several minutes, the parents calmed down, while the motorist tried to assist me. The counselor left with the child. After the parents had calmed, I released them. They left and were able to negotiate the return of their child after a day or so and they left the area.

The interest of the management of the National Park had somehow prevailed in an illegal and unprecedented case that allowed several employees, including me, to become principals in violating the law. As the years passed, I witnessed many questionable management practices that violated procedures and the law.

11

_____

Snakes Alive!

*T*hings around the seashore were usually routine but I was still excited to be a Park Ranger. Working on the beach had become my home for many years. Although the pay was sad, working as a taxidermist offset my financial difficulties.

Early Patrol Vehicle

Law enforcement activities increasingly got more intense and dangerous. There were suicides, a couple murders, lots of burglaries, serious vehicle accidents and lots of intoxication problems. The

Rangers handled most of the minor instances and minor vehicle accidents, but due to the legislative Proprietary jurisdiction, the major crimes were handled by the local authorities or the FBI. We were still substandard in training and equipment and lacked support from the management of the National Park Service to recognize us as law enforcement officers. We still drove 4-cylinder K-cars that were built in the 70s and early 80s as "energy efficient" commuter type vehicles.

Radio communications were barely minimal with Law Enforcement Rangers sharing the radio with the maintenance and other divisions within the park. To get back-up or emergency medical assistance, we got the dispatcher (who might be anyone near a telephone) and they called by telephone to our local agencies for assistance. Sometimes when an emergency occurred, I couldn't get through on the radio due to the maintenance staff talking about cleaning a restroom and needing more toilet paper. One may think this is exaggeration, but it is a fact.

I enjoyed the free rein and being able to patrol the seashore where there were plenty of activities to keep me busy. The wildlife consisted of racoons, skunks, foxes or other small animals. Every now and then, an alligator washed out of the rivers and ended up on the beach. Snakes were also on the seashore, where the canals had lots of moccasins and water snakes. Eastern diamondback rattle snakes were also numerous, with some of them reaching six feet in length. All the wildlife was protected, including the snakes.

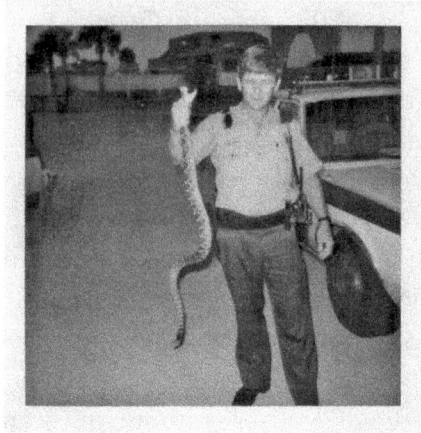

Ranger Grubb relocating a diamond back rattlesnake from Ft. Pickens Campground

Right before I was hired as a Ranger at the Seashore, while I was still in the Coast Guard, a park visitor from Georgia encountered a large diamondback rattlesnake crossing the road and he ran over it with his car several times and killed it. Not only did he kill it, he reported he killed it to a seasonal Park Ranger. When the Ranger got there, he proceeded to write the guy a ticket for killing wildlife in the park. The guy became very upset in getting the ticket and thought he was doing everyone a favor by killing the large rattlesnake. The National Park Service had its rules, but so did a rural country boy from Georgia. That rule would be killing every snake that crossed your path. Being from rural Georgia, it's just instinct to kill all snakes, and the visitor, I am sure, did not know the snakes were protected in the National Parks. If this would have been a person he had killed, there would not have been much news reported. This incident became national news and the National Park Service tried to do damage control to mitigate the incident. The superintendent had a new fishing boat and he was out for the day when he was called to come and meet a barrage of reporters. He tied the boat to the Coast Guard dock, and I met him and walked with him to my vehicle where I took him to his office. The superintendent was livid over the incident and pissed that the

Ranger had written this guy a ticket and it had turned into national news.

The local Chamber of Commerce got involved because the guy threatened "never to come to the area again" and all the negative news reported the Pensacola area was no place to come unless you wanted to get arrested for a trivial matter as killing a snake. The Chamber of Commerce appeased this guy by paying for another vacation to the Pensacola area. However, the Ranger was right in writing the ticket because of the Federal Codes that protected everything in the park. The superintendent had no choice but to back his Ranger, even though he thought it should have been handled differently. The story remained in the news for several weeks before it finally went away. Even though the seasonal Ranger had done his job, for some reason, he never landed another job with the National Park Service.

If a snake or other nuisance animal got into the campground or around people, we would catch it and relocate it in a remote area away from the people. It looked good when we caught a snake or other animal and told the visitors we were going to relocate it, although they didn't have a clue we took the critter less than a half mile and released it, for it to return to where we caught it. We didn't have any Resource Management Specialist to supervise and monitor the environmental aspect of the seashore for many years. If an incident happened, the Rangers took care of it in any way possible. We became wildlife specialists on our own. Today, the National Seashore includes many turtle whisperers, bird counters, and numerous environmentalists such as wildlife specialists and other science related divisions. They study and deal with everything from the three-toed Perdido Key Dune mouse to sea turtles, and a wide range of invasive threats to a variety of natural and cultural resources.

I had been given a Park Ranger title somewhere down the line from a Park Technician. There weren't any ceremonies, pay raises, special training, or headlines in the papers or news media when this had happened. As a Park Ranger, the visitors and other agencies expected you to know everything about anything. I had been a

Ranger for two to three years when I got a call of a large sea turtle laying eggs next to the Holiday Inn on Pensacola Beach. The turtle had come up on the beach and made a nest within 30 feet of the boardwalk steps. This was quite a distance from the seashore jurisdiction. It created a huge spectacle as the turtle tried to get her eggs laid with all the people crowded around her. At this time, there were no turtle rescue centers or turtle whisperers or anyone who knew or cared about the sea turtles. If this occurred today, the entire beach would be closed off, there would be 24-hour monitoring, with sea turtle midwives brought in to assist in the delivery of the turtles. There were Florida Marine Patrol officers assigned to the area and they responded to the turtle call that was in their jurisdiction. Unbeknownst to me, the title Marine Patrol was just that. A title with no expertise, sort of like a Park Technician turned Park Ranger. One of the officers called me to come and assist them in removing the turtle eggs from the beach because it was right next to the Holiday Inn boardwalk, a very congested area, and the nest would be trampled and destroyed. When I got there the chore of handling the turtle was turned over to me, because the Marine Patrol officer had absolutely no clue what to do with the turtle eggs.

I did not know anything about it either, but I had read a little about the sea turtles and found they cried while they laid their eggs. Sure enough, when I got down and looked at her eyes, she was crying. I was amazed I had gotten to see a sea turtle this close. I was intrigued at the size of it, and watched it cry, but I found out later, they weren't crying but getting the sea water out of their eyes while they laid their eggs. We had no sea turtle whisperers to confirm this at the time, but as far as I was concerned, she was crying. I had read somewhere, when the turtle came onto the shore to lay the eggs, the eggs had to be removed and relocated to a safer location other than on a congested beach, where they would certainly be destroyed.

The turtle was about the size of my Datsun pick-up, and finished laying her eggs, covered the nest and lumbered inch by inch back into the Gulf of Mexico. I got a large Styrofoam cooler from my house and went back and uncovered the nest. I don't remember if someone told me, or I remembered from hatching chickens, you marked the eggs where they were positioned in the nest, upright, to avoid drowning the embryo. Anyway, I was careful removing the eggs from the nest, marking each egg, and carefully placing it in the cooler, placing sand around them. There must have been over a hundred eggs in the nest. After I got them removed, I took them back to the beach across from the Coast Guard Station, dug a hole and placed them back in the sand. I didn't have a clue as to how long it would take the eggs to hatch, or if they would, in fact, hatch at all. It didn't matter much at all at the time if they hatched, but the people on the beach were impressed that a Park Ranger knew so much about seas turtles and rescued them from the danger of being trampled or destroyed.

I occasionally checked on the nest, but never observed the eggs hatch. After a couple of months, I gave up on them, and one day, I saw where it looked like the nest was disturbed. The disturbance appeared to be a day or two old, and I couldn't tell if they had hatched or a racoon or other critter had disturbed the nest. I dug into the nest and found pieces of shell, along with eggs that didn't hatch and concluded some of the eggs may have hatched, but there was no way to determine how many made it. I later read that a relocated sea turtle nest has about 60% hatching success, so I figured if I assisted the turtle population and got any eggs to hatch, it would have been miracle turtle births. Now there are turtle scientists, turtle rescue responders, turtle hotlines, and it's a big production in handling and monitoring sea turtles. I just hope I didn't alter the genetics and behavior by taking the eggs from the mother who cried painfully, laying her eggs, and is now searching the ocean floor for her babies over at the Holiday Inn rather than over by the Coast Guard Station.

I tried to focus on being a real Park Ranger and doing other things besides law enforcement. There were not many resource projects in the park because of the lack of expertise and the lack of funding. The focus was on visitor enjoyment, protection, maintaining order in the campground, and collecting fees to enter the park. The Ft. Pickens campground was inherited when it was converted from a state park. It was a popular campground, and stayed full almost every day of the spring, summer and early fall. Most of the camp sites had electricity, with bathhouses, and there were other camp sites for primitive or tent camping. Anyone staying in the campground in the early days when it was full may have had to camp in the Fun in the Sun camp sites where there were no trees and nothing more than a parking place to pitch a tent in the sand and sand spurs. These sites were hot.

One winter, I decided I would plant some trees in the campground and especially in the Fun in the Sun sites. Back then, there was no specialist in the park and no impact studies, and no money to fund these projects. Slash pine trees were native on the island with stands of the pines throughout the park. Black Water State Forest was located close by and they had a nursery where they cultivated pine seedlings. I contacted the forestry supervisor and he supplied me with a couple thousand seedlings, at no cost. The only thing standing in the way of me establishing a forest was one of the maintenance supervisors. He was adamantly against me putting out these seedlings because maintenance would have to mow around them in the campground. I thought it to be a pretty lame excuse and my supervisors didn't say anything, so I went ahead with my project, putting out at least a thousand seedlings in the Ft. Pickens campground. The maintenance supervisor was pissed because I planted the trees, but I was friends with the maintenance chief, and he helped keep the maintenance supervisor in check. It was hard to get these babies to live from the thousands of campers stomping around, lawn mowers, and environmental hazards.

There were several hundred of them that survived for about 25 years, growing upwards of 80 feet, providing shade for the campground, and other environmental benefits. Then along came a large hurricane, and all the trees standing on the islands were flooded by saltwater, causing them to die. Only a few of the planted trees remained in the campground, but for years, they provided for a better camping experience and gave me a sense of pride, creating my own National Park Forest, that was unofficially named after me. In the years to come, some tree planting continued. This was after the seashore established professionals with science degrees and not to forget, college education. Before they could be planted, there would have to be environmental impact studies, soil studies, and archeological studies, and approved by a long list of other experts, to get the same results I got, and where another hurricane would destroy the trees again.

At the onset of the National Seashore, there were very few experts assigned to monitor the resources of the newly formed park. In the beginning, there were efforts to protect the seashore's natural environment. Dune preservation was a top priority. Law enforcement campaigns stopped vehicles and pedestrians from destroying the dunes and harvesting the sea oats that, at the time, were sought out for florist's decorations. Some of the dunes were 40 to 50 feet high, prior to the 1979 hurricane Frederick that leveled the dunes and destroyed the vegetation. Vehicles had been allowed to drive on the beaches and dunes and quickly destroyed what took nature many years to produce.

It was difficult at the onset to get compliance from some of the good ole boys with dune buggies and pick-ups who had abused the beaches and dunes for years. The beaches were sugar white sand, stretching for miles. The Florida districts of Gulf Islands National Seashore were broken into four different areas: Fort Pickens and Santa Rosa were divided by Pensacola Beach, which is a popular, developed tourist destination. Further east was the Okaloosa area where there was only a small picnic and day use area. West of Ft. Pickens, across the inlet to Pensacola Bay, was the Perdido Key area. In the beginning, that area was called Johnson Beach. Johnson Beach had been owned by Escambia County, and the county named the beach after a black soldier killed in the Korean War. When Gulf Islands National Seashore was formed, Johnson Beach and a portion of undeveloped land was purchased to form the Perdido Key area of the Gulf Islands National Seashore.

By the mid 1980s, more resource management was introduced to Gulf Islands, and we got our first Resource Management expert.

Actually, the expert was a political appointed position with no science background, but he coordinated with the real scientist, making sure the policies and procedures were followed.

One of the duties was the restoration of the Perdido Key dune mouse that was becoming extinct. The Perdido Key dune mouse looks identical to the Santa Rosa dune mouse but with genetics that makes them different. Regardless of what they look like, no one would ever see them to begin with because they were nocturnal, only coming out at night. If they became active in daylight, they would be eaten by sea gulls and other daytime predators, even though they were white and camouflaged by the white sand.

The Perdido Key dune mouse was later called the Perdido Three-Toe mouse. When the mouse was captured and counted, they looked just like their cousin across the inlet and a quick DNA test couldn't be done to determine the difference, so the mouse lost a toe so they could be identified later when caught again. Because the habitat loss on the Perdido Key, the mouse was becoming extinct. There were a lot of predators that feasted on the mice, like feral cats, skunks, and the red fox.

Ranger Mike Farley was the Perdido Key Ranger. Because Perdido Key was across the bay and out of the way, there was little interference by park management. It was strange that the island was named Perdido. Perdido means "lost" and would be incidental that it identified Ranger Farley, the dune mouse, and most everything associated with Perdido Key. Being lost was a good thing because you would be the furthest away from 'hindquarters' and would be forgotten for most of the year.

When the scientists converged on Perdido Key, Ranger Farley was saddled with monitoring the dune mouse project, catching or killing the red foxes and feral cats that feasted on the little dune mouse. Capturing red foxes proved to be difficult. The foxes had apparently studied Wiley Coyote's Acme training manuals, and no foxes were trapped. Different types of traps and baits were used, along with different scents to attract them, but Wiley Coyote's manuals were effective for the foxes.

I had killed several red foxes when I hunted them, back in my earlier days. The red fox could be called by a predator call. The call resembled a dying rabbit and the foxes quickly identified where the call came from. I only had a short time to aim and shoot. The young foxes came straight to the call without hesitation, but older foxes would circle the area, staying obscured until they were comfortable there was a meal available. I suggested we try this, and I began to hunt the foxes. The island was five-and-a-half miles long, and I took the ATV down the beach where I could cover more ground. I set up in the dunes, where I could see for a hundred yards and see the foxes slipping around investigating where the call came from. To kill them, you need a large caliber rifle with a scope. The island was desolate in the winter and there were no visitors around. There was ample dune protection to stop a stray bullet.

The first day proved effective and I think I killed two. I brought them back and Ranger Farley put them in a freezer. I repeated the hunt several times and killed red foxes like the Resource Management gurus wanted. Then, they found out how I killed them, and I was restricted to many government oversights in how the foxes would be shot. I used my .270 caliber rifle, where I could make a good, clean kill. I didn't think about checking their plumbing, how fat or skinny they were, or if they were old or young. In true government fashion, rules were made for the proper protocol for killing foxes.

First off, I could not take the ATV on the beach to get to where I could find the foxes, even though we used the ATVs for patrols on the beach. Then, I had to use a small caliber .22 rifle that was ineffective, even if you could hit one. A checklist was kept identifying each sex, age, and hours that would be allowed to hunt the foxes. Needless to say, no more foxes were killed, and I wouldn't be a part of the Perdido Key dune mouse project that was soon compromised after Hurricane Fredrick flooded the island and all the little tunnels the mice used in the dunes. Being a part of these projects was very interesting and gave us a break from law enforcement that consumed most of our time. Even though we weren't scientists, we were quasi-scientists because we were Park Rangers, which meant we were a jack-of-all-trades and a master of none.

In the coming years, the parks got college-educated Park Rangers with specialty degrees, studying everything that moved or crawled in the National Parks. As a result, the traditional Park Ranger would only protect the species and have very little involvement in the actual Resource Management division activities.

Horn and Ship Islands were barrier islands in the Gulf of Mexico, in the Mississippi District of Gulf Islands National Seashore. Both the islands were designated as Wilderness areas of the seashore because of the uncommon birds, wildlife, and remoteness. The islands, at the time, were scarcely visited and visitors were brought to the islands by tour boats. There were few facilities on the island when I was there, with a small cabin on Horn Island, where the Rangers would stay. In the mid 1980s, an eagle hatching project began on Horn Island. A large tower, about 30 feet high, was erected. The tower consisted of a cage to contain the hatched eagles, a platform and an observation room. The eagles were half grown and needed to be fed throughout the day. It was imperative the eagles would not see humans and were fed by a puppet. We had convinced one Ranger we had to wear a chicken suit to feed the chicks and he wouldn't be able to participate because he couldn't fit in the suit. He was depressed when we told him, but he soon found out there was no chicken suit.

Rangers were assigned and took turns staying on the island for a week, where we fished all day. We used gill nets or cast nets to catch fish to feed the baby eagles. After the hard work of net fishing was done and the babies fed, I resorted to fishing for myself. Pretty unbelievable I had a job where I got paid to fish all day. The pay was lousy in the beginning of my career, but participating in a variety of activities, going on special details, enjoying the natural environment, and being part of history was a special time. There weren't any overbearing supervisors, and opportunities were given to enhance the enjoyment of being a Ranger. The laid-back atmosphere at the Mississippi District had come to an end, and I went back to my regular routine at Fort Pickens.

I always reveled at the chance to get a special detail in another park because each park had its own unique history and purpose. If a problem occurred that needed extra law enforcement security, we could get lucky and be selected to participate. One of my fondest memories was participating in a law enforcement detail at Independence National Historic Park. This detail was in the late 1980s and there was extra security needed where people protested where a Congressional delegation was held. The event was nothing special and nothing significant occurred. The highlight of the event allowed me to travel to the Independence Hall, which I had visited almost 20 years earlier. Back in 1970, on my way to Coast Guard boot camp in Cape May, New Jersey, I traveled through Philadelphia, where I spent the day, waiting on a bus to pick me up. I managed to wander into one of the buildings. I had no clue where I was, and I remember the building turned out to be Independence Hall. The doors were unlocked and when I went inside the place, it was decorated with displays depicting the American Revolution. There wasn't anyone around and it was amazing that all these displays were not secured nor the doors locked. In one of the rooms, I found the Liberty Bell displayed. There were no barriers around it and you could walk around it and touch it. I remember trying to reach around the bell, sticking my finger in the crack, and just hanging around for a few minutes. The bell wouldn't last 20 minutes today if it was left unsecured.

Now, 20 years later, I returned to Independence Hall as a National Park Ranger and the Liberty Bell was encased in a glass display on the Independence Mall. It was my job to provide security and greet visitors as I reflected on the days where I actually touched the Bell. The Mall was now crowded with thousands of protestors and people. Quite different from my first encounter with the area. This was just another moment of being a National Park Ranger that was special to me.

12

Tragic Accident

I encountered more difficult situations as I worked nights and visitation at the seashore grew. I still had my trusty .38 caliber Ruger six shooter. Bullet proof vests were available, but expensive, and the management of the seashore would not purchase any vests for us. I was concerned enough for my safety, I bought my own personal bullet proof vest which, at the time, was called a "Second Chance" vest. The vest was bulky, one size fits all, but they were effective. The main concern was getting your weapon taken and used against you, and the vest would stop a .38 caliber bullet, especially the rat shot I carried in my gun. I was also able to get a portable radio from the Sheriff's department where I could talk directly with a real emergency dispatcher. These radios were older radios that had been upgraded by the Sheriff's office, and through some friends of the department, I was able to get one. Our patrol vehicles were being upgraded in the early 80's, getting larger vehicles that were getting markings, identifying our vehicles as emergency police type vehicles lettered with PARK RANGER, with upgraded emergency lighting, sirens, and prisoner cages. We no longer drove patrol cars that looked like they had come off a used car lot.

Vehicle accidents in the seashore were plentiful. There were several accidents that included fatalities that were handled by the Florida Highway Patrol who maintained jurisdiction in the park. Park Rangers handled all the minor vehicle accidents. Fort Pickens Road, in the seashore, was about 7 miles in length. It was a straight, desolate road, and excessive speed on the roadway was not uncommon. Late one night, there was a horrific crash on Ft. Pickens Road. I worked alone when I got the call and was only about two miles from the crash. I arrived within minutes and the carnage I witnessed was unbelievable. A crash like this would be common had it been on an interstate or a large highway, but on this road, it was something one would not expect. There had been crashes that had killed people on the roadway, east of Pensacola Beach, in the Santa Rosa area of the park, but they were usually single vehicle crashes.

This time, the crash included two separate crashes together, five vehicles involved, nine victims seriously injured, with one fatality. When I arrived, one of the vehicles was on fire. There was oil and fluids running out of the overturned vehicle. I quickly got a fire extinguisher from my patrol car, but before I could get to the fire, it miraculously went out on its own. I ran up to the passenger side of the vehicle, which was a van, and an individual was crushed and trapped in the passenger seat. The seat back was broken and the individual's legs were crushed, pinning him in the wreckage. I cannot forget the gruesome image as this individual tried to sit up in the seat. It was complete horror with his face covered in blood and he looked straight at me, as I told him I was trying to get him out of the vehicle. Within seconds, the individual fell back onto the seat, where he died as a result of his injuries. Every so often I still remember that horrific image that was ingrained into my mind, almost 40 years ago. These kinds of things, whether you like it or not, will stay with you and be triggered by the least little thing, jogging your memory. As a Park Ranger, or any other emergency worker or law enforcement officer, this is a given and part of the job. In the early days of my career, there was no such thing as CISD (Critical Incident Stress Debriefing) and you bit the bullet and went on with the job. Nowadays, if someone cuts their finger or knew someone who had cut their finger, there must be counseling.

There were seven juveniles in the van, and it had overturned several times. The back of the van had no seats and all the occupants had been either sitting on the floor or on a cooler, unrestrained. There were several other occupants inside the overturned van who were unconscious. All the occupants of the van suffered injury and trauma as a result of the crash. My adrenaline was over capacity as I tried to get this scene managed and get rescue, medical vehicles, and more law enforcement assistance. The occupants of the other vehicles sustained no injuries and the focus was on the van in getting the injured taken care of. I had very little vehicle accident training, dealing mostly with minor vehicle accidents. This was an unprecedented crash and required a lot of expertise. I immediately contacted the Florida Highway Patrol for assistance. All the emergency services in the area responded, including Life Flight medical helicopter. I remember a bystander walking around with a 35mm camera taking pictures. I didn't have a camera, so I commandeered the camera from the bystander and began snapping pictures. Meanwhile, emergency services and more law enforcement personnel arrived. My supervisor arrived and was of little help as he didn't know any more than I did.

The Florida Highway Patrol officer arrived as I snapped pictures. The officer told me he could not help me because it was in the National Park jurisdiction. It was, without a doubt, in his jurisdiction and responsibility to investigate this crash, but he declined. No one would assume responsibility in investigating and left it up to me to take care of it. Meanwhile, all the victims were transported to local hospitals by either ambulance or helicopter. But I could not account for one of the victims. After many times of counting victims who were being transported by various medical ambulances and helicopters, I still came up short one victim. There were two victims in an ambulance at the scene who were conscious, and I went to the ambulance to talk with them. I was met at the doorway of the ambulance by an emergency worker who told me I couldn't talk with the victims in the ambulance due to the trauma they had suffered. I explained to the worker I was the investigator of the crash and I was going to talk with them, and he again blocked me from entering the ambulance. My adrenaline was over the top and when he interfered with me entering the ambulance, I grabbed the fat ass about belt level and jerked him out on the ground and yelled to him I was going to put his ass in jail if he interfered. I guess he realized he had pissed me off and got out of my way.

I interviewed the two victims and they helped me account for everyone in the van. We drew a diagram where everyone sat in the van with their names and after trying to account for everyone transported to the hospitals, one kept coming up short. By now all the emergency vehicles and other agencies left the scene and left me to investigate the crash. I was completely lost trying to put this together. My college-educated Park Ranger supervisor left, telling me to "just take care of it." The only person that I could rely on was a seasonal we called Jim Bob. Jim had worked at the Great Smoky Mountains as a seasonal Park Ranger and had vehicle crash experience from the many wrecks that occurred in the Great Smoky Mountains, and he helped me with the crash investigation.

I was not satisfied we had accounted for all the victims, due to the chaos of the event. It had been a couple of hours at the crash scene, and the person unaccounted for still had not been located. One of the Pensacola Beach volunteers had a 4-wheel-drive vehicle and I asked him to drive down the beach before he left, to make sure someone had not walked away from the crash. Thank God I had remembered from my rookie accident investigation training that victims would sometimes leave the crash scene, either in shock or just trying to get away. The volunteer drove west about a mile along the beach from the crash scene and found one of the juveniles of the crash lying next to the dunes, unconscious and bleeding due to severe head trauma he had sustained from the crash. He was airlifted to the hospital, where he recovered. Had he not been found, he would have died.

This crash was over my head, but I had to try to put it together the best I could. It took me about a week to get the report together. I was frustrated that the report was incomplete, and I went to a staff meeting where the department heads met with the superintendent. I took the report and laid it on the meeting table and explained to the superintendent my frustrations trying to deal with this serious accident. The superintendent politely told me to call the Highway Patrol. I informed him I had contacted them and they declined to investigate. The superintendent told me, "By God, I'll call the governor." The governor, at the time, was Bob Graham, and the superintendent had his number on speed dial. The next day, after the phone call to the governor, there was every high-ranking Highway Patrol officer in the Northwest Florida area at the seashore. They were so high up the ranks they had gold trimming on every inch of their uniforms. We sat down to the meeting and the Highway Patrol officers were pretty cocky about their presence. After the situation was explained to them, one of them replied that if I would have called them, they would have worked the crash, but they were not notified and all the evidence had been removed from the crash scene, almost a week earlier.

At this point, I pulled an 8x10 glossy photograph I had taken with the commandeered camera. In the photo, standing, looking at a big skid mark with his hands in his pockets, was none other than " a Florida Highway Patrol officer." When they saw the photo, they were dumbfounded and tried to mitigate their embarrassment and arrogance. It was at this point they explained they would do an investigation. At the time, there was a required Florida Homicide report that went along with the traffic accident investigation, if there was a fatality. I had completed it best I could, and it was included in my report. The next day the local Highway Patrol officer came to me and told me he had been assigned to investigate the crash and asked me for all my information. I took this opportunity to get back at the Highway Patrol for leaving me stranded at the crash and told the patrolman I was not giving him my investigation and to do his own. Looking back, it was really stupid, but I ignored the patrolman like they had ignored me. The case was almost a week old and it was impossible to go back and collect all the evidence and information of the accident without my report. The next day is when being stupid was identified. The superintendent was notified of my arrogance, and I was called into the office. I don't know how I kept my job. I heard cuss words I didn't even know. The superintendent was livid to the point I thought I was going to have a stroke. I was literally kicked out of the office with instructions to accommodate the Highway Patrol with everything I had or knew about. I gained a lot of experience in stupidity in just one day that I couldn't gain in a career. I gave the report to the Highway Patrol and they went through some motions and turned the report over to the Florida State Attorney, referring charges for Vehicular Manslaughter against the driver of the van.

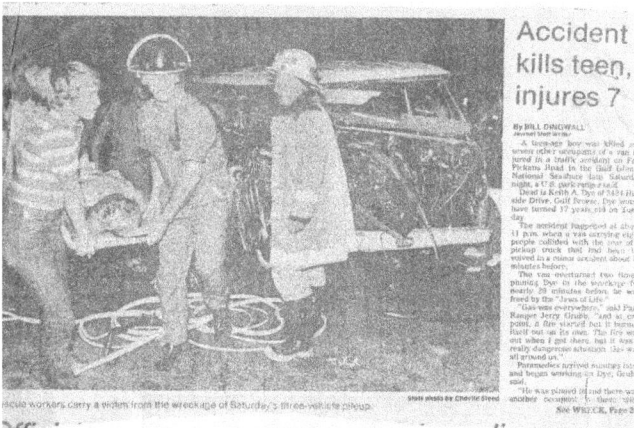

Birthday ends in tragedy

The cause of the crash was found to be alcohol related. These were local kids, celebrating the seventeenth birthday of the kid who was killed in the crash. The driver was his cousin, either 18 or 19 years old, making him an adult under Florida law. These kids had a cooler full of Kool Aid mixed with grain alcohol, they called "Kickapoo Joy Juice" and they headed into the park. The other vehicles involved in the crash were stuck in the sand with another vehicle trying to pull it out. Another vehicle stopped, facing the oncoming van and flashed his headlights to warn the approaching driver. Instead, the driver of the van flashed his lights back and sped up at a high rate of speed hitting one of the vehicles with the passenger side, front quarter of the van, shoving the engine into the passenger compartment. The 17-year-old passenger had impacted the windshield and side windows, after the van had flipped and rolled over several times, and became pinned in the wreckage.

As it turned out, the report I had done was exceptional and was commended by the State Attorney for doing a very complete report that was presented to him through the Highway Patrol. The driver of the van was prosecuted for vehicular manslaughter and sentenced to seven years in prison. It was many years afterward; I was at a convenience store on the beach outside the park and greeted by an individual. I did not recognize him, but it was the same individual who had been driving the van and was out of prison. With tears in his eyes, he emotionally apologized to me for his behavior and actions that night. The encounter stuck with me for a while, and throughout the years this would be repeated many times from working many serious incidents involving death and serious injuries.

13

New Dispatchers and the Navy

*M*anagement of the seashore reluctantly and slowly was upgrading our law enforcement capabilities and established a radio communications dispatch. This was a result of a program where physically challenged people were utilized, through programs administered by the state, that allowed them to be employed. There were no upgrades to the radio system, and the only improvement was dedicating a room for the dispatchers to use to answer phone calls, monitor the radio, and call the appropriate agency for emergency assistance, or assisting a division in the park that included getting toilet paper to the bathrooms. The first two dispatchers hired under this program were both blind. At the onset, everyone thought this was ridiculous, but it soon proved the validity and dedication of these guys. Although they were blind, they had braille writers to log all calls and information, and were quick at getting calls in and out and got the needed back-up Law Enforcement Rangers needed. They had a lot of pride and were very trustworthy. After a while, they were included as federal employees, getting full benefits and hired under the Affirmative Action program. Once they were hired, the Park Service management touted their achievement in hiring the handicapped individuals. What they didn't acclaim was denying them the opportunity for career enhancement and advancement, or training and equipment. They were basically placed in a room and given a job, to be forgotten. The program was not funded to include transportation in getting to work, or training, and were employed because of the Federal Disability act that made the government employ them, only to be ignored. They were invaluable to the operation of the seashore. To get these guys to work, the Rangers would pick them up at their homes, in our personal vehicles, and get them home at night. There was no extra pay or benefits, but it didn't matter. It became routine for us to do this, and it provided us with more protection in getting law enforcement back-up and assisted them with their difficulties that most people take advantage of every day. Even though the dispatch operation was upgraded, sometimes, there was no dispatch available at all and we relied on someone at their home to casually monitor the radio. I would get lackadaisical and sometimes not be aware of my situation, that at any moment, could mean the difference between life or death.

There was an incident where a group of Navy sailors came to the seashore late at night. They drank and became intoxicated at an area known as Battery Worth picnic area, that was right next to the Fort Pickens Campground. The old, concrete bunkers, built by the military, had a picnic area nearby where the sailors came and played around the bunkers at night, getting drunk, shooting fireworks with a lot of noise that disturbed the campers. There were no patrols after midnight and the campers had no one to call to report the noise. I drove through the campground one afternoon, and was approached by several irate campers, who reported the ongoing noise and disturbance that had occurred almost every night. They told me they had reported it to the campground office, but nothing was done about it. The law enforcement patrol was off duty at midnight, and I had not been aware of it until now. I assured the campers that if it occurred anymore, I would come and take care of it. I gave them my card, with my home phone number, for them to call me if it occurred again. I was pretty sure it was a random thing and I wouldn't get called. That night, my phone rang and it was the campers. They were back, intoxicated, shooting fireworks, speeding around in the parking lot, and again causing a disturbance.

I immediately responded from my home, about 15 miles away, and went to the Fort Pickens Ranger Station to get a patrol car. It was about two o'clock in the morning when I arrived at the Ranger Station, and there were several people there. It was part of the group of sailors from the Naval Air Station, and they had come to the Ranger Station looking for help, because one of their friends had fallen off the concrete battery onto the concrete floor and was severely injured. I didn't have a dispatcher, so I called from the Ranger Station office for an ambulance and a back-up from the Escambia County Sheriff's deputies. The only back-up I had was Nick and Karleen Taylor, who were campground hosts at the campground. I don't know if it was because of stupidity, or just an everyday response, as a National Park Ranger, where we would always go into situations alone. These were the days of no cell phones, no dispatch coverage, or communications, to gain any assistance. We had to figure it out as we went. I went to the picnic area and there were about 25 people there from the Pensacola Naval Air Station, most of them intoxicated. Their friend, also intoxicated, fell about 12 feet onto his head on the concrete from atop the concrete battery and was paralyzed. I didn't come to the area for a medical emergency, but to arrest the people who were causing the disturbance. With the assistance of Karleen and Nick, we got the victim immobilized, waiting for the ambulance. The ambulance arrived before the deputies and loaded the victim in the ambulance and left.

There were about 20 or more sailors, four females and one wife, with a small baby. I got them all gathered in front of my patrol car, in the headlights. They thought they were going to be briefed on their friends' condition, but instead, I decided to arrest everyone for the disturbance they had created every night. My back-up was on the way.

Now, one may think, one crazy ass Park Ranger could not arrest this many people at one time. The secret was, they were all members of the Naval Air Station, and they all were students in a classified training program, with security clearances. Any breach of their conduct would get them terminated from the school, where they had a lot of time invested for a promising career with the Navy. I really thought most of them would run and try to disappear, which was all right with me. Instead, they elected to let the alcohol start talking. I began gathering military I.D. cards to identify each of them, if they elected to run or disappear. None of these guys were criminal, but the intoxication level of several of them, made them sidewalk lawyers, including their instructor, who was with them. I was already committed, and I was determined to follow through. I herded them into the headlights, where they sat on the pavement in the parking lot. They were guarded by the campground hosts, Karleen and Nick, while I tried to sort through the identifications, still waiting on my back-up from the Escambia County Sheriff deputies. I needed the deputies to be able to call for the Navy Shore Patrol to come to the area and pick up these guys, because I didn't have any way to call them, and they were too intoxicated to drive.

I had come up short an identification and asked the subject where it was. He told me he had given it to me. I told him I couldn't find it, but it really didn't matter at the time. It was at this time the student's instructor came to me and threatened me with arrest. He told me he was a Petty Officer with the United States military, and he would have me arrested for losing the identification card. This guy was already on my last nerve, and he began to incite the rest of the group. I hadn't handcuffed anyone, but when he began his threat, I handcuffed him, placed him in physical custody and put him in my patrol car. The rest of them remained quiet as I waited on my back-up. Another subject stepped up to protest for the group and I quickly got him handcuffed and placed him in my patrol car. After a few more minutes, another one of the subjects stepped up to protest their detention and I loaded him in the back of my patrol car.

Everyone now is relatively quiet, except for the drunk mother with the baby. She was not as intoxicated, but she was just plain obstinate. She became disorderly and refused to cooperate. She didn't have any security clearance and nothing to lose except being thrown in jail. I didn't care to oblige her and put her in jail, except I didn't want to have to take care of a small baby. She continued verbally assaulting me, beginning to incite the others. I decided I would get her handcuffed and restrain her until my back-up arrived. Back-up sometimes took 30 minutes or longer, and I didn't have a radio or telephone to see if they had been diverted to another call. I had the female subject by her arm to handcuff her, and she pulled free, using a large garbage can as a shield between us. As I pulled on her, her drunk husband came to the rescue. He came up behind me and hit me in the back of the head with his fist. The momentum from her pulling me and the momentum of being plummeted in the back of the head, sent me flying over the garbage can, landing on my back. I got up just in time to see the deputies grab the husband and drag him just out of reach as I swung my large Kell light, trying to connect with his drunk ass. They loaded him and his wife in their patrol cars, while one of the females took care of the baby who was asleep in one of the vehicles. I had the deputies radio for the Naval Shore patrol to respond to the parking area to pick up the drunk sailors.

With the military, instead of arresting these guys, we could detain them and turn them over to the shore patrol as a civil turn over. It would then be up to the military, in this case the Navy, to take custody of them rather than put them in jail. Each of them would be cited for Disorderly Conduct, to appear in Federal Magistrates court, except the one who hit me in the back of the head. This was a direct Assault on a Federal Officer, and carried a significant penalty, including imprisonment. The shore patrol showed up with three vans to get the subjects, but still did not have room for all of them. They called for another van and we all went to the Ranger station, waiting for another van to get the prisoners I had in my patrol car and the Sheriff's patrol cars. The female was a civilian and was issued a violation notice to appear in court and released with her baby. Wreckers were called and all their vehicles were hauled off.

When I got back to the Ranger Station, and took the subjects out of my patrol car, I noticed what appeared to be water in the rear floor-board of my patrol car. It was not water, but urine from one of my prisoners. The shore patrol was there, waiting with us for the other van, and were going to watch and wait with the prisoners. I was pretty sure the cocky instructor had peed in my patrol car. I got the one of the students out and took him in the Ranger Station where he and I had a quiet conversation regarding the pee in my floor. I reminded him of his security clearance, and how he was in the balance of being a regular swabby if he didn't tell me who peed in my patrol car. He politely told me he couldn't lie; it was the Petty Officer Instructor who had intentionally peed in my patrol car. I had the sailor carry a large mop bucket of water, some soogie powder, and sponges out to my patrol car. The Petty Officer Instructor volunteered to clean out my patrol car in the presence of all his students, giving them a lesson in leadership. It was now almost daylight as the Shore Patrol hauled off the hungover sailors to the Naval Base.

I contacted the JAG (Judge Advocate General) office at the Naval Air Station and informed them I had violation notices for all the sailors of whom I still had their military identifications. They accepted the identifications and citations for Disorderly Conduct for all the sailors to appear in Federal Magistrates court. I had spoken with the U.S. Attorney about the assault charge and he would make a federal complaint and warrant for the Assault on a Federal Officer. I didn't get hurt from the assault and the sailor's demeanor was over-taken by his intoxication. I considered the guy's career status and where he committed a bone-headed mistake because of his intoxica-tion. It was his crazy wife who was the remaining factor if he was to be charged with the more serious crime of Assault. Another Ranger and I, along with an Escambia County deputy, went to his residence where I met with him and discussed his future. He was very apolo-getic and sincere and because of his intoxication he had made a bad mistake. The next step was talk with his crazy wife. When she came to the door, she had apparently just gotten back from bible study. She was very polite and apologetic and much different from the night before. I explained to them, they would be cited for Disorderly

Conduct and the serious crime would be dropped. They were happy and relieved, and I was happy for not having to deal with a long, drawn-out judicial process.

All the sailors received their violation notices through JAG and appeared in Federal Magistrates Court with their legal representation. The courtroom was already to capacity when 20-plus defendants entered in the court room. They lined each side and back of the courtroom wearing their Navy dress uniforms. When the U.S. Magistrate entered the courtroom, he hesitated and looked around shaking his head and looked directly at me and said, "This must be yours," as he seated himself at the bench. The proceedings went very quickly, as all the defendants had been instructed to plead guilty to Disorderly Conduct by the military officials. They were each sentenced to pay a $50.00 fine and withholding adjudication of guilt, where there would be no record of the offense charged. This would insure they could continue their training and classified status.

I received some letters from the Navy Commander at the Naval Air Station and the defendants after the court was over. The Navy Commander applauded me for handling the situation as I did with a very nice complimentary letter. The Navy students followed up with about 26 complaint letters to the Chief Ranger, concerning them being harassed. They were all bundled in a nice manila envelope, handwritten and signed by each defendant, except the guy who had hit me in the head and his wife. We decided not to answer nor turn the letters over to the Navy and I kept the letters. The incident prompted the Navy to include in its training and correspondence, the penalty for being Disorderly in the National Seashore and for years there were no more problems with any of the Navy personnel, except for six others that I caught being disorderly and trashing the park.

They had been drinking and had trashed one of the picnic areas with beer cans and other trash. I made them clean up the trash and didn't have time to deal with them. I told them they were all under arrest, but I couldn't get all them in my patrol car. I instructed them to drive up to the Pensacola Beach sheriff sub-station and I would meet them there. Again, I called the shore patrol to come and get them and

I would detain them in the beach jail holding facility. They left and I had forgotten about them and didn't consider they would do what I had told them. One of the Pensacola Beach Deputies called me by phone. He asked me what in the hell are you doing. I joked with him and thought he had just called to talk. He said he had six guys in a car, sitting in the parking lot of the sub-station, and said they were all under arrest by a Park Ranger. I told him that could not be true, but I did tell them to go to the sub-station. He said they were there waiting, and I drove to the sub-station and found them. I had to follow through with my instructions that they were under arrest to save credibility. I took them inside the jail and locked them in the cell and called the Shore Patrol and they came and picked them up and took them back to the Navy base as a civil turn over with written warnings only.

As the years passed and I transferred to a supervisory position, I had one of my subordinates get a complaint letter from a visitor. Everyone gets complaint letters if they do their jobs, but this Ranger was upset because he had never gotten a complaint letter. As he complained to me about his complaint, I pulled out the manila envelope from my desk with all the complaint letters I had received years before from these students. I handed them to him and explained to him when he got 30 letters at a time we would talk about his complaint.

14

The Grand Canyon

*I*n 1982, I was selected to attend the "Ranger Skills" training program at the Horace Albright training center at the Grand Canyon National Park. At the time this was acclaimed to be a premier training program to prepare Park Rangers with experience and motivation to become Park managers throughout the National Park Service. This was supposed to be an elite program, and only certain Rangers qualified to attend. This was done by a nomination process where supervisors submitted a request for their subordinates, based on merits and other factors. The nomination required very articulate writing to be nominated. My supervisor, at the time, was Park Ranger John Bradberry. He had risen through the ranks and was selected to the Ranger Intake program. The Ranger Intake program was designed to take certain, highly educated Rangers and place them into supervisory positions to become park managers.

Ranger Skills was instituted to gain qualified Rangers to train and become park managers also. Ranger Bradberry was highly educated and experienced and through his creative and articulate writing, I was selected to attend the program. Ranger Bradberry was too intelligent and motivated to be just a Park Ranger, but he loved it. His calling came, and he resigned to become a medical doctor and went on to be the Senior Medical Director of one of the largest medical facilities in the southeast. His articulate narrative and nomination were submitted to the training center and that was how I qualified, with little education and park service experience. I was excited to get this opportunity and looked forward to getting some real Ranger training, riding horses, fighting fires, jumping out of helicopters, white water rescue, and all the other things that came with being a National Park Ranger. It was a standing joke, the Park Rangers east of the Mississippi weren't really considered Park Rangers, and only real Park Rangers worked in a western park like Yosemite and Yellowstone. Now I would be training with "real" Rangers in the National Park Service.

It turned out; Ranger Skills was not exactly what I thought it would be. It was a five-week program where there were classroom hours, with discussions and instructions concerning how the National Park Service management should evolve in the future. At the onset, one of the major discussions that came up was firearms being carried by Rangers in the National Parks. There were only a couple of us in the class who were actual Law Enforcement Rangers and carried guns. There were very intense discussions about guns and the use and need for guns by National Park Rangers. A lot of the class was very liberal and condemned Rangers carrying firearms, stating they were not needed in the National Parks. Most of the people in attendance were not actual Park Rangers but were management types with backgrounds in resource management, or interpretive rangers, or other science and social employees that would throw their mothers under a bus to get a management position. These are the people who had never put their lives on the line and provided actual service to the park visitors but later became Chief Rangers and Superintendents, and the leaders who dictated how each park would run.

There was no actual hands on training, and most of the activities were classroom related, getting indoctrinated and programmed to carry out future park service plans. There was no firefighting training, but one day, the Grand Canyon firetruck was brought out as if it were a show and tell school day. If a class member wanted, after class, they would be allowed to ride with a Law Enforcement Ranger on patrol, but unarmed, and only as a passenger. The staff of the Ranger Skills did arrange for rescue training and we spent a day rappelling off the ledges of the Grand Canyon. Now I'm thinking we're getting ready for some real action, but the next day we went back to the boring classroom to be indoctrinated with park service policies and programs and more discussions about firearms. One week was dedicated to Interpretive training where we colored Bambi with crayons and cut out pictures of the National Geographic and pasted them to posters to hang on walls and bulletin boards. We also went outside and played some children's games to help plan for interpretive programs. One game consisted of all the class in uniform, standing around, holding a parachute and throwing a pinecone in the middle of it. We kept shaking the parachute to get the pinecone to fall in the hole in the center of the parachute. For some reason, this really didn't appeal to me, and I wanted to get back and chase some more bad guys.

The only thing that made the trip satisfying was spending five weeks at the Grand Canyon itself and enjoying the scenery. The staff really went overboard to make our stay pleasant, with noon volleyball and after-hours potluck dinners. This was a family affair and arrangements were made for husband, wife, and children to stay in apartments at the Grand Canyon during the training period. Most of the class members eventually meshed, and the stay at the Grand Canyon was pleasant.

The highlight of the trip was hiking into the Canyon. Other classes prior were scheduled to hike into the Canyon as part of the training program, but it was discontinued. According to the staff, it was because one class member fell to his death off a canyon ledge and the program was stopped. However, provisions were made to allow the class to volunteer to hike into the canyon on a weekend and camp to experience a wilderness environment. To justify the hike, we were required to take notes, observe the canyon's resources and when we returned, prepare a 20-minute program to be presented to the class on how well the Grand Canyon management was doing to preserve the environment and provide visitor use of the Grand Canyon.

We were briefed on getting a Wilderness experience, making sure we carried plenty of water and other survival gear, should we become lost. We carried large packs that had to weigh 45 pounds and we weighed on scales to make sure someone wasn't fudging. The packs contained anything one would want to carry but had to weigh 45 pounds. Some carried large pots and pans and provisions to cook spaghetti at the campsite at the bottom of the Canyon. I elected to carry my fishing rod, some cooking grease and corn meal. I had found out the fishing was pretty good, and I was going to have fried fish instead of freeze-dried pasta. This hike into the Grand Canyon was something I had never experienced, and I looked forward to getting started.

We loaded our large packs and headed down the Kaibab trail that was nine miles getting to the Phantom Ranch campground. As we got down the trail a little way, I began noticing toilet paper behind the rocks and then realized that when you 'gotta go,' you gotta go. I had not even considered this. There was a lot of paper because of the large number of people hiking the trail daily. Due to the dry desert environment, the deposits would not deteriorate. There were no restrooms of any kind available along the trail, and this was the only place to go. Everyone disregarded the rule of scooping the poop and packing it out. As we trudged on, carrying our large packs, the wilderness experience was not so novel anymore. Especially when there were hikers and runners, running to the bottom of the canyon and back to the top, wearing nothing but tennis shoes and shorts. I just figured they weren't getting the wilderness experience we were going to get and kept going.

When we got to the bottom of the Canyon, we walked across the Bright Angel Creek on a 10-ton pedestrian bridge that spanned the creek to the campground. The creek wasn't very wide and could be easily forged but there was a huge bridge built instead. The rocks of the creek were stacked and held in place by wire and the campground was strewn with water hoses watering the plants and trees planted around the campground. There was a strong odor of marijuana drifting in the air throughout the campground as people lay around smoking dope out in the open. There were few campsites available, due to the large number of people who were pretty much residents of the campground, which resembled a hippy commune or a homeless shelter. It was getting late and we found a sleeping spot to throw our sleeping bags. For some reason, the ground at the bottom of the Grand Canyon was much harder than any ground I had ever slept on, but after the nine-mile hike, it didn't take long to get to sleep. After a little while, in the night, there were little visitors running around that would wake you up as they scurried over your face and sleeping bag. There were a lot of mice and they ran around looking for crumbs dropped by campers and hikers. They were very annoying and carried the hantavirus that could make you very sick, so you really didn't want them running across your face. Trying to sleep was tough, but the guy playing a guitar and singing in the middle of the night made it even tougher.

I made it through the night and was up early. I hit the Colorado River for some fishing action. I was at the river's edge, fishing, when one of my classmates yelled to me if I wanted a cold beer. I didn't know someone had brought beer and thought he was joking, and I told him to just 'bring me one' and continued fishing. A little while later, he brought me a cold beer. I asked him where he got it and he replied he bought it at the Phantom Ranch concession. I was confused and he explained to me there was a store with cabins around the corner. I had not noticed them. I had to check this out. I found there were developed facilities, including overnight rental cabins, a restaurant serving hot soup and hamburgers, and a large satellite dish for making phone calls from the bottom of the canyon. I was amazed at what I saw, as I thought we were in a wilderness area, fixing to get a 'real wilderness experience.' And the guitar man, was the local drunk that played music and sang during the night. My visions were definitely blurred from what I saw but it didn't surprise me. At no time during the class room instructions did they tell us there was an established, commercial concession at the bottom of the canyon, and since I was from "east of the Mississippi River" and not a "real" Ranger, I didn't know this was the way the parks in the west were operated. They also didn't tell us we could have stayed in the cabins, but the plan called for us to sleep on the ground, with sick mice, to gain a wilderness experience.

I returned to the river where I caught a nice rainbow trout. Since I was a taxidermist, I prepared the fish to be mounted. After I caught the trout, I returned to the campground where

Rainbow Trout

I skinned the trout, saving the skin to mount later. To mount a fish, all that is used is the skin, and I preserved it with salt and packed it out. I saved the meat of the fish and took it to the river and washed it, so I could cook it. Several of the classmates watched me while I skinned, gutted and prepared the fish. Some of them were squeamish and thought this was nasty as I had bloody hands, fish guts and fish smell. The trout was about two pounds and had quite a bit of meat, but I had to cook it with a small Sterno cooking burner. I had enough grease and corn meal to cook it, but had to cook it in small pieces, so it took longer to cook. When the grease got hot and the smell of fresh fried trout fillets filled the air, everyone gathered around and sampled the fish I cooked. The fried fish disappeared faster than I could cook it with everyone getting their sample, including the squeamish ones. I really didn't get much of my fish as it disappeared quickly.

The next day, I was nominated and designated to catch enough fish for the class, and we would have a fish fry. This was a pretty tall order, and I didn't have any more grease or corn meal to cook any fish. Not to worry, because we were in a "wilderness environment" and getting a "wilderness experience." Nature would supply us with the needed items to cook fish. I caught many fish to fry and when I returned to the camp, I found someone had gone to the concession store, where they borrowed a large pot, grease, and cornmeal, just like nature would supply us in a wilderness environment, to maintain our survival. We cooked fish in the afternoon, drinking cold beer, and surviving a true wilderness experience I would never forget.

The next morning, we packed up and headed back to the south canyon rim, hiking the Bright Angel trail. The Bright Angel trail was all uphill about 12 miles in length. The Kaibab trail was 9 miles and downhill. As we hiked up the trail, I took more mental notes to include in my presentation I would present to the class, justifying our weekend wilderness experience. I observed the canyon walls where green slime ran down the walls. We were met by hundreds of visitors, hiking into the canyon and the famed mule trains that brought people by mule into the canyon. The mules were a traditional and iconic part of the Grand Canyon. They could be rented by visitors that had money and couldn't or wouldn't otherwise hike into the Grand Canyon. The mule skinners would lead 8 to 10 mules carrying the visitors. The Bright Angel trail was not very bright, being it was very dusty. One would also have to hike through the green alfalfa poop that was left by the mules the length of the trail. The wranglers made regular stops at the switchbacks that were sharp turns on the trail that changed elevation. Where the mules stopped was a cesspool of mule urine that covered the trail leaving muddy and wet ponds and it was difficult to impossible to hike around it. The stench was overwhelming. As a result of these cesspools, the urine ran off the trails along with the alfalfa poop and down the canyon walls causing the walls to become green with slime. This, in turn, polluted all the canyon water supplies making the water unfit to drink. Drinking any of the water in the canyon without being treated would cause dysentery or worse.

The Bright Angel trail was not a difficult trail and it took about six to eight hours to hike out to the South Rim of the Grand Canyon. The class was strewn out from one end to the other and the time to hike out depended on each person's physical condition, dictating a pace and desire to get off the trail as quick as they could.

We had a couple of days to prepare our presentations. There was a podium set up (as if we were going give a political speech) and each classmate delivered their presentation. It was obvious my presentation was going to be a little different than what was presented by the first classmates. Most everyone in the class aspired to be a park manager, Chief Ranger, or supervisor. They aligned themselves with the management of the Grand Canyon, confirming the great job that was being done by the management of the Grand Canyon in preserving the resources of the park. I hardly agreed with their analysis but had to consider they wanted one of those management jobs and had to remain status quo.

I went up to the podium and gave my presentation of what I had observed in the canyon. It was my place to be truthful and share constructive criticism concerning the state of affairs in the canyon. I started off by saying, "The first thing I would do would be to sell this place to Disney World, put in a tram with restrooms to deliver people up and down the canyon and shoot them stinking mules and clean the nasty place up."

Wow! You could hear the staff's jaws dropping and the audience stared intently at me in disbelief of what I said about the Grand Canyon. It was the truth. There was no wilderness experience, the trails were littered with poop and walking through mule manure the entire length of the Albright trail. The profound changes that continued to occur were a result of more and more visitation, requiring a different approach in managing this many people in this environment. But nothing has changed, and the stinking mules still erode the canyon trails, providing the rich nitrogen fertilizer that grows them big trout in the Colorado River.

The creek was held in place by chicken wire, a bridge erected that was big enough a tractor trailer could drive on, the campground was more like a homeless camp or a commune with all the dope smokers smoking dope in front of the Rangers. There was a small city at the bottom of the canyon, complete with a town drunk that thought he could sing. We didn't have to provide solutions to the problems we addressed, but present mere observations. I had broken the ice, and some of the Rangers agreed with my observations and they tailored their presentations to reflect and align themselves with what I had presented. The great part of Park Service training is there are no tests! I blew through the presentation unscathed and I'm pretty sure the management of the Grand Canyon didn't take my suggestions under advisement. I don't think I went away from the Ranger Skills program with any special skills, but It did provide me with a better under-standing of National Park Service philosophy. The main thing I took away from Ranger Skills training was the Western Rangers were no more 'real' than the Eastern Rangers.

Law enforcement in the National Park Service was evolving quickly, but the Park Service Management would not recognize the volatile and serious threats Rangers faced every day. Federal Legisla-tion identified Park Rangers as Law Enforcement Officers but were denied 6c Law Enforcement Enhanced Pay and 20-year mandatory retirement at a maximum age of 57. The reason for the enhanced retirement was maintain a young and vigorous work force for the strenuous jobs. Although law enforcement was very strenuous, the other jobs of a Park Ranger also included strenuous jobs of Wildland firefighting and Emergency medical response and technical rescues. Park Ranger jobs were unlike any other law enforcement agency. At any given moment the Park Rangers could be investigating a murder and stop and go into a different mode and perform a rescue or respond to a wildfire. I know this from experience, and I wouldn't have wanted it any other way, retirement status or not. I loved being a Park Ranger and if we wouldn't have succeeded and gotten the retire-ment options, I was okay with it. It just seemed fair that Rangers who were performing in these jobs should be afforded the retirement when a clerk or secretary with other Federal Law enforcement agen-cies received the 6c retirement. The management of the Park Service and Office of Personnel Management would not support 6c retirement even though Federal Law mandated this. In the mid-eighties, Rangers came together, demanding the Park Ranger jobs be covered under 6c.

Reluctantly, some parks and managers started a dialogue with the Office of Personnel Management to consider the 6c but only as a narrative that would stall and confuse the issues regarding the law enforcement retirement. Rangers, although commissioned, armed, doing investigations, still had to jump through many bureaucratic hoops and each Ranger had to personally justify specific arrests, investigations, law enforcement contacts and such. This was a bureaucratic boon doggle and created a lot of unnecessary administrative interference and animosity within the Park Service Ranks. In the end we succeeded in getting the retirement options with mandatory retirement at age 57. Even at age 57, Rangers were still given the option of freezing their retirement status and going into a non-law enforcement position, be it maintenance, or park administration, and did not include direct law enforcement supervision. On the other hand, the Superintendents of the National Parks directly supervised and oversaw the law enforcement operations of the National Park Service but were not included in the 6c retirement mandatory retirement. This allowed the government employee to gain a higher grade and gave them more years of government service, adding more dollars to their retirement checks. I was lucky while I was a Park Ranger at Gulf National Seashore, working for two different superintendents who did a good job of managing the National Seashore. They kept the park open to the visitors, allowing for full enjoyment of the Seashore. They had to balance the need for a law enforcement operation where only minimal funding was allowed by the Department of the Interior, to each National Park, for a law enforcement program. As a result of their collective efforts, Gulf Islands National Seashore became one of the most visited National Parks in the National Park system. Law Enforcement officers are expensive, and the National Park Service had to deal with escalating criminal activities.

15

Exxon Valdez

*M*y best bear adventure was when I was selected as a Resource Protection Officer, during the Exxon Valdez oil spill at Kenai Fjords National Park. The Exxon Valdez disaster occurred in March of 1989 in the Prince William Sound in Alaska, where 10 million gallons of crude oil were dumped in the water after the oil tanker ran aground. This was one of the worst environmental damages ever. The oil quickly spread into the bays and sounds of Katmai and Kenai Fjords National Parks. The oil was sticky and gooey and covered everything. The sea birds and marine wildlife were quickly overwhelmed as the oil began to come ashore. The encroaching oil devastated, killed, and injured the sea birds and marine life that were surprised and trapped by the thick, sticky petroleum. Everyone scrambled to get control of the disaster, but it was impossible to manage. Exxon began a clean-up campaign, and they got clean-up crews to try to stop the oil flow to the shore. There were thousands of workers hired who tried every technique possible to clean up the oil. As a result, the crews worked on the beaches of the National Parks with the area wildlife and bears. The bears would come onto the beach to feed while the workers tried to clean up the beach.

Jerry guarding the beach

At the onset of the clean-up, a bear was shot and killed by an Exxon employee, working on the National Park shore. He had carried his gun for protection and when the bear came out to get dinner, it was shot and killed. Most of the bears in and around Kenai Fjords were black bears. The black bears were not as aggressive and dangerous as the grizzly bear. These black bears were wild and really didn't pay much attention to the humans. There was plenty of food for them, and the nasty taste of a human wouldn't take the place of the fresh salmon and other aquatics supplied by the waters in Alaska. These beaches were their homes, and now they had unwanted visitors. It was unlikely the bear attacked the worker who shot and killed it. This prompted the National Park Service to quickly assemble teams of Park Rangers, bringing them in on detail from across the country to protect the bears and the workers. At the beginning, the Park Rangers were identified as "shooters" who would stand guard over the workers and shoot the bears, if need be. I can't imagine the management ever calling us "shooters" and somehow it was probably conceived by the Exxon workers when Rangers showed up with shotguns. Our roles were Resource Protection Officers. We had shotguns with slugs and oo buckshot, and we monitored the activities on the beach, essentially protecting the workers should an aggressive bear show up. There were very few bears where I was assigned, mainly because the salmon run hadn't started yet. The crews were all brought ashore by boats and they worked throughout the day. Later, they were picked up by a boat and taken back to their crew boat. The oil mess was impossible to clean up as the workers loaded up millions of pounds of pebbles and rocks onto wheelbarrows and hauled the rocks to a barge.

Exxon Clean-up Crew

This proved to be another environmental disaster by removing all the rocks, going through the motions of being washed and dumped elsewhere, leaving the beach bare without the rocks. It was all a futile motion that was implemented to show the beaches were being cleaned up to appease the public. The fact is, the oil had already seeped through the rocks onto the beach and was impossible to get to. It had stained the rock walls and stuck to the vegetation and shoreline litter. The incoming tides continued to slosh the oil around and re-oiled the places that were cleaned. Another tactic was applied where the rocks were no longer hauled off, but the workers used paper towels to wipe the oil off the rocks.

Utilizing the Bounty Quicker Picker Uppers

The Bounty Quicker Picker Uppers were deployed, and workers went around sopping up the visible oil on the beaches.

This was just another motion that was incapable of producing any results. The daily routine found workers lying on the beach, dressed in disposable hazmat suits, wiping off individual rocks and placing them back where they came from as the Park Rangers watched for wandering bears.

The workers no longer carried guns for protection and the Resource Protection Officers kept watch over the crews to monitor any bear activity. At the onset, the workers thought if a bear came onto the beach, we would automatically shoot it if it wouldn't leave.

The reality was, if the bears came onto the beach, the workers were loaded up and taken back to their boats until the bears were finished with dinner. There was a lot of down time for the workers, where they couldn't clean up the beach due to weather and other conditions that kept them off the beaches. Just as I arrived to my crew boat, there was a worker who was allegedly overcome by the oil fumes. The clean-up operation ceased until Exxon could fly in a safety management crew to determine if it was safe to clean up the oil.

This was good news for us Resource Protection guys. If they didn't work, we didn't work. That gave us a lot of time to go fishing. We stayed on contracted crew boats with a captain and his crew. The operation had shut down because of safety problems. I stepped off the bush plane that had brought me to the boat and I was met by my friend, who had gotten me my Park Ranger job and whom I hadn't seen in years. He told me to hurry up and come on, that we were going fishing. My Alaskan trip was already fascinating and now I was going on a fishing trip, within minutes of arriving to where I was supposed to go to work. Three of us Park Rangers and one park police officer loaded into a small fishing boat our crew boat captain loaned us. We didn't have to go far to find the fish. The boat captain had also loaned us fishing reels and equipment. We started fishing using cut bait. I had no idea what we would catch, but it didn't matter, I was in good company, and the weather was unbelievable, with a picturesque and panoramic view of the Alaskan mountains and bays.

When I lowered my bait to the bottom, Boom! A huge halibut grabbed the bait and almost pulled me out of the boat. I was on the front of the boat fighting the fish while the others watched. I hadn't been in Alaska an hour, and I'm on the fishing trip you could only read about in a magazine. I got the huge halibut up to the boat and it looked like it was five to six feet long, and weighed a couple hundred pounds. There was no way the fish would fit in the boat and there was no way of killing it unless you are a Park Police officer. As I got the fish up to the boat, I heard him yell "I'll get it" and he had whooped a .357 revolver from his shoulder holster and shot the halibut in the head. I didn't know he had a gun, and I didn't know you could legally shoot a fish in the head. He had killed the fish and it was hanging on my rod. One of the Rangers decided to use a rope and tie it around the tail of the halibut, and tow it back to the crew boat. I was still holding the rod in amazement while the rest of them tried to get the fish turned around so they could get the rope around the fish's tail. Like most of the fish in Alaska, they have teeth. They have lots of razor-sharp teeth, and this halibut was equipped with them. While the line was being used to hold the fish, it cut the line with the razor-sharp teeth. The dead halibut started sinking in the crystal-clear water while all we could do was watch.

This Halibut didn't get away!

At the same moment it looked like fighter jets under the boat as several sea otters attacked the halibut as it sank. The clear water became blood red where the otters attacked it. We had not seen any otters and had no idea where they came from, but they arrived like jets appearing out of the clouds. I remember standing in the front of the boat stunned and amazed by what had happened, still holding my empty rod. After a few minutes of regaining our ability to fish again, the otters popped their little mustached heads out of the water a few yards from the boat as if they were thanking us for the meal. This would be one of the many fishing adventures in Alaska we had while being Resource Protection Rangers for the National Park Service. For three weeks we suffered through the agony and other Rangers came in and relieved us. I had always fantasized about Alaska and had put in for a transfer to Alaska when I was with the U.S. Coast Guard. The National Park Service had facilitated my fantasy with an all-expense paid fishing trip to Alaska.

My crew of Resource Protection Rangers had fulfilled their duty with no workers being injured by the bears and no bear casualties. By being a Park Ranger, we were allowed special privileges. There was an otter rehabilitation facility in Seward, where the otters that had been cleaned of the oil were kept. No one was allowed in the facility in order to maintain an environment without human interference. As Rangers, we were able to breach the security, and we could view the otters up close. A lot of the wildlife and birds could not have made it without these rehab facilities. As Rangers, we were able to be a part of, and see, the real Alaska by getting up close to the action. I rode my crew boat back into Seward and the boat captain pointed out a colony of sea lions. He asked me if I wanted to see them up close and I was all for it. I didn't realize there was a distance to view the sea lions and the captain violated the rules and took me up next to the sea lions.

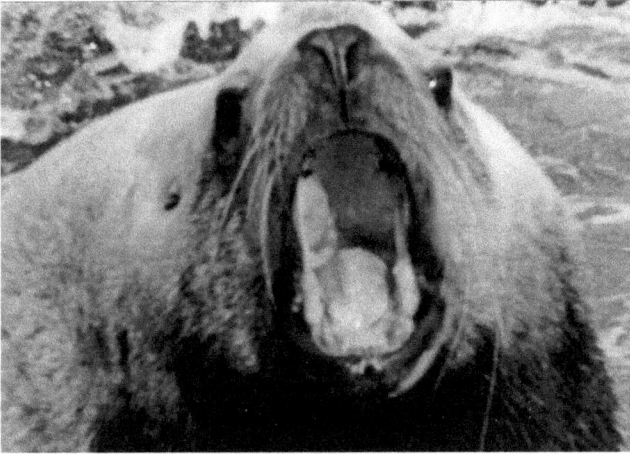

An Old Survivor

There was an old bull, weighing about a thousand pounds, on a rock by himself. He had war wounds all over him from fighting the younger bulls trying to take over his harem. I was on the bow of the boat with my camera, trying to focus in on a good picture. I didn't realize how close the captain had gotten the boat to the sea lion as I looked through my camera. I heard the old sea lion growl loudly as I snapped a picture. I was literally feet from the old guy as he opened his mouth, and I got a picture of his tonsils. I call it a perk of being a Ranger, but in the real world it would be a violation of the law. I could never be satisfied being a tourist, seeing the area from a pair of binoculars. I was blessed to have been a National Park Ranger, being able to see behind the scenes of one of the best movies in the world.

16

Park Ranger Robert Lewis McGhee, Jr.
End of watch May 26, 1990

Bob McGhee

hen it happened. A National Park Ranger was gunned down. I expected it to occur in some of the larger, highly visited parks, but it happened to my friend and colleague, in my Park, at the Mississippi Ocean Springs district of Gulf Islands National Seashore. Ranger Bob McGhee had worked in the park for about 10 years. Bob was a Ranger dedicated to the profession and was one of the friendliest Rangers you would want to encounter. The Ocean Springs district of Gulf Islands National Seashore was in Mississippi, about two hours away. The district included Horn Island and Ship Island. Ocean Springs was no larger than a city park with picnic areas and a campground. I did not work with Bob on a daily basis because he was in a different district. There was very little crime in the Ocean Springs District. Bob was present as an armed law enforcement officer in the Ocean Springs District, but the park had very few serious problems, mostly related to campground disputes. The park was adjacent to the City Limits of Ocean Springs, Mississippi and Law Enforcement back-up was readily available if they were notified.

A couple of months prior to Bob's death he had come to the Florida District of the Seashore, where he partnered with me to work a large concert that was held on Pensacola Beach, adjacent to Ft. Pickens. This was an all-night event, and a lot of alcohol and large crowds were anticipated. We had boosted our patrols, and brought in more law enforcement personnel. I recall the night Bob and I rode patrol and a conversation came up about our weapons. Bob had been issued a .357 revolver, while I was still carrying my trusty .38 caliber revolver. My ammunition had been upgraded to jacked hollow point rounds and I was no longer carrying the rat shot I had first been given. These bullets were factory rounds and no longer loaded by the district Ranger in his basement. As the discussion began, I told Bob I wished the park would issue all of us .357 weapons. Bob replied to me, he didn't know why we even carried guns because nothing ever happened. Bob was just the opposite of me when it came to law enforcement logic and awareness. Bob was a good guy and didn't recognize people as bad guys, whereas when I put on my uniform, I automatically was apprehensive there were real criminals lurking and preying on innocent people. I had encountered a lot of serious incidents, from assault, murder, rapes and a host of other crimes, whereas Bob only encountered everyday nice people who enjoyed the laid-back activities of the Ocean Springs District of the Seashore. It was neither Bob's nor my fault of the circumstances. There was a huge curve in law enforcement responsibilities that left us with different mindsets, but both of us had the same responsibilities. I told Bob the Florida district was different than Ocean Springs, and at any given moment we could run into a serious problem because of the alcohol and beach activities.

After a short while, we drove past the campground. There was a campground store at the entrance of the campground, and I observed an individual leaning against the store wall. The store was closed, and things were JDLR (Just Don't Look Right). The individual saw us and ran up to my patrol car, yelling he had been robbed. He explained to us he was just robbed and the people who robbed him had driven into the campground. He quickly described the vehicle, occupants, and what happened. He told us the subjects had a gun when they robbed him, but later after we arrested them, we were unable to find one. The campground had only one way in and out and he said they had not come out of the campground yet. Bob and I went in the campground and found the two people in the vehicle described by the victim. They had become stuck in the soft sand as they tried to turn their vehicle around. I had my spotlight on the subjects and ordered them, at gunpoint, on their knees with their hands over their heads. Both subjects complied and I told Bob to cover me while I went up to handcuff the subjects.

I approached them and got the first subject handcuffed, patted him for weapons and laid him face first on the ground. I only had one pair of handcuffs on me, and I called back to Bob to give me his hand-cuffs. I had the subject by his hands over his head and waited for Bob to give me his handcuffs, but Bob was not there. I looked behind me and saw Bob in my patrol car. Turns out Bob did not have his hand-cuffs and went to the patrol car to get a pair of Flex-Cuffs. These are plastic straps used as temporary restraints when there may be several arrests. I had a couple of pair of cuffs hanging on the steering column of my patrol vehicle. Bob went and got them, and we secured the second subject in handcuffs. Bob explained to me he had left his handcuffs in his room.

I am not writing this in any way to condemn Bob, or fault him for a mistake that was made that night. Everything was a mistake in Park Service Law Enforcement and the mistake was made by the management of the National Park Service, not equipping Park Rangers with knowledge, training, and mental awareness, that there were bad guys in the National Parks. The truth of this matter occurred only a very short time after Bob had returned to Ocean Springs.

The previous Park Ranger shot and killed was on August 5th, 1973. Ranger Ken Patrick was before my time with the National Park Service. I was with the Coast Guard at that time and aware of his death because of my relationship with the Park Rangers. Ranger Patrick was shot and killed at the Point Reyes National Seashore by a group of Black Panthers. I don't know the full details, but I hope he was not killed due to tactical limitations that had him unarmed or unequipped, because of the National Park Service policy, in limiting the use and display of firearms at this time. In the 26 years I worked as a National Park Ranger there four Rangers shot and killed in the line of duty. I personally worked with three of them. Having worked with these guys, I know the details of their deaths, and their deaths were perpetrated by poor law enforcement management and support by the National Park Service. You may think I write this as being angered and dissatisfied. I had the opportunity to quit, but being a National Park Ranger was exactly what I wanted to do, and regardless of what was thrown at us, real Rangers persevered despite the obstacles, and continued with the main mission of keeping the parks and the visitors safe. The real facts cannot be changed, and as I continued through the years, it became more difficult to deal with the mismanagement of the National Park Service. Chasing bad guys, dealing with difficult tourists, rappelling off cliffs, fighting raging fires, and dealing with human tragedies was the easy part of being a Park Ranger. Dealing with management that suppressed and interfered with the Ranger's duties was very difficult.

On May 26, 1990, Bob McGhee lost his life after he was shot and killed by two escaped convicts that Bob had casually encountered, early in the morning, as he opened the gates to the park. The convicts tried to escape pursuit by the local police and Jackson County Sheriff.

They entered the park where they encountered Bob. Bob didn't have any idea the pursuit was happening, and the vehicle the convicts were driving went through a stop sign without stopping. Bob was out of his vehicle and went up to the convicts. As Bob approached the vehicle, the driver turned and shot Bob point blank, three times. Seems the first round hit Bob in his chest. From what I remember, the first round did not penetrate because the gun was stolen during their escape from a prison guard and supposedly the prison guards did not load their weapons with a full powder charged bullet. I was told the reason the bullet did not have the full capacity charge was to prevent a discharged weapon in close prison quarters from exiting a body during a shooting situation in a crowded prison. Guess it makes sense, but it makes more sense now, that no guns are allowed by just anyone in a prison environment. I also thought about the ammunition I had been carrying for years, that wouldn't stop a rat, much less some drug crazed lunatic.

Regardless, Bob was shot. A Jackson County Sheriff deputy who pursued the convicts drove by Bob's location just seconds after he was shot. The deputy saw Bob's patrol vehicle, which resembled a golf cart, parked opposite where Bob was. As he drove by, he failed to see Bob, who lay in a ditch on the opposite side of the road from his vehicle. Bob was in the wrong place at the wrong time. The convicts had escaped from a Florida prison the day before and had kidnapped a woman, holding her hostage in a motel adjacent to the park. The convicts had also stolen a large Dually pick-up truck. In the early morning, the woman escaped from the motel and summoned the local authorities, where she gave them the description of the vehicle and what had happened. The vehicle was soon spotted by law enforcement officers and a pursuit was initiated. The local authorities pursued the vehicle when it entered the park. The Jackson County Sheriff deputy who had driven past Bob caught up to the vehicle just a short distance from where Bob was, still inside the park. As the deputy pulled up behind the truck, the driver put the truck in reverse and rammed the Jackson County Sheriff patrol vehicle, disabling it. The deputy was stunned by the impact and saw two subjects come out of the truck toward him. The deputy then fired three shots with his .357 revolver through his windshield causing the convicts to run into the woods. The deputy gave chase on foot and encountered one of the subjects, hiding behind a tree in the woods. The deputy took the opportunity and blew the convict's leg off. The other convict ran into the woods and out the other side, in a subdivision where he was apprehended.

During this time, no one knew where Bob was. Bob had no dispatcher, but one of the park employees, at their residence in the park, had heard the gunshots and went out and found Bob, who was deceased, as a result of his injuries. Bob had a radio that he had gotten from the local authorities in case he needed back-up, but the radio was on the seat of his vehicle and he was outside his vehicle, unlocking a gate. This would be a common scenario working in the park environment, where everything is supposed to be serene and peaceful. I know from experience, the number of times I was stupid and left my radio on the seat instead of having it with me. I repeated the same scenario as Bob, within a short while, that could have very well gotten me killed.

The shooting death of Bob McGhee prompted an immediate response from the National Park Service management, that included a review of the National Park Service Law enforcement procedures. There were many changes that slowly came from Bob's death, but it took many years to recognize the dangerous job of Law Enforcement Officers in the National Park Service. I had been working for about 12 years and experienced the struggles of the law enforcement program of the National Park Service, that was conceived as a result of Federal legislation in 1976, that required Rangers to be commissioned. The legislation did not require the preparation and mental awareness that would be required in dealing with serious law enforcement issues. Over the period of 12 years after I became a National Park Ranger, I had gone from carrying my gun under the seat, driving multi colored, used cars for patrol vehicles, to wearing a bullet proof vest, equipment belt, driving larger, marked law enforcement sedans, but still carrying my trusty .38 caliber six shooter even though semi-automatic weapons had already been transitioned and issued to most Federal and State law enforcement agencies. I was still apprehensive I would piss off somebody in Park Management that was still against Rangers, wearing guns and doing law enforcement. I was an aggressive law enforcement officer, but I would have to second guess situations that would have to be tailored to suit park management. Many times, situations required sound, tactical law enforcement responses that were watered down to appease the park management and peers within the other park divisions.

Gulf Islands immediately took some measures to upgrade the law enforcement program. Everyone was fitted with a custom, bullet proof vest. Firearm and other aggressive law enforcement procedures were being incorporated in yearly in-service training. Bullets were upgraded to copper jacketed +P rounds, instead of wad cutters we used to shoot at paper targets to qualify. Law enforcement procedures were addressed, and more aggressive training was implemented at the Federal Law Enforcement Training Center. We had already upgraded to larger police type vehicles in the Florida District of the Seashore, but in Ocean Springs where it was a quiet and serene park, Bob still drove a small compact K-car, not much bigger than a golf cart, with a little, portable blue light attached to a cord that ran along the outside of the door and windows and held by a magnet to the top of the vehicle. There were no markings on the vehicle, and it was used this way, mostly to keep from intimidating the park visitors who came to picnic and camp in a make-believe world that criminals would not dare enter. Each park superintendent and other Park managers had different backgrounds, with most of them not having a clue about law enforcement or visitor protection, but still were charged with the law enforcement programs in the park. Superintendents usually had backgrounds of administration, historian or maintenance backgrounds or maybe an interpretive background. If this was the case, the agenda was usually set around their expertise, keeping law enforcement and visitor protection on the back burner. Enabling legislation required the Park Service to "protect" the resources for "now and future generations." I guess there was a clause in there I must have missed where it required you to use a stick or hold a rally and yell loudly to protect the visitors from any real harm.

Bob's death occurred at the time all law enforcement agencies in the country were transitioning from the .38 caliber and .357 caliber revolvers, to the semi-automatic pistols. Most old police officers liked their .357 six shooters that hung off their hip like an old west gunslinger. It looked bad ass, but there was no arguing that six rounds versus the high capacity magazine of the semi-auto was no challenge. The deputy who pursued the convicts in the park, that had shot Bob, was one of these old timers, who liked his six shooter, until he was confronted by the convicts and he had to shoot. He fired five rounds during the pursuit. This left the deputy with one round in his gun and a suspect still at large. He was faced with unloading the one round and trying to reload.

Speed loaders were the only option for reloading a revolver, unless you carried your extra ammo in your pants pocket. A revolver held only six rounds and you usually carried 12 more rounds in two separate speed loaders. To perform a reload, the bullets had to be dumped from the revolver, while simultaneously reaching for a new speed loader that was attached on your equipment belt. The next step was to position the speed loader in the correct position and insert the bullets into the revolver cylinder. This deputy was faced with trying to watch for a suspect, listen to the screaming and crying of a wounded suspect, with his vision clouded with stress and adrenaline, and a physical impairment, by hoping he wouldn't drop the speed loader. He had to reload by lining up the bullets with the little tiny holes in the revolver cylinder. A lesson was learned, and when the deputy returned to work his next shift, he had a high capacity 9 mm semi-automatic pistol. Even so, and with Bob's death, semi-auto pistols were not issued until sometime later after I left Gulf Islands and transferred to the Great Smoky Mountains National Park where the Rangers there also carried .357 six shooters.

Being a Law Enforcement Ranger in the National Park Service was fraught and exciting. We had poor equipment, worked alone with no back-up, and an administration that could care less. Still, I was just excited to be a National Park Ranger as I had envisioned when I was 12 years old, and struggled to maintain a sense of professionalism, trying to survive in an environment that was certain to get you killed.

A couple of months after Bob was shot and killed, I was on night patrol and encountered a situation where I believe there was a "God's Moment" and I had been assigned a guardian angel. After being a part of Bob's situation and seeing the discrepancies that caused Bob's death, I repeated the same mistakes that could have easily gotten me killed on this night. I was ending my shift about midnight and my dispatcher had already left. As I drove toward the Ranger Station, I saw a vehicle sitting alongside the road that looked disabled. I stopped and observed the windows down and a lot of female clothing hanging in the vehicle. My first thought was the vehicle was disabled and the occupants were walking, looking for help. I continued to drive further up the road to see if anyone walked along the road to get help. I had planned to continue home if I didn't see anyone, but as I left the vehicle, and got a couple hundred yards down the road, I saw taillights in my rearview mirror at the vehicle I thought was disabled. I don't know why, but I turned around and drove back to the vehicle. There was another vehicle parked behind the vehicle I thought was disabled. I pulled alongside them and turned on my vehicle side lights that lit up the side of the vehicle and the people. There was a large male individual leaning onto the window of the disabled vehicle, blocking my view of the driver. I inquired in a friendly Park Ranger greeting if everything was okay. The male subject turned slightly and replied everything was okay. I still could not see the driver of the vehicle and I again inquired if they were sure they didn't need any help. This time the male subject turned to where I could see a female driver in the vehicle, and she appeared to be crying.

At this point, I exited my vehicle, leaving my portable radio that I could use to contact the local authorities for back-up, on the seat of my patrol car. I was alone, had no dispatcher, and could not call in information. Out of habit, I left the sheriff's radio lying on the seat beside me. I didn't have room to carry two radios on my duty belt, and most of the time, I would have my own dispatcher. This time, I did not have a dispatcher, and the scenario looked like just one of hundreds of disabled vehicles we encountered, and I disregarded the warning signs where the female was crying. I went around to the front of my patrol car and ordered the male subject back to his vehicle that was parked probably 30 feet behind me. As I approached the driver, I could see the male subject standing next to the front of his vehicle. I leaned over to the female driver and she was crying hysterically. My first thought was a domestic quarrel, being it was late at night and the bars had emptied, and there were usually some intoxicated individuals encountered after the bars closed. When I asked the female, what happened, she was very anxious and excited and cried uncontrollably. She explained to me she had to get out of here because the male subject had dragged her out of her car, and he was going to kill her. Again, my thoughts were this was a domestic quarrel. I asked her to explain to me what happened. She shook so badly, she could hardly talk. It was then I realized I got myself into a serious situation and could not call for help. The female driver explained to me she did not know the male subject and he had kidnapped her at knifepoint. The male subject then became belligerent and began to approach me. This guy was about twice my size and unbeknownst to me at the time, he had just been paroled, after serving 15 years in the penitentiary for rape and kidnapping. As he aggressively approached me, I pulled my trusty .38 caliber revolver, pointed it at him, and yelled at him to stop. It was at this time the female subject also screamed. She screamed so loudly, next to me, I almost threw my gun down. The male subject got more and more belligerent and tried to approach me. I began screaming at him to get on the ground or I would "shoot your ass."

I had learned this phrase from a video of a Georgia Trooper who kept yelling at a subject, "I'll shoot your ass," before he shot a suspect reaching for a gun. I found this phrase to be very useful over the years, getting the attention of the thugs, there was a crazy bastard behind a gun and the way he screamed probably caused a physiological effect in the behavior of the thug, who really didn't want to get his ass shot.

I was literally screaming, and the subject turned away from me, but he would not get on the ground, but he did, however, go to his knees. I was apprehensive in approaching the subject alone and tried to handcuff him in this position. I had no other choice but to get him handcuffed or shoot his ass if he didn't comply. I don't know, to this day, what made this subject comply with me. He had a lot of experience with law enforcement intimidation and was a violent felon. Me thinks the reason he submitted was because he thought I was bad ass and was going to shoot him, but in reality, it was the guardian angel telling him this little crazy bastard is fixing to shoot you, and he submitted to let me get him handcuffed and placed in my patrol car. I got my radio and called for some back-up and an Escambia County deputy responded. Out of dozens of Escambia County deputies I had worked with, there were only about two, I can remember, that I wouldn't personally call for help, but they were better than nothing. These guys loved to back me up, whether they admitted to it or not. On this night, I got one of those deputies for back-up, but things were under control.

The female subject was a young 22-year-old student from Mississippi State University, who came to Pensacola Beach for vacation. She was in a bar and met the male subject and she explained to him she was unable to get a hotel room. The male subject told her he knew of some good hotels, and if she would follow him, he would lead her to them. The naïve female left with him and he drove to the park, as she followed in her vehicle. After several miles the female realized how desolate the area was and she was uncomfortable going any further. As she stopped along the roadway the male subject also stopped behind her and got out of his vehicle and approached her. She tried to tell him she was turning around and the male subject then grabbed her through her car window and dragged her out of her car and around to the rear of her vehicle, where he fought to subdue her, while brandishing a knife. The female then submitted and got into the male subject's vehicle and he drove further into the park. It was at this time, the female subject saw me driving past them in the opposite direction heading toward her vehicle. She saw the emergency light bar on top of my patrol car and told the male subject she needed to go back and roll up her car windows because the police would be looking for her. It was at the same moment I stopped and checked her vehicle and drove away. For whatever reason, the male subject turned around and drove the female subject back to her vehicle to let her roll up the windows of her car. When she got to her vehicle, she jumped in her car and attempted to get away, but again was forcibly removed from her vehicle by the male subject. It was at this very moment, I pulled up as this unfolded. How I recovered from all the mistakes I made, and was able to apprehend this guy, and save this girl's life could only been an act of God. There were literally seconds that had occurred that made the difference in a life or death situation.

Before my back-up arrived, I found where the young girl had fought with the subject behind her vehicle, as she tried to get away. I also found the knife the girl had described the subject had lying on the ground behind her vehicle. Gulf Islands Seashore jurisdiction was still Proprietary, and therefore all the serious crimes, like this, had to be handled by either the FBI or the local authorities. Although serious, it still did not rise to the level of the FBI involvement. When the local deputy arrived, I had to turn the subject I had arrested over to him. The girl left on her own and went home, never to be heard from again. I thought this was over, except for having to prosecute the guy in court, but I was wrong.

This was a capital crime that involved Kidnapping, Assault with a Deadly Weapon, and Violation of Parole by a Felon. The deputy took custody of the subject and left. It was the next day, I found out the deputy had only charged the subject with simple assault and allowed him to bond out of jail immediately. I was livid that this occurred. It was too easy for the deputy to let this guy go, rather than do extra paperwork, and to appear in court. There was nothing I could do to get the proper charges filed.

I was in the process of moving within a couple of days to my new

duty station at the Great Smoky Mountains National Park. This
serious crime was mitigated by my move, with no motivation by
anyone to go forward and get the proper charges filed for a serious
crime. Later in the afternoon, the officer in charge of the Pensacola
Beach Sheriff substation came by my house and asked me if I had any
information regarding the subject who had been jailed for the
assault. He had reviewed the incident and realized how dangerous
this guy was and told me there had been a mistake made regarding
the charges and the subject's release, and they had to find him. I told
him my frustrations and told him I could not help finding him or
knew where he was. I was officially off duty at Gulf Islands National
Seashore and did not get involved with the search of this dangerous
individual, as badly as I wanted to.

I was at my home the next day, watching the movers pack up my
belongings to be moved to the Great Smoky Mountains National
Park. As they packed, I watched TV and a newsbreak came on about
a manhunt that was being conducted in the north end of Escambia
County for a subject who had kidnapped and raped a woman and
was a fugitive on the loose. This was the same subject I had arrested
the day before for the same offense. I didn't know if this crazy bastard
would come looking for me, and most of my guns had been packed
away. I dug out a shotgun, just in case this bastard wanted me to
"shoot his ass." The subject was not found that day but the next
morning, the crazy bastard appeared in the Escambia county jail
parking lot with his bail bondsman to turn himself into the jail. As
they approached the entrance of the jail, the subject told his bail
bondsman he had to get something from his vehicle. He walked back
to his vehicle, got in, with the windows rolled up, and retrieved a
sawed-off shotgun. He stuck it under his chin and blew his stupid
head off.

When I heard about this, I had some serious emotions reflecting
on the circumstances I had encountered with the crazy bastard just
days before. Everything turned out good. I gained a better perspective
in law enforcement techniques and dangers of being in law enforcement. I also realized I was not there alone, as I dealt with a very

dangerous individual. The young girl was safe and did not have to be subjected to further proceedings, dealing with this in the courts, and it saved a lot of money by not tying up the criminal justice system. Another thug was removed from society without a law enforcement officer having to shoot his ass!

Gulf Islands National Seashore was a great place to be. Especially having a Ranger job, living and working on the beach. Between my Coast Guard time and National Park Service time, I had lived and worked on the beach for almost 20 years. I had mixed emotions about leaving the seashore but needed career enhancement and a promotion. I had not really considered anything other than being a field Ranger and did not long for a desk job. A position in the Great Smoky Mountains National Park came open. It was a supervisory position, and a field position with a promotion. This was a perfect job, except there were over a hundred applicants for the same job. The Park Service always looked for Rangers that were college educated, instead of experienced, and I didn't think I would have a chance in getting a position in one of the largest parks with the most visitation in the National Parks. The only thing that got me in the running for the job, was again my friend, Ranger Len, who was transferring from the Great Smoky Mountains National Park to another park. He was able to convince the supervisor doing the hiring for the position, I would be a good Ranger. The assistant superintendent of Smokies at this time, had also been the superintendent of Gulf Islands, when I first hired on as a Ranger. I had known the superintendent for many years, even before I was a Park Ranger, working with the U.S. Coast Guard. The assistant superintendent knew of my qualifications. With the influence of him and my friend, and traveling to the Smokies and interviewing with the district ranger at his home, I was selected and began working at the Smokies in July of 1990.

17

Car Clouts

I was no stranger to the hillbilly culture and the transition from beach bum to hillbilly was not very difficult. I arrived at the Great Smoky Mountains on a Saturday in July, 1990. I moved into a Park Service house at the headquarters area of the park, in Gatlinburg, Tennessee. The movers dropped off all our possessions, and we lived out of suitcases and cardboard boxes until we settled in. The next day, Sunday, I had planned to drive around the park with the family, exploring the new area where we would be living. Around noon, one of the Rangers came to my house and told me my supervisor had planned stake outs in all the parking areas in the Little River District, in Gatlinburg, and asked me to help them. There were ongoing car burglaries or 'car clouts' that occurred in the district and no one could catch them. My supervisor was going to try to get the people responsible, arrested. There weren't enough Rangers to cover all the key parking areas, so they asked me if I would participate.

I was apprehensive in participating, since it was my day off. I wasn't scheduled to begin work until the next day, and I had plans for the afternoon. I was a new supervisor to the district, and I didn't want to alienate any of my coworkers or new supervisors, so decided I would go out for a couple of hours, make some over time money, and be a part of my new family. I figured the chances would be slim if we caught anyone, anyway, and I still would have plenty of time to enjoy the afternoon. I had turned in my trusty .38 caliber revolver and law enforcement equipment at Gulf Islands National Seashore when I transferred to the Smokies. I was hurriedly issued a revolver, hand-cuffs and bullets before I went to the area I would be staking out. To my surprise, it was a .357 caliber revolver and not a trusty .38 caliber pea shooter. Now I was ready to shoot somebody's ass.

I had no idea where I was going except one of the parking areas called Rainbow Falls trailhead. I drove my personal pick-up to the trailhead, where I found the parking area packed with vehicles, with people steadily coming and going on the Rainbow Fall trail. I was in plain clothes with a camo t-shirt and my .357 revolver, concealed and tucked in my waistband. I couldn't figure how anyone would be able to commit a crime in this parking area, due to the number of people present, but I continued trying to find someplace to conceal myself and observe the parking area. I concealed my radio in a small fanny pack with my handcuffs. Before I left for the stake out, I got my personal video recorder and took it with me. This was the earlier version video recorder, the size of a suitcase, you held on your shoulder. I thought if I was going to do surveillance, I needed the video recorder to capture the event, should I see a car burglar.

As I sized up the place and the parking area, sitting in my pick-up, a red sedan pulled in front of me and the driver of the vehicle looked directly at me eyeball to eyeball. The vehicle was an ordinary one, and there was nothing especially suspicious about it, and there was no sign on it indicating the person inside was a criminal. This was JDLR (Just Don't Look Right). The vehicle continued out of the parking area and I gathered up my equipment, got out of my truck, and proceeded to locate a place to set up surveillance. As I walked away from my truck, looking the area over, I turned and saw the same individual I had made eye contact with from the red sedan, standing in front of my truck about a hundred feet away. It was again another

JDLR moment. He looked at me and the parking area. I was at a large blackberry thicket at the edge of the parking area. The blackberries were blooming with a lot of flowers. I turned again and the subject stood watching me. At this time, I got my video recorder up onto my shoulder and started videoing the blackberry flowers, looking like an excited tourist, observing nature. I watched the subject as I walked off out of sight of the individual, still filming with the recorder. When I got out of sight, I dove into the woods and found a place to conceal myself from view of the parking area. I belly crawled to where I could see the individual and was only about 75 feet from him and the parking area. This wooded environment was quite different from the seashore, and instead of sand spurs and sand, I was lying in poison ivy. I was pretty sure I was not allergic to it, but it was already too late, so I lay still and watched the parking area. I was not in position for more than five minutes, and the individual who was JDLR approached a Honda vehicle parked directly in front of me. The parking area did not have any people in it at the time, as everyone was on the trail away from their vehicles. The subject was now less than a hundred feet away from me and he retrieved a Slim Jim from under his shirt and unlocked the vehicle. A Slim Jim is a flat piece of metal fashioned to go between the glass and door of a vehicle to manipulate the locking mechanism and unlock the vehicle. Some vehicles would readily unlock, and some vehicles took more time and expertise in unlocking them.

When people arrived at the trailhead, 'car clouters' or burglars watched them as they put their belongings in the vehicles before they began their hike. When the purses and valuables did not go into a locked truck, or were carried with the hikers, they knew the vehicle contained a purse that was readily available for the taking. They also knew tourists carried money and valuables. In this case, there was a purse tucked in front of the passenger seat and visible. The subject tried to unlock the vehicle, so I began filming him with my video recorder. I was so close to him, when I crunched a leaf or twig, he could hear it and began looking into the woods. He struggled with the lock, and people began returning to the parking area. He would put the Slim Jim back under his shirt and greet people in the parking area as they came and went. The subject tried in vain to unlock the Honda but was unable to get the vehicle unlocked and the parking area became busy.

My supervisor had a plan that would include operating procedures if a suspect was identified. The plan called for all the major parking areas to be surveilled. If there was a hit, the plan called for letting the suspect get into his vehicle and drive off, where there would be a catch car or patrol car available to make a stop on the suspect, once they left the parking area. I found out quickly, the Smokies had the same problem I had experienced at Gulf Islands.

The radio system was terrible, and due to the mountains, the radios were not effective or reliable. As I watched the subject try to unlock the car, I tried to radio that the burglary was going down and for the patrol car to move in. This was when I found the radio system in the Smokies was useless. When he could not get the car unlocked and he backed away, I called for the patrol not to come in. The radio was working, and everyone could hear me, but I couldn't hear them. It was frustrating, and as this scenario continued for about an hour, the subject was unable to break into any of the vehicles in the parking area, and all the Rangers tried to figure out what the new crazy Ranger was doing. Without him breaking into a vehicle, we could not arrest him. After he tried for about an hour, the subject started to leave the main parking area and go out of sight around a curve, where there were other cars parked along the shoulder of the road. He then came back to the main parking area and watched the vehicles for a few minutes, greeted some of the hikers, and left again. I did not know what was around the curve, but after about 20 minutes, I decide to go through the woods and see if I could see where the subject headed. When I got to where I could see the subject, he stood alongside the vehicles parked on the shoulder of the road. He was on the opposite side of the vehicles, and I could only see his upper body. I had trouble seeing through the trees and vegetation, and the subject then disappeared. I was about a hundred feet from him and I heard a loud crash and the breaking of a car window. The subject had taken a large rock and smashed in a car window. When I saw him the first time, standing by the vehicle, he had a shirt on, but after he smashed the window, he took his shirt off and wrapped a purse that he had taken out of the vehicle, with the shirt, and proceeded to walk down the road. This was not the plan that was supposed to occur.

As he walked down the road, away from the parking area, I tried to get someone on the radio to get the patrol car to move in. I was unable to talk with anyone, including the dispatcher, and the subject got further away from the vehicles. Fortunately, my back-up and dispatcher could hear me, and I could hear the patrol car coming down the mountain. The suspect also heard the car coming and ran, jumping into the woods, running away from the roadway. At this time, I ran parallel to him in the woods and caught him about 75 yards from the road.

He was surprised at my presence, and when I got to him, I drew my pistol and screamed to him I was a police officer and to get on the ground. The suspect stood still, and I could see him look around for an avenue to escape, and I knew he wanted to run. We could hear the patrol car coming as it got closer to us. He still clutched the purse, wrapped in his shirt, as he looked around to see which way to run. I then yelled at him, "I see the gun, I see the gun and I'll shoot your ass" and to 'get on the ground.' I'm guessing this guy must have thought I was psychotic, not having a badge or uniform and pointing a pistol at him, telling him I was going to shoot him. At this time, he threw the purse and shirt forward and dived to the ground on his belly screaming he did not have a gun. I kept telling him I saw a gun and if he reached for it, I was going to "shoot his ass". My back-up arrived and parked at the bottom of the hill. The Ranger got out of his vehicle, racking a round in his shotgun and tried to figure out where I was. The sound of that shotgun echoed up through the woods as the ranger racked and loaded the shotgun. It had a clear, distinct sound that business was going to be conducted. My adrenaline pumped as I held the suspect's head down with my foot, waiting for help to get to me. The suspect lay motionless, scared shitless, and he was handcuffed and arrested.

So much for a quiet afternoon on my first day at the Great Smoky Mountains National Park. I spent the rest of the day doing reports and processing the crime scene and getting the subject booked into jail. I read the suspect his Miranda warnings and asked him if he wanted to give me a statement. He told me he was going to confess to breaking into the vehicles because he saw me going into the woods with my video camera and it was no use to lie about it. I had told him I had videoed the whole thing, so he gave me a written statement and confessed to the breaking and entering of the vehicles. The suspect told me he had a car payment due and he was trying to get money. On that day, I learned the art of using a video camera to record these types of incidents. When I played the video back, I found the video camera recorded the closest thing to the lens, that turned out to be nothing but blurs and tree leaves, but I did have some really neat blackberry blooms. The subject pleaded guilty to the charges and I didn't have to use the video as evidence.

The next day, I officially began my new adventure with the Great Smoky Mountains National Park. This park was what I had envisioned as a child and being in this environment. My district was the Little River District and next to the City of Gatlinburg and City of Pigeon Forge. Little River district was the busiest district in the park due to the Foothills Parkway Spur that was a four-mile, four-lane highway split by the Little Pigeon River that connected Gatlinburg and Pigeon Forge. There were cheap hotels in Pigeon Forge, liquor and bars in Gatlinburg, and thousands of vehicles traveling the road back and forth between the two cities. The Little River district also shared Highway U. S. 441 with the Oconaluftee District, with about 16 miles of the highway being in the Little River District. This was the main two-lane U.S. highway connecting North Carolina and Tennessee at the top of the mountain, at an elevation of about 5,500 feet. After I was there a short time, the Cherokee Indians built a casino in Cherokee, North Carolina, adding to the traffic flow even more, as people traveled to Cherokee to gamble and come back to

Tennessee to their cheap hotels in Pigeon Forge and liquor in Gatlinburg.

I left the relatively quiet National Seashore that was a barrier island with an elevation of sea level. It was only about 6,000 acres in size and the annual visitation about two to three million. The Great Smoky Mountains was about 500,000 acres with a yearly visitation of 10 million. The law enforcement, Emergency Medical, Search and Rescues, traffic accidents, wildfires, and any other thing one could think of, were numerous in the Great Smoky Mountains. I had never seen so many vehicle crashes, drunk drivers, and fatalities. There were suicides, continuous calls of nuisance bears, and wildlife incidents, staking out marijuana patches, ginseng and wildlife poachers, lost individuals, and medical emergencies occurring on the backcountry trails. The park districts were divided into areas of the Little River District at the Gatlinburg Tennessee entrance, Oconaluftee District at the Cherokee, North Carolina entrance and the Cades Cove District at the Townsend, Tennessee entrance. Rangers were assigned to these districts as their duty stations but would assist in all areas of the Great Smoky Mountains.

The Great Smoky Mountains on the Tennessee side of the Smokies had Exclusive law enforcement jurisdiction unlike Gulf Islands Proprietary jurisdiction. The North Carolina area of the Smokies had Concurrent jurisdiction and allowed for state and local jurisdictions to enter and investigate and enforce any crimes. Any crimes committed in the Smokies on the Tennessee side of the park were handled exclusively by the Rangers and prosecuted in the Federal District Court in the Eastern District of Tennessee. If it was a capital crime of murder or rape, the FBI may assume the lead in the investigation, but most of the investigations were handled and prosecuted by the National Park Rangers. The State, or local authorities had no jurisdictions to investigate or make an arrest on the Tennessee side of the Smokies. There were mutual aid agreements made with local and state law enforcement authorities and Emergency Medical providers to allow them to come in the park and assist us. The four-mile section of the Foothills Parkway spur, connecting Gatlinburg and Pigeon Forge, was Concurrent jurisdiction and allowed for the local authority to make arrest and investigate crimes and vehicle accidents on the spur. Although they had the jurisdictions, none of the local authorities wanted anything to do with what was happening in the Smokies because they had their hands full with their own responsibilities, and the federal government was not paying them extra to do the Park Service job. The emergencies, and law enforcement activities were overwhelming, but it was an action-packed adventure every day and this was exactly where I wanted to be.

I was also beginning a new job as a supervisor, overseeing district operations and supervising about a dozen employees. I had supervisory responsibilities in the Coast Guard, but I had limited supervisory experience in the Park Service before coming to the Smokies. I was soon enrolled in formal supervisory training. I really didn't know how I would be accepted by the Rangers and management at the Smokies, because I was new, and they were mostly old timers who had been in the park for some time. I quickly realized that supervision in the district was nothing more than a title. I had the same responsibilities as the rest of the Rangers I was supposed to supervise. The Rangers knew what their jobs were and were motivated without interference by a bunch of needless supervising. This made my job very easy and I was able to stay out in the field more. Besides, there were enough supervisors at the Smokies to conflict with the Rangers who just wanted to do their jobs as Park Rangers. The Ranger job at the Smokies was just what I was looking for, but I soon realized, the government bureaucrats would ruin the greatest job in the world.

18

Poachers

*I*t was January of 1991 and I had been at the Smokies for about six months. It was early morning, just getting light, and I was beginning my daily patrol up the mountain. As I got a couple miles up the mountain on Newfound Gap road, I heard the Tremont Ranger calling on the radio to one of the Cades Cove Rangers. The Tremont district was in the far end of my district but closer to Cades Cove. I was a supervisor of the Tremont District and supervised the Tremont Ranger, although he did not need any supervision, like most of the Rangers in my district. He was supposed to be off duty when I heard him calling on the radio. I thought he had gotten called out during the night for an incident, that was not uncommon, because there were no 24-hour patrols, and Rangers could typically be out without anyone knowing about it. I radioed him to see if he needed assistance and he told me to call him right away at the Tremont Ranger Station. We did not have cell phones during this time, and I had to drive back to the office and called him by telephone. He told me he had been working with the Cades Cove Rangers for three days on a poaching case, and he had been out all night, watching for a vehicle that was supposed to be poaching deer in Cades Cove. He watched Laurel Creek road that was one way in and one way out of Cades Cove. He told me he had to take his wife to the hospital that morning and he had to leave and could not watch for the suspect vehicle. There were no more Rangers close by to assist and radio traffic was kept quiet in case the suspects monitored the radio. I told him to wait for me and I would come and take his place. He told me he had to leave immediately, so I took off to get to his location, 15 miles away, driving on twisting and turning dog leg roads. I had no information about what was going on and I couldn't call on the radio to get any information without risking the poachers hearing me. I intended to get the information from my Ranger when I arrived, but he had already left.

The Cades Cove district was considered by some of us Rangers to be a separate park. You had the Cades Cove National Park and then you had the Great Smoky Mountains National Park. Cades Cove had their own operation and would be apprehensive in sharing anything going on there. This was the case this morning. There was an active poacher investigation going on, and they had not shared any information with me or my district supervisor. I took a chance and radioed to the District supervisor of Cades Cove to get some information as to what to watch for. All the Cades Cove Rangers were in the woods or at the other end of the park trying to catch these guys poaching deer. He related to me they were watching for a tan, Ford Bronco, with a Florida tag and a CB antenna on the roof. He said the vehicle had entered Cades Cove earlier in the night and no one had seen the vehicle leave. There was about a 20-minute lapse between the time I arrived at the location where the road was being watched and the other Ranger leaving the area that watched the road. The poachers could have slipped out before I got there, but there was no way of knowing.

I was there no more than five minutes when I observed the suspect vehicle leaving the park. It was January, and there were no vehicles on the road, especially this time of the morning, and I was sure this was the vehicle they were looking for. I immediately got in behind it and started following it. The vehicle left the park, and I didn't know any information except the occupants were suspected poachers, and I was unsure of what we were doing. I radioed the Cades Cove supervisor and told him I was following the vehicle and it was leaving the park and what was I supposed to do. I wasn't pursuing the vehicle with any blue lights on, but the vehicle traveled at a high rate of speed as it left the park, with me just a few car lengths behind it, in a marked Park Ranger patrol car. Without a doubt, the suspects knew things were fixing to get difficult with a Ranger on their ass. The Cades Cove supervisor asked me how many people were in the vehicle and I couldn't see inside through the rear window, because of a screen across the back of the window. As we left the Park, we entered the valley and the City of Townsend. I could see two people with the early morning sunlight shining in the wind-shield of the Bronco. The Cades Cove supervisor then told me to stop the vehicle.

Now I was a little concerned with his request. I had only been in the Smokies for about six months, and I had never met a real-life poacher. I had read a little about them, seen stories about them, and warned in my law enforcement training that these guys were mean and would kill you. I intended to keep following them until I could get a back-up for assistance. When I called my dispatcher for a back-up, my dispatcher told me there was no back-up available as all the nearest Rangers were 20 minutes getting to me. I needed to get the vehicle stopped before it turned into a high-speed pursuit, with the occupants getting more nervous and making plans for an escape. I radioed to my dispatcher to get the nearest local agency for back-up and I had no choice but to stop the vehicle to keep it from getting further away from the park.

I stopped the vehicle alongside the highway in front of the Best Western Motel in Townsend. The vehicle immediately pulled over and the driver exited the vehicle very quickly and approached me. I quickly got out of my patrol, drawing my weapon and maintaining cover behind my car door. I still carried a .357 revolver. I did not point my gun at the suspect, and he did not see my gun, as I was behind my car door with my gun concealed by the door. I yelled at him to stop and raise his hands and he complied, somewhat, but was still not reaching for any stars. I still did not know if there had a been a crime committed and I tried to be careful displaying my firearm, when I didn't know if this was a camper or a poacher. The suspect was dressed in full camouflage clothing and appeared to be wet. I tried to get the suspect to turn around with his hands up and he asked me why he was being stopped and some other gibberish that I could not understand. He kept his hands up but still wanted to approach me and not follow my orders to turn around. He got to about the center of his vehicle and I yelled at him to stop and turn around and keep his hands up. It was at this time, he looked around and began to turn around, and at the same time he dropped his right hand to his waist, as if he were going for a weapon. I pointed my gun at him, putting about six pounds pull on the trigger and yelled at him I'm going to "shoot your ass!" The suspect turned and looked at me and saw my weapon with a look of shock and fear on his face. It was at this moment the suspect reached into the air for those stars. He then turned away from me and I had him back up to the back of his vehicle, while yelling, "I'm going to shoot your ass if I see anything that resembles a weapon." I had now gotten the suspect's attention and compliance. I guess when he turned and saw the business end of my gun, with a crazy little bastard yelling, he was going to kill him, his instinct for survival kicked in. I still maintained cover behind my door because there was a second suspect in the vehicle, and I didn't know if he had a rifle or some other weapon pointed at me through the back of the suspect's vehicle. The suspect vehicle was an older SUV type vehicle with a back window. I ordered the suspect to place his hands on the roof of the vehicle and got him in position to cover the back window of the vehicle and block any weapon that the other suspect may try to shoot me with. The first suspect complied with my orders and blocked the view of the other suspect. I was able to retrieve my .870 Remington shotgun loaded with oo buckshot, that I carried on a gun rack, mounted on the prisoner cage of my patrol car.

I switched weapons and kept the shotgun trained on the vehicle and suspects while I was able to get my PA (public address system) microphone. I then called the second suspect out of the vehicle. He was apprehensive to follow my orders and it wasn't because he didn't hear me, because later on, some of the employees of the Best Western motel on the hill said they could clearly hear me telling the suspects I was going to "shoot their ass."

The second suspect finally exited the vehicle, but I could not see him until he got to the rear of the suspect vehicle. He had his hands up as he peeked around the corner of the suspect vehicle and saw me. He then jumped back out of sight as I was racking and loading a round in my shotgun, screaming at him not to run, or I was going to shoot your ass! My adrenaline was above maintenance level now. The second suspect then came back to the rear of the suspect vehicle and showed me his hand as he came around the back of the vehicle. He was nervously saying, "M-mm-man, put that shotgun down, you're scaring the shit out of me." I yelled at him to get his hands over the top of the vehicle like his partner, that would completely block the view of me if there was someone else in the suspect vehicle.

I had two suspects positioned where I could control them or shoot their asses, if they attempted to get a weapon. I still had not heard if I was going to get a back-up from my dispatcher, and very apprehensive to approach two poachers that may be armed and possibly another suspect hidden in the vehicle. I kept them at gun point for a few minutes and decided I was not getting a back-up, and I attempted to arrest these guys by myself. I had arrested many bad asses by myself without incident, but this time was different to me because of what I had learned, that poachers would kill you and take you to a taxidermy shop where they would get you stuffed.

As I attempted to handcuff them, I heard a vehicle stopping in the roadway. It had no blue lights or siren but was a Crown Vic cruiser that belonged to the Police Chief of Townsend, Freddie Ledbetter. When I first met Freddie, I was amused by his hillbilly name and recollected the days of Jerry Clower, when he talked about the Ledbetters in his stories. Freddie was much older than me and was from hillbilly descent. He had the typical "old man police belly" that I have since acquired. At that time, there was only one police officer in Townsend, and he was the Chief of the only police. My dispatcher had contacted Freddie at his home and told him of my situation. Freddie was in his blue jeans, with his t-shirt wrapped over his belly and bedroom slippers, and when he heard I needed help, ran out of his house, leaving his gun belt and other equipment, and hurriedly came to my rescue. Freddie didn't have his service weapon but had a very small derringer he kept in his patrol car for a back-up weapon. He had not taken the time to get his weapon as he left his house, but he did take time to get him a "chaw of tobacco," before he got to me. If a gun battle broke out, Freddie was a dead eye spitter, and could have taken out at least one of the suspects with a spit in the eye. Freddie pulled his derringer out and kept the suspects at a half of a gun point. The suspects were pretty much frozen in their tracks, afraid to move or flinch. I gave Freddie my shotgun and proceeded to move in and handcuff the suspects.

The first suspect was named Travis. He was wet and dressed in camo. I handcuffed him and did a quick pat down for weapons and found .22 bullets in his pocket and a knife that was covered with blood and what appeared to be deer hair and blood on his hands. I placed Travis in Freddie's car. The second suspect was named Bubba and was dressed casually and did not appear to have been outside in the woods, like Travis. I handcuffed Bubba and put him in my patrol car, to keep them separated, so they could not compare stories. I then secured the suspect vehicle to see if there were more occupants and I found in plain view, the head of a large whitetail deer lying in the rear of the Bronco. Lying between the horns of the deer was a .22 Hornet rifle, with a silencer to muffle the shots and was used to kill the deer. It was at this time, the Cades Cove Rangers arrived, and they finished processing the evidence of a planned poaching expedition in Cades Cove by these two suspects.

I took the suspects to jail and the Cades Cove Rangers completed the investigation that uncovered the wild and planned scheme to kill trophy deer in Cades Cove in the Great Smoky Mountains National Park. It turned out the two suspects weren't the dangerous poachers I had been warned about, but instead, two stupid and ignorant fire-fighters with the St. Lucie Fire department in St. Lucie, Florida. One of them was a lieutenant and paramedic, and the other was a fire-fighter and EMT, and the son of the St. Lucie, Florida, County Sheriff. The subjects had planned the trip to Cades Cove to kill a trophy deer each and they shared their plans with all the firefighters at the department. The firefighters told them if they did this, they would turn them in to the authorities, but they ignored the warnings and proceeded to go hunting in the Great Smoky Mountains National Park.

They followed through with their plans and arrived in Townsend, just outside the National Park. The St. Lucie firefighters made good on their word and contacted the Tennessee Wildlife Authorities and reported to them these guys' plans. Their names, type and description of their vehicle, and where they would be staying, was given to the Tennessee Wildlife authorities who, in turn, gave it to the Cades Cove Rangers. Their vehicle was spotted immediately at the Docks Motel in Townsend. Surveillance was set up, and the Rangers watched it as it came into the park and left. The subjects drove around the Loop road in Cades Cove where there were deer by the hundreds, grazing in the fields with tourists snapping pictures and walking around them. There were two large bucks in Cades Cove, and the subjects spotted where they were. The deer in Cades Cove, and these bucks, were semi-wild as they encountered thousands of people who would walk up to them to take pictures. For the most part, the deer stayed in the same general area each day.

The two bucks were also celebrity bucks and had been named Streamer and Tim's Ten. Their pictures had been featured on the covers of Sports Afield and other magazines. There was a freelance photographer who worked with the U.S. Forest Service and came to the park and photographed the deer many times, and he sold the photographs to the magazines. After he learned of the poaching of the deer, he brought us the photographs he had taken of the deer just prior to them being killed. The pictures included in this book are photographs of the deer just before they were shot and killed.

After the deer had been located, the subjects kept surveillance on the bucks. The Loop road was closed to vehicles after dark. Bicycles were still allowed to enter and ride around the Loop after the gate was locked. This was in January so there were not many visitors in the park during this time except maybe on the weekends.

The two subjects had gone down to Wal-Mart and bought a new bicycle to ride around the loop and keep surveillance on the two deer. They used the bicycle to get to the location at night where they had found the deer earlier. They also had a large camera where they had photographed the deer each day. When it got dark, the subjects would drop each other off at the Loop road, communicate with portable radios, and then individually go to the location where they had last seen the deer. The other subject would then leave the park and return during the night and pick up the suspect that was hunting for the deer. They used powerful spotlights and walked around in the woods where they had previously located the two big bucks. It was hard to imagine how they were able to identify the deer from the thousands of deer eyes reflecting in the spotlight, but then again, the deer were tame, and they were able to walk around them without the deer being too concerned, and they were able to find the two big bucks in the dark. The rifle they used was a .22 caliber bull barrel Hornet. The rifle had an exclusive, custom-made silencer attached to the barrel to suppress the sound of the gunfire. Bubba was the first to score and he shot Tim's Ten. He was close enough to the gate where they loaded the meat of the skinned deer in a cooler, along with the head and skin of the deer to be mounted. The Rangers went off duty at midnight and there was no one in the park throughout the night, giving them plenty of time to take care of the deer. Rangers were out in force to catch these guys, but could not find them or their vehicle in the park because it was driven back to the motel, where one of the suspects waited and would go back and get the deer and pick up the other suspect later in the night.

Tim's Ten

They repeated their plan the next night. Bubba drove Travis into the park and dropped him off. Apparently, Travis had a hard time finding Streamer, as they left the park in the dim light of the morning, instead under the cover of darkness. The only thing they had was the head and skin of the deer to be mounted, leaving the meat behind. The Rangers had spotted the vehicle as it drove into the park but were unable to find him in the woods as he hunted for Streamer.

There was only a five-minute difference in these guys making their getaway and getting caught. If I hadn't gotten involved, driving like a bat out of hell, and getting set up to spot these guys, the entire case would have been lost. The subjects had killed their bucks and it was deer season and the possession of these deer would have been legal outside the park, should they have been checked by a wildlife officer. The only thing that wasn't legal was that Silencer. The possession of a Silencer by itself is a Felony defined by the ATF (Alcohol Tobacco and Firearms codes) and getting caught carried a mandatory minimum Federal Prison sentence of 18 months.

Streamer

I don't know if it was their stupidity or arrogance that made them drive around on a public roadway, and especially in a National Park, with a Felony Silencer and a rifle laying across the horns of an illegal deer in plain view.

The Cades Cove Rangers got a search warrant and located the other deer, Tim's Ten, that Bubba had shot and was in the motel room, in a cooler.

They were packed and ready to head back to Florida. After their arrest, their vehicle was seized along with the firearm, bicycle, money, cameras, flashlight, and everything they had in the vehicle, related to killing of the two deer. These guys were so caught and had to appear in court where they were charged with numerous offenses related to hunting and killing wildlife and firearm possession in a National Park and, felony possession of a silencer. The silencer was a homemade silencer and was turned over to the ATF where they tested it and confirmed it to be a silencer. It had been designed and fabricated by a machine shop, and one of the most effective silencers they had seen. ATF charged the subjects with Felony Possession of a Firearm

Silencer. This was a pretty open and shut case, with the subjects being caught red-handed with a firearm, killing and possession of a deer in the Great Smoky Mountains National Park, and the felony possession of a silencer.

There was no criminal record found on Travis and Bubba and they appeared to be squeaky clean with no prior arrest or violations. Both subjects were skilled firefighters and emergency medical providers. About a week after the smoke cleared, I talked with my dispatcher at Gulf Islands National Seashore and related to him what had occurred. When I told him they were firemen from St. Lucie, Florida, he told me his cousin worked at the same fire department and I should call him to get the lowdown on the two subjects. I called the cousin, and he had no sympathy for the two subjects, and told me how the staff of the fire department told them not to come to the Smoky Mountains to kill the deer, and if they did, they would report them. Travis and Bubba disregarded the warning. The cousin told me further that this was common activity of a group of them, as they would ride up and down the interstate with a vehicle in the front with a radio and a vehicle in the rear with a radio and the middle vehicle with a radio and would shoot deer along the roadways. He further told me Travis had been arrested for night hunting, although there was no criminal record indicated by NCIC (National Crime Information Center). By paying a fine there was no adjudication of guilt and there would be no criminal record for the offense. I contacted the County Clerk of St. Lucie County and asked them if they had a record of a fine being paid by Travis for night hunting and they found a ledger where he had been cited for night hunting and paid a fine of $500.00. This was significant information that could be used in sentencing after the trial and furthered their contempt of the law.

They hired a prominent Knoxville lawyer to represent them and they came to court to enter a plea of guilty or not guilty. Their lawyer was arrogant, and we were preparing for the court hearing, and the lawyer came into the lobby and sat with us. He explained to us he "had us ole boys" indicating he had devised a defense for the subjects. It was clear to me and the rest of the Rangers and our U.S.

Attorney the suspects were caught red-handed and the only way to mitigate their actions was to make a plea agreement to lessen their penalties. Everyone was surprised when they pled not guilty after being caught red handed. Their attorney argued I had made an illegal arrest by arresting the two subjects before I had seen the deer in the vehicle, that constituted a misdemeanor arrest not committed in my presence, and I had to have a search warrant to look in the vehicle. Therefore, anything that was found would be considered "Fruit of the Poisonous Tree," and all evidence would have to be dismissed and the charges dropped against the individuals. Their attorney entered a motion for the case to be dismissed, but the case was bound over for a probable cause hearing that would be held on a later date.

At one point in the court proceedings, a recess was made for lunch. As I walked out of the court room, Bubba, who was one of the defendants, came to me and asked what I was going to do for lunch. I told him I was going over to Pete's, which was a little diner across from the courthouse, and get a sandwich. To my surprise, Bubba asked me if they could join me for lunch. I had come to realize, after dealing with Bubba and Travis, they weren't hard criminals and I was not threatened by their presence. We sat together at lunch and discussed a few things. Bubba was an aspiring taxidermist and we talked about taxidermy and skirted the conversation regarding the court proceedings. Bubba then asked me how I felt about their situation. When the courts would recess, witnesses were instructed not discuss the case of an active hearing and I was apprehensive to talk with them about the case. I explained to Bubba I thought their attorney was ripping them off, but it was their decision to go forward. Bubba told me they had to try something and try to be found not guilty. They told me they didn't have any animosity towards me even though I had threatened to shoot them. They laughed about them being stopped and the intense confrontation and Bubba asked me if I would really have shot them. I don't think they were trying to set me up and get me to make any statements that would benefit their case and I simply told them I was trained to take whatever action I had to and survive.

We ended our conversation and went back to the courthouse where more arguing and testimony occurred. These guys were professionals, being paramedics and EMTs, but made their bone headed decision because of their arrogance. Bubba's father was the Sheriff of the county and I am sure Bubba felt entitled and protected by his father in the county and didn't realize it didn't work that way in the Federal jurisdiction. Even when they came to the Federal Court, they were escorted to the proceedings by two of his father's deputies from St. Lucie County, Florida. The deputies were quickly versed on Federal Court proceedings when they arrived in uniform and armed as they came into the courthouse. No one in a Federal courthouse could enter being armed, including all law enforcement officers. These guys were turned away to store their firearms and allowed to sit in the courtroom with the rest of the spectators and defendants.

The court proceedings weren't anything out of the ordinary. If you had enough money, an attorney would twist the facts, question reasonable doubt, and make a motion, hoping to get a ruling for an unconstitutional action and getting the case dropped. These guys had enough money to get that far, but it was in vain because the Federal District Courts ruled in favor of the government that the arrest was constitutional. A lot of money was spent by the individuals to only come back to the court and arrange a plea agreement. Being convicted of the Felony Possession of the Silencer, would result in immediate suspension, and dismissal from their firefighter positions, as well as having to serve 18 months mandatory minimum in a Federal Penitentiary. Although it was a lame defense, the judge had to consider their defense attorney's motion and it was bound over for a trial. In the meantime, a plea deal was reached, and the subjects pleaded guilty to the misdemeanor offense of hunting and killing wildlife in the park and possession of a firearm in the park. They each paid significant fines and restitutions for the two deer resulting in thousands of dollars, forfeiting their vehicle and other equipment. They got off lightly by paying the fines, but the silencer was going to ruin their careers. A trial was held in Federal District Court for the Eastern District of Tennessee for Felony Possession of the Silencer and they were found guilty and sentenced to the 18 months in Federal prison. Their lawyer again convinced them they could still win an appeal and have the sentence overturned. He charged them more money to take it before the Federal appeals court. This delayed them from going to prison, awaiting the appeal in the 5th Circuit Appeals Court.

January 1991

Ranger Grubb with Streamer

The appeals court upheld the verdict of the district court and they were confirmed guilty of the offense of felony possession of the silencer. Instead of the subjects conceding to their guilt and serving their time, they were again convinced by their lawyer to appeal the 5th circuit court decision. The lawyer again charged them a lot of money to appeal the decision. The appeal process had taken years getting through the 5th circuit court and now the case would go before the United States Supreme Court. The Supreme Court Justices ruled from the bench with no further discussion that the stop and arrest I had made was constitutionally legal and the defendants went to the Federal Penitentiary for the mandatory 18-month prison sentence. There was no way these guys could win this. The U.S. Attorney representing us argued at the beginning, the stop that I had made was an investigative stop. There was reasonable suspicion a crime was committed, and the totality of the circumstances resulted in a detention for officer safety rather than an arrest for the offenses they were later charged with. Their arrest came after seeing in "plain view," the deer and gun inside the vehicle.

These guys did it to themselves by not confessing and mitigate their actions and serve their sentences. I really think these guys got a bad rap from their lawyer. Their lawyer was aware of the 4th Amendment of the Constitution concerning Search and Seizure but went forward and charged them thousands of dollars taking them on a wild goose chase, basically ruining the rest of their lives, because they made a bone headed mistake. I was told later the guys lost everything, including their homes, wives and jobs over a stupid stunt, killing a deer and especially after they were warned by their co-workers of the consequences. This was one of the biggest poaching cases made in the Great Smoky Mountains National Park and I was proud to be able to participate and fulfill my ambitions of being a National Park Ranger.

19

Bear Hunters

There were a lot of wildlife problems, interactions, and misdemeanor violations, harassing wildlife in the park, relocating nuisance wildlife, and keeping the visitors from harassing the wildlife by getting too close to them or feeding them. One day, as I drove by an overlook parking area by Fighting Creek gap, I saw a half dozen people outside their cars and a deer standing with them. As I drove past, I saw a middle aged man holding his hand out, feeding the deer a cookie. Every adult who has ever watched an episode of Yogi Bear knew feeding wildlife in the park was strictly prohibited. Being fed cookies and other items only caused the animal to be habituated to humans, and the interference would likely cause the death of the wildlife.

This deer was acclimated to the presence of humans because he had been fed a lot and the deer would approach the visitors for a snack. I stopped and walked up to them and asked the man to walk over to my patrol car away from the other people to lessen his embarrassment of being cited for feeding the deer. I didn't see anyone else feeding the deer, but I am sure they were, and they could not be cited unless I saw them feeding the deer. As I wrote a violation notice for feeding the deer, the subject became irate, complaining I singled him out and all the others there, also fed the deer. I explained to him I had to see them and unfortunately, he was the only one I saw. He continued to berate me as I finished up the ticket. To get him quiet, I asked him to walk back over to the where the others were present, when the incident occurred. He was adamant I should write the others a ticket. I then told him in front of all the others, to show me which ones had fed the deer and I would write them a ticket, like he wanted, and he could be called as a witness. This guy was not going to make any new friends here today, as the other visitors looked at him in disgust and exasperation. I could tell he was mad as hell for being put in this situation, but he shut up, took the ticket, and left. Later on, he put his check in the mail to pay the fine, which was a pretty significant fine, for feeding wildlife in the park.

Then there are the bears. Bears are everywhere. Everyone wanted to see bears, and hunters wanted to hunt bears. There is a fall bear season on the lands adjacent to the park. This is a local tradition, and especially, hunting the bears with dogs. The hunters turned the dogs out next to the park boundary and tried to run the bears out of the park, where they could legally shoot them. Every fall, there would be a lot of animosity between the hunters and the Park Rangers, as the dogs always ended up in the park, and were caught by the Rangers and impounded until the hunter came and got them. Some of the hunters would slip into the park and tried to kill a bear, but most of them abided by the law, and the Park Ranger's job was mostly to keep the hunters honest but arrest any violators.

When I arrived at the park, I was a supervisor in my district, and this was my first bear hunting season around the park. I was contacted by the Chief Ranger. Hunters on the park boundary had reported to him they had shot and wounded a bear and it ran into the park. This occurred at the Townsend area of my district, and the bear hunters had camped atop a steep mountain next to the park boundary. I was instructed to go and find the bear, but if the bear was wounded in the park, it would have to be shot and left in the park. I went with the Tremont area Ranger, up to the location where the hunting camp was. When we got to the camp, we were greeted by four hunters who were excited we were there to help them get their bear. They were from Louisiana and had their hunting license out for us to check, but they were hunting outside the park, and we didn't care if they had hunting licenses. These guys were the nicest, most polite hunters one would want to meet. I told them we would try to track the bear, but if it was in the park, it would have to stay in the park. Their excitement drained, and they didn't understand why they couldn't get the bear they legally shot outside the park. As an avid hunter myself, I didn't understand the instructions given by the Chief Ranger, either. After we had some coffee with them at the campsite, we started to track the bear. It was already dark, but if the bear had left a blood trail, or was seriously wounded, we should find it quickly. I told the guys, if we found the bear, we were going to take it out of the park, regardless of my instructions, and they would get their bear. They quickly became excited again. We left the camp and all the hunters had their rifles. Since it was dark and there were too many rifles to watch after, I told them they had to leave their rifles behind. Besides, it was illegal to possess a firearm in the park. Again, they were perplexed, and told me the bear was big and they needed the rifles if we found the bear wounded. I told them the Tremont Ranger and I had our sidearms, (.357 caliber revolvers) that could kill a wounded bear, and for them to leave their rifles behind. They asked if they could bring their sidearms and we agreed they could bring them, if they stayed in the holster. They dug out their pistols that resembled the old west O.K. Corral six shooters, and other pistol types that I didn't think would even fire, but I elected to let them bring them. We tracked the bear until we ran out of a blood trail. Where the bear had gone was straight off into a deep ravine. Even if we had located the bear, it was too steep to get the bear back to the top and it was in a very remote area, where the bear, most likely, would not encounter any park visitors. We ended the search and returned to the camp, where the guys thanked us for trying to help them.

The next morning, the Tremont Ranger contacted me by telephone, and told me the bear hunters we had contacted the night
before, were in the parking area of the Tremont Ranger Station. He
said they had a large bear in the back of their pickup they had killed
early in the morning. The hunters told the Tremont Ranger they had
gone out early in the morning, hunting for another bear. I had heard
of many hunters that encountered game animals, while they were
preoccupied. One of the hunters had to take his early morning
constitutional and was squatted behind a big log when the bear
appeared. The hunter was somewhat incapacitated but was able to
get his gun. He was able to squeeze off two rounds, with one of them
being from his gun, bagging the bear. They were proud of their
trophy and had brought the bear by the Ranger Station to show us
the bear.

"WHAT?" I asked the Ranger. These guys have got a dead bear in
the back of their truck, in the Great Smoky Mountains National Park.
Having a dead bear in your vehicle, in the park, would surely cause
panic if someone saw it. I don't think they had their guns, as I had
lectured them the night before that firearms are illegal inside the
park. The Tremont Ranger and I were confident these guys didn't kill
the bear in the park and they only came by to show us their trophy. I
told the Tremont Ranger to escort them and get that bear out of the
park as fast as they could. The bear was covered by a camper shell
and wasn't visible unless someone looked inside, but nonetheless,
they had to get that bear out of the park, damn quick.

To make things even worse, the hunters had come by the Tremont
Ranger Station earlier and found no one at the Station. They
decided, while they were near the Cades Cove area of the park, they
would drive around the 11-mile loop road taking in some sights while
they waited on someone to get to the Ranger Station. They drove the
truck with the dead bear in the back all the way around the Cades
Cove loop road, stopping at the overlooks and looking for a Ranger.
They were oblivious to what they were doing and returned to the
Tremont Ranger Station hours later. It was unbelievable they were
able to pull this off. Had any Ranger besides the Tremont Ranger, or

myself, found them with this dead bear in the park, they would have been arrested. The Tremont Ranger gave them a quick lesson that hunting in the National Park was a little different than hunting in other places. Because the Tremont Ranger was a levelheaded and practical Ranger, everything turned out well. The hunters got their bear and a great bear story and got out of a serious violation for having a dead bear in the Great Smoky Mountains National Park.

Bear jams in the park were very common. This would be when traffic would come to a complete halt, backing up for miles, as people at the head of the line stopped in the road and exited their vehicles to get a picture of a bear. These people were oblivious to their surroundings, and dumbstruck when they saw a bear. Traffic was halted for long periods of time, with tempers flaring, and especially, when the motorist knew it was probably a bear jam and they were stopped two miles behind. We had to get around all the traffic with our emergency lights and sirens to get to the end of the line, where cars were parked and abandoned, causing complete chaos. Even as the people knew we ordered everyone back to their vehicles, to clear the road, many of them were still apprehensive to clear the road. As the traffic began to move, the next cars down the line stopped and we repeated this over and over until the bears went out of site. Sometimes the bears would sleep in the trees along the road or have a special acorn tree they would feed under and it was hours, trying to manage the traffic, until the bears decided to go out of sight.

The bears were the iconic symbol of the Great Smoky Mountains National Park and Rangers knew what to expect, and especially in October, when the fall of the year approached. As frustrating as it was, this was one of the reasons we became Park Rangers, playing the role of "Ranger Rick," chasing the elusive "Yogi." Visitors were fanatic over bears, wanting to get close to the bears, and get a picture of them. Sometimes the visitors got very close and surrounded the bears to get pictures. Of course, some of them took some groceries from their "pic-a-nic basket" and fed them. The large crowds were difficult to manage, and were oblivious to what was going on, paying little attention to the Rangers trying to get the area cleared. When people fed the bears, I occasionally took off my uniform shirt, or turned it inside out, and infiltrated the crowds to identify who was feeding the bears. They would be incognizant and focused on getting close to the bears for the picture. Once someone was identified, then I would turn my shirt round and approached the violators and cited them for feeding the bears. This was the fastest way to get people back to their cars, because they did not know who would be next and the bear jams cleared up very quickly.

One of the main questions visitors would ask was, where can they see a bear? Of course, they wanted to see a bear out of their car windows instead of hiking and looking for a bear in its natural habitat. I explained to them, if they got up very early and hiked into the woods, sitting quietly under a big white oak tree, where there were acorns, they would most likely see a bear in the wild. When I told them this, they looked at me as if I was crazy, because they meant they wanted to see a bear out of the car window. If visitors wanted to see bears the easiest way, I directed them to downtown Gatlinburg. This is where the city bears live. I gave them directions to the dumpster locations around the city, where they were almost certain to see a bear, and would not have to leave their vehicle. Most visitors did not care if the bear was in a natural environment, they just wanted to see a bear.

There were lots of White Oak and other oak trees with acorns that were a favorite of the bears. Bears love mast, that is fruits, berries, acorns, and other natural foods of the forest. They usually preferred these foods better than picnic baskets, if they hadn't already been habituated and became garbage eating bears. In the fall, when the acorns began to mature, the bears became more active, feeding on the acorns, trying to get fattened up for the winter. Acorns are staples for the bears, and in good years, when there was a good acorn crop, the bears were not a nuisance as when there was a shortage of mast. If the mast was scarce, bears became hungry and resorted to raiding them picnic baskets. As the towns around the park developed, bringing in more and more development, the bears became acclimated and habituated by people feeding them and leaving their garbage unsecured, making it easily accessible for the bears to get to. Once these bears became habituated, getting the tasty garbage, they would undoubtedly become a problem bear.

The Wildlife division in the park had recently made major changes on my arrival to the Park in 1990. The staff began to grow and was led by a very motivated, supervisory Wildlife Biologist, Kim Delozier. As a result of his short staff and growing problems in managing the bears, Park Rangers had to assist in dealing with the problem bears. The wildlife division also had to manage wild hog eradication in the park and other wildlife incidents as well. They were spread thin as they had to deal with problems in the entire 500,000 acres, rather than just a district. It was an overwhelming task as the park visitation and wildlife interactions with visitors increased. The cities around the park boundary developed rapidly, bringing the smell of more steaks and hamburgers cooking. We had a significant number of rogue bears in my district that was surrounded by the boundary of the City of Gatlinburg. Bears frequented the picnic areas and campground where there was food and garbage. The bears that lived next to town would slip over the invisible line that separates the park from the city and dine in the numerous dumpsters available at nearby restaurants. They would then come back to the park to get a nap, before going back to the dumpsters for another snack. At the time, there were no real bear proof garbage cans, and little education in removing and storing the garbage or food in the campgrounds, picnic areas, or in the cities. The wildlife staff grew and focused on getting the natural habitat for the bears restored, mandating food storage rules, bear proof dumpsters, and educating the public and cities in helping manage the bears to keep them habituated in their natural environment. The cities soon followed suit, establishing rules to secure the garbage in bear proof containers. It was difficult to manage the bears where there were millions of people in the area, making it impossible to keep the bears from trying to get the people food. As a result, they entered people's homes, broke into the vehicles, and attacked people when they learned people were a source of food.

The wildlife biologist began a campaign to stress and educate the public in removing and properly securing the garbage and food. As a result, the bear problems in the park were drastically reduced in the picnic and campground areas. Backcountry campsites were designed to store backpacks and food overhead on cables, so bears were unable to get to them. If there was a problem bear, it was immediately dealt with by the wildlife division. The bears were trapped and taken from the area, campsites were temporarily closed, and other techniques used to make sure the bears did not become habituated. It took years to get the public better educated and the compliance needed to manage the wild bears in the park. The surrounding cities also adopted the program and began a more aggressive program to secure the garbage in the city. Slowly but surely, the public became more aware for the need to alter the bears' behavior by not feeding them and keeping the garbage secured.

The wildlife division created a slogan GARBAGE KILLS BEARS, and it was included in the park brochures, seminars, bulletin boards, and the news media. Bumper stickers were placed on all the bumpers of the parks' vehicles and offered to the public to be placed on private vehicles. People became concerned the garbage was killing the bears. The narrative that was created that garbage kills bears was a little misleading and visitors asked what kind of garbage killed the bears, and how did it kill them. The fact of the matter was, the garbage itself would not kill the bear, but once the bear became habituated it relied on human intervention to get the garbage. It was more than likely to be trapped and removed from the area, or in the worse cases, it would be euthanized. If the garbage directly killed the bears, there would have been a serious decline in the bear population around the Great Smoky Mountains National Park from the number of restaurants and dumpsters located around the boundaries of the cities next to the park. I never once saw a bear feasting in a dumpster, climb out and drop dead from obesity. Garbage made them fat, just like people. They may not have been as healthy, but most garbage bears were big and fat. They had become habituated and unafraid of human presence that was only going to fill up their buffet again. This would only lead to aggressive behavior and they would have to be removed.

There was a bear incident that occurred when we got a call of a man dancing with a bear at the Newfound Gap parking area, at the Tennessee/North Carolina state line on U.S. 441. There were always calls coming in that got misinterpreted and this seemed to be one of these calls. I drove up to the parking area, which was about 12 miles from my location and met with a couple of other Rangers. Sure enough, there was a man petting a bear. As the bear stood on its hind feet, it followed people around in the parking area. Some of the people there described the bear dancing with the man. When we saw this, we yelled, the bear was going to kill him and eat him, and for him to get away from the bear. As the man tried to leave the bear, the bear followed him. It was obvious this bear had been tamed and was not a wild bear. The bear was about 200 pounds and had been well taken care of. It was apparent someone had the bear in captivity and brought it to the park and released it. I'm sure we could have ridden it in our patrol cars to remove it from the area, but instead we tranquilized the bear with a dart gun and took it to the wildlife building and put it in a holding cage.

After checking the bear, we found it had been de-clawed, confirming the bear had been in captivity somewhere. Due to its size, it was probably getting too big to manage and had to be relocated by the person who had taken the bear from the wild. The bear was probably taken when it was a newborn and most likely, while the mother was still asleep, hibernating. The babies are born while the mother is asleep and sometimes crawl out of their den and get lost or wander off. Even though they would cry out, the mother would not go out and retrieve them if she was still asleep. I found two newborn bears at different times, no bigger than both your fists, that had crawled out on the roadway with no mother present, but I was sure they were close. I removed them from the road trying not to handle them and pushed, tossed, and rolled them down the steep embankment to get them from the road. They would be handled the same as a baby deer where they were removed from danger and left for nature to take its course.

This bear was probably the victim of circumstance, where it was found and taken from the wild. After it became habituated in a captive environment with its claws removed, and its natural abilities altered, it was dependent on humans and unable to take care of itself. The persons who took this bear had no aforethought that this bear would not remain a cuddly teddy bear but grow into a massive animal that required high maintenance and territory to roam. This bear did not exhibit any aggressive behavior and cried and moaned like a dog, wanting attention. It lay against the cage, where it welcomed being rubbed or touched as if it were a dog. The sad part was the bear could not be released into the wild. Rules regarding the bear's adoption allowed it to be turned over to a wildlife park or zoo, but most of these facilities were over capacity with bears and we could not find an adoption facility to take the bear. The bear remained in the wildlife building in a cage for about a week, at which time, it was decided the bear would have to be euthanized. It was almost like a prisoner on death row as time neared for the bear to be executed. At the last minute of the last hour, the bear was given a reprieve and was adopted by the Cincinnati Zoo in Ohio.

Acclimation, an altered environment, and physical habituation resulted in the first death of a local resident schoolteacher in May of 2000, where she was killed by the bears. This occurred in the park and was the first bear fatality that occurred in the Great Smoky Mountains National Park and the southeastern United States. The end of the book will detail how and why the attack occurred as well as the mismanagement and negligence and false and misleading information by the management of the National Park Service that may have attributed to the fatal bear attack.

A large black bear at the smokies averages in weight 300-400 pounds. The bears that had been habituated by the presence of people were dangerous because they lost their fear of humans. The wild bears would run at the sight of a human, but there were a lot of bears that were acclimated to the presence of humans and would frequent the roadways, picnic areas, and campgrounds, where they eventually became a problem. One afternoon, I was at the Jakes Creek and Little River trail. I was out of my car walking around and there was an old apple orchard about a hundred yards away. There were several visitors walking around and hiking on the trails. They had come to the apple orchard and had spotted a small buck deer grazing in the old orchard. There was also a large bear there. Most of the time, the bears and other wildlife co-exist, but on this afternoon, the bear had venison on his menu.

I heard people yelling and screaming across the woods and I ran to see what was happening. When I got there, a bear that weighed probably 300 pounds had caught and killed the deer. The deer was not a big deer and had antlers but was a good size for an afternoon meal. The bear had the deer by his throat and began dragging it into the woods. When I ran up, visitors yelled to me to shoot the bear because it was killing the deer. I don't think the visitors liked my response when I told them the bear was getting dinner, but there were others there that agreed with me, so I didn't have to kill the bear. Later in the afternoon, I went back to where the bear had dragged the deer into the woods to see if I could maybe get me a loin off it, but the bear had already processed it. Once the bear got through feeding, it will cache the kill by covering it with dirt and leaves. There must have been another dinner guest from the amount of feasting on the deer and probably by the next morning it would be gone either by the bears or coyotes.

According to the visitors who watched the bear catch the deer, the bear was just ambling up close to the deer and attacked it before the deer could engage his running gear. Black bears are fast, running upwards of 30 mph, but in this case, it appeared to be the element of surprise that enabled the bear to catch the deer. I was only minutes from seeing a rare, natural phenomenon, where the bear caught the deer, but by the time I got there the bear had the deer incapacitated. This still didn't deter the visitors from staying clear of the bear, snapping pictures, and getting as close as possible. If people only knew they were within seconds of being a bear's next meal, they would stay away. It is a matter of time before another visitor is killed by a bear attack in the Smokies. The bears are multiplying and there are more bears than ever in the Great Smokies, according to the bear counts. There are also more visitors with over 11 million people visiting the park each year. Park Volunteers now try to referee the massive bear jams and visitor encounters, where they surround the bears and disregard the volunteers. I have spoken with three different volunteers and they all have told me they rarely call for a Park Ranger to assist them in trying to keep visitors away from the bears. Now that the elk have been introduced into the Smokies, they became habituated and caused more problems. When I was a Ranger, the bear calls were handled like any other disturbance. Volunteers could assist us, but now the Park Rangers assist the volunteers that are doing the jobs of armed Park Rangers, without the authority to cite the violators and take immediate action if there was a violation or a bear attack. If a bear chooses to attack, the person will be dead before the radio call could be made. The volunteers have told me they can only threaten the violators by telling them, they will call a Ranger, and it was difficult to get the visitors to comply. This is the same scenario that got Glenda Bradley killed, when a park fee collector assumed the responsibility of a Park Ranger.

When a rogue bear entered and stayed in these areas and became a nuisance, they would be captured and taken to another area of the park and released. The bears would usually be captured by a large culvert trap, that looks like an oversized metal barrel baited with food. The bears were like most humans and loved bacon and Krispy Kreme doughnuts. You could tell when there was going to be a bear trapped in the Great Smokies. When you entered the basement of headquarters and found a big sack of Krispy Kreme donuts and the smell of bacon being cooked in the microwave by the Wildlife Technician, you knew a bear was going down. If a bear kept returning, it would be captured and removed from the park to an area much further away in a remote area of the Cherokee National Forest, or a State Wildlife Management area. The bears did not have exclusive protection in these areas like the Great Smoky Mountains National

Park and could be hunted during an established hunting season. Once the bear became a problem bear, it had to be dealt with. If the bears could not be trapped, then they were tranquilized by a dart gun. They were tranquilized using Ketamine, that was a powerful sedating drug and would put them to sleep very quickly. While they slept, they were loaded on a gurney or stretcher and carried out to a trap.

We caught little bears, big bears, baby bears and old cranky bears. Seems the most problem bears were juvenile bears or bears weighing about 100 pounds. We responded to the Chimney's picnic area one afternoon, where an old cranky bear was terrorizing the picnic area. When we arrived, the bear had trashed the picnic area, turning over all the trash cans, including the large green dumpsters that were used at the time and were not anchored to the ground. The bear was an old male bear and weighed 400 pounds and was having a rough night. He picked up one of the large green dumpsters and threw it down the roadway, very aggressively. There were garbage cans strewn over the picnic area. We finally got him tranquilized and on examining him, we found he did not have any teeth and what teeth he had were abscessed and causing the bear a lot of pain. There was nothing that could be done for the bear and it was euthanized.

20

Odie

Most of my staff of Rangers in the district at the Smokies were old timers. There were very few new hires, with new seasonal Rangers occasionally added to the staff. In 1994, the "Ranger Future" calamity ended my supervisory duties and I could not hire and supervise anyone. Several new Rangers came on board. One Ranger made an impact in the district. His name is none other than Kevin Moses. The first day I met Kevin, we were on the firing range at the Oconaluftee district on the North Carolina side of the park. Kevin came "bouncing" down the drive to the shooting range, happy and gay with a semi-punk doo. He introduced himself to everyone and his accelerator was stuck. I thought to myself, 'where the hell did this come from?' A lot of times, you get a first impression when you meet someone. My first and immediate impression was this guy looked and acted like the dog, "Odie," in the Garfield cat cartoon, and I thought "Odie" was more defining than Kevin, and while he was at the Smokies, his name was "Odie."

There can be a complete book written about Odie. Odie was an airborne soldier and was now a National Park Ranger. Absolutely no one in the National Park Service could match the drive and enthusiasm Odie brought. Being a newbie, he was naturally going to be subjected to many pranks. He arrived at the smokies, driving an old, rough Nisan Pick-up with stickers all over it. I later call this the "suspect vehicle." Odie wanted to be involved in every definable aspect of being a National Park Ranger. Odie was simple but hungered for complexity. No Ranger could keep up with him and he became one of the best Rangers in the Smokies, and remains a Park Service favorite today, being the District Ranger in the Shenandoah Valley.

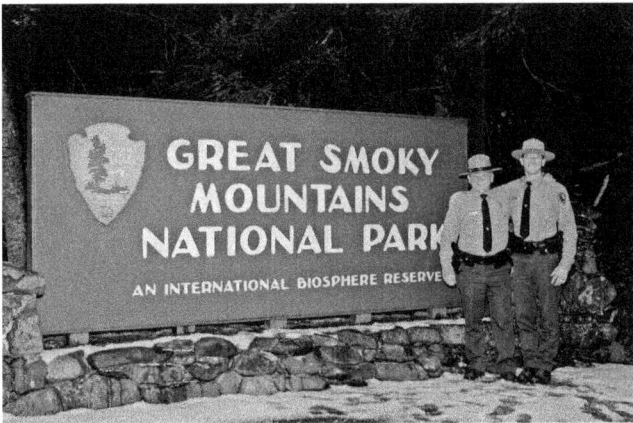

Ranger Grubb and Ranger Moses

I constantly kidded Odie, and his early days brought gullibility for a prank. He had gone to the swimming hole at Elkmont and had seen a lot of snakes on the wall by the river. He came to the office declaring the place was infested with copperheads. I knew there were a lot of water snakes that would be on the wall next to the river, but Odie insisted they were copperheads. I went with him to the swimming hole and sure enough it was infested, but with water snakes. I got down on my belly, hung over the wall, and got hold of one of the snakes. I told Odie he was right; this place was infested with copperheads. He leaned, looking over the wall, and I tossed one of the snakes around his legs. He could have won the Dancing with the Stars Competition and singing for America's Got Talent. The best part of pranking Odie, he never got mad and never tried to get even. I always kidded him about wearing his kerosene socks to keep the fire ants off his candy ass, and he has never forgotten it.

A lot of the Rangers were just no fun, but Odie put the fun into being a Park Ranger, along with his dedication in becoming one of the best Park Rangers I have ever known. Odie is one of the best trained Park Rangers in the National Park Service. If there was any type of training, Odie was sure to be in the class or in the field. He reveled at his own shortcomings and determined to learn every aspect of being a National Park Ranger. I reflected on my early days, and see myself as Odie, full of piss and vinegar, wanting to be one of the best Park Rangers ever. Odie was able to achieve and maintain his positive attitude, but I fear he will succumb to becoming one of "them" in Park management and forget his roots in becoming a National Park Ranger. My enthusiasm began to wane due to the political pressures that made it more difficult to be a National Park Ranger, thanks to the Ranger Future disaster the National Park Service created.

Even though the Smokies was one of the largest parks, with the most visitation of the National Parks, with 10 million visitors and waxing, the Law Enforcement program was still sub-standard with minimum funding. The vehicles were old and worn out with hundreds of thousands of mountain miles on them. We still carried .357 revolvers, with speed loaders. Bullet proof vests were issued, but they were one size fits all, and hand-me-downs from other Rangers that transferred to other parks, turning the vest in. My vest was an exception. Because of Ranger Bob McGhee's death at Gulf Islands, we were issued custom-fit bullet proof vests and I carried it with me to the Smokies. The communications system was a dinosaur and because of the terrain, very ineffective, depending on your location. We still worked alone covering hundreds of thousands of acres, and hundreds of miles of roads, along with hundreds of miles of back-country trails in the one district alone. The closest Ranger back-up could be at least 15 miles away having to respond from another district, driving on steep mountainous, dogleg roadways. It was not much different getting back-up from the local jurisdictions where their manpower was also diminished due to departmental budget restraints and departmental policies. Radios were still maintained in the park residences as back-up communications, where Park Rangers' wives would listen to the radio.

Even with these shortcomings, the Ranger jobs at the Smokies were still dangerously exciting. We knew this, but this is what Rangers were used to and what we did and didn't expect it to be any different. As time went on at the Smokies, the job kept getting more dangerous and stressful, responding to the assorted emergencies that occurred. The management of the Park had to maintain a Protection Division in the Park, but also was obligated to fund other divisions such as wildlife, fire, fisheries, interpretation, as well as the massive administration structure and cost. Every division complained of not being funded to operate and a lot of animosity resulted throughout the park divisions.

It was nonstop action at the Smoky Mountains, driving fast on crooked mountain roads with blue lights flashing and sirens screaming and echoing off the mountains, responding to river rescues, high angle technical rescues, and numerous medical emergencies that would be complex and difficult to manage. I encountered situations I had never dealt with at Gulf Islands National Seashore. Even as busy as the park was, there were patrols only up until midnight and everyone went home. If there was an incident, it would be reported to the local authorities and they would call us at our homes, and we would respond, without a dispatcher. Gatlinburg Police department and Pigeon Forge Police department had our radios separately from theirs, because the federal government had higher frequencies that would not be compatible with the local agencies. They would listen for us unless they were busy, and they would turn our radio down and maybe forget about us, leaving us without any communication. The other issue being the radios would not work in the remote and higher elevations. If we were called out in the middle of the night by any of the local agencies, they would monitor our radio and dispatch for us and provide back-up for any emergencies. It was a pretty screwed up operation, but it was better than nothing and the Rangers had learned how to cope with their situations and still respond to all emergencies.

21

New Guns

$\mathcal{O}$n or around 1992, Christmas came for the Law Enforcement Rangers of the Great Smoky Mountains as well as most of the Law Enforcement Rangers in the National Park Service. The old service revolvers were being replaced with semi-automatic pistols. When we learned we were getting new pistols, we were apprehensive in the quality and makes of the pistols. I figured we would be issued the lowest bid and grade of pistols that could be made in China. The Park Service management decided they would provide us with one of the best pistols available. The Sig-Sauer semi-automatic pistol was chosen. They went one step further to allow the Rangers to choose the caliber of pistol each would want to carry and set up a day at the range where each caliber of the semi auto pistol could be fired. The calibers were 9mm, .40 caliber, and .45 caliber that were available at the time.

The Great Smoky Mountains Rangers spent an entire day firing thousands of rounds of ammo from each caliber until each Ranger was comfortable with the weapon he would choose to carry as his service pistol. There was the lightweight 9mm for lightweight Rangers that had a high capacity magazine for extra ammunition. Then there was the heavyweight .45 for heavyweight Rangers but only had a 9-round magazine capacity. It was high velocity weapon where if you could hold on to it, and you shot a guy in the lower ear lobe, it would blow his head off. I was a lightweight ranger but chose the middleweight pistol and I decided on the .40 caliber based on the fact it was double the capacity of a revolver loaded with 13 rounds with two magazines as back-up. This gave me at least 36 rounds of fire power versus 18 rounds with a revolver, with quicker reloading capabilities. Even though I did not have to shoot a man, I experienced the stopping power of the .40 caliber when I had to shoot several wild hogs and bears that will be discussed in further chapters of this book.

Slowly, the Park Service tried to catch up to modern law enforcement technology and practices. Even though we had been given bigger and better firearms, the superintendents, who had little or no law enforcement experience or training, still controlled the law enforcement program. Most park managers were more concerned in counting hoppy toads and lizards than providing the Rangers with the needed equipment and training and personnel to safely protect the visitors, Rangers and the hoppy toads. With the new semi-automatic weapons, more Rangers were trained firearm instructors. The firearm training was being enhanced with more aggressive shooting and role-playing scenarios to enhance the reality of a confrontation, rather than just shooting at a piece of paper. I had been a firearm instructor for years, conducting firearms training and qualifications but was not given the opportunity to continue when the new semi auto pistols were introduced. Being an instructor came with no extra pay and was very strenuous, and required a lot of preparation, so losing the certification was not a bad thing. I thought I was not elected to maintain my firearms certification because of the new weapons. I was also pretty much burned out in firearm training anyways, so it didn't matter. Unknown at the time, this turned out to be a small piece of my responsibilities being taken away by a vindictive park management, to end my leadership position at the Great Smoky Mountains National Park, to be replaced with diverse employees in the reorganization that was upcoming.

Firearms Qualifying

22

K-9 Ammo

I recall an incident that occurred after one of the firearms qualifying days when the Kentucky Highway Patrol was requesting assistance in locating a firearm used in a murder in Kentucky. The suspect in the murder was arrested and he confessed he had thrown the weapon off one of the steep overlooks on the Tennessee side of Newfound Gap on U.S.441. The overlook had massive rocks and boulders and was very steep. The officer had brought his K-9 partner that specialized in bomb and gunpowder residue. It was a long shot to find a gun in this terrain and I was very apprehensive whether this dog would be able to smell a gun in this environment. We spent the best part of the day searching for the gun, and finally suspended the search and went back to our patrol vehicles. The Kentucky trooper wanted his dog to end the search with a find and wanted to plant the K-9's toy in the trunk of my patrol vehicle.

My vehicle was a large, Chevrolet cruiser with a big trunk. In the trunk was everything needed for most any emergency, including a chainsaw, emergency medical equipment, repelling gear, blankets, firefighting equipment etc. There was very little room in the trunk, but the trooper proceeded to place the K-9's toy in one of my hiking boots and closed the trunk. He brought the dog back to my cruiser, walked it around and to the trunk where we opened the trunk for the K-9 to find his toy. The K-9 jumped in the trunk sniffing around, but instead of going to the shoe, he went to the opposite side of the trunk and sat down. The trooper was pissed the dog would not find the toy and took the dog out of the trunk and scolded the dog and walked him around again putting him in the trunk where the dog did the same thing. He made a third attempt where the dog would sit down and not retrieve his toy. The trooper scolded the dog and got the K-9's toy and put the K-9 in his cruiser. The trooper told me he had never had his dog to act this way, and I just figured the K-9 was just having a bad day.

The trooper had just left, and I was talking with one of the Rangers and told him about the dog. It was at the same time, I finally realized why the K-9 had acted like he did rather than find his toy. I had left the firing range a couple of days prior and had put a full case of .357 ammunition in the trunk of my patrol and it was under all that gear. The K-9 had located the ammunition and did what he was supposed to do by sitting down when he made the find. I immediately got in touch with the Highway Patrol officer and explained to him he was dealing with a very smart K-9, but a stupid Park Ranger who should have had enough sense to know that finding bullets is what K-9s like this do. I went and met with the trooper who had not left the area yet, and apologized to him and apologized to his K-9 partner. We met in the Dollywood parking area and we let the K-9 search around the perimeter of the parking area and led him back to my cruiser. We didn't use the toy but opened the trunk and the K-9 jumped in the trunk and again sat down over the ammunition. We dug out the case of ammo and the dog was praised for the find and everything was made right. The only thing I was dreading, after the trooper put the K-9 back in his cruiser, that he was going scold me like he did with the K-9 and make me find the toy. He was professional and understood the mistake that was made, but I guarantee when he got back to his friends and coworkers, he was fast to tell them of his experience with a dumb-ass Park Ranger.

23

Ranger Future

*I*n 1994, the Park Service was pressured in recognizing that Law Enforcement Rangers retirement were covered under the 6c, Law Enforcement legislation. Rather than just declare the Law Enforcement Rangers the 6c status, the management of the National Park Service came up with a new plan called "Ranger Future." This gave Park Service management the justification to rearrange, demote, replace, and reorganize its employee structure that allowed picking and choosing who got career status, based on diversity, gender and personal friendship. This was a defining moment in my career and a lot of other Rangers' careers who held career supervisory positions. I was relieved of my supervisory responsibilities, that took away any enhanced opportunities to be upgraded in the future. My supervisor lost his supervisory responsibilities and was replaced by a "diverse" employee who had very little supervisory experience and no law enforcement experience but had a law enforcement commission. The individual had made no arrests or investigated any serious crimes. Because of the Ranger Future, this could be done by the will of the management, because the demotions did not interfere with the pay status that allowed the demoted individuals' pay to remain the same, but at the same time, it took away the ability to compete for an enhanced career position. By returning to the field it took away all the enhanced training, management of district operations, and personnel supervision. I would have preferred to remain in my supervisory position because I could compete for a higher position much easier due to the experience I had accumulated. But then again, just being a Park Ranger was fulfilling and was, after all, what I had dreamed of doing. Sitting in an office, shuffling paper to keep up with park management policies, dealing with personnel issues and a long list of other duties was not my kind of job. I was quite comfortable just being a Park Ranger, where I had the personal satisfaction of being in the action and making a difference in people's lives.

It was at this time the Park Service upgraded their Law Enforcement Officers pay grades and pay status. However, as Park Service management would have it, it was decided by the powers that be, all Park Service employees would be upgraded in pay status that would equal each Park Ranger's responsibilities at certain grade levels. The law enforcement officers got a 1.5 % pay incentive over regular employees and could retire at 50 years old with 20 years law enforcement service and mandatory retirement at age 57, just like all the other Federal Law Enforcement agencies. A lot of Law Enforcement Rangers retired with 6c status that had never made an arrest or conducted any investigations.

The superintendents of the National Park Service were paid at the General Service pay grades that were usually GS-15. As a result of this re-organization, the Superintendents quietly slipped into Senior Executive Service positions that boosted their pay on the same level of what the vice president's pay is.

Along with these promotions came more administrative support staff and especially Public Information Officers, who drafted all news releases and information concerning the activities in the park. These Public Information releases were carefully crafted to create a narrative that distracted from what was really happening in the parks and especially law enforcement situations the Park Service did not want the public to know about. The Public Information Officers basically wrote the news story for the media and included what the Park Service wanted to be disclosed. There was no journalism involved, and the media did not question any of the information given to them, usually resulting in mitigated and false and misleading information to the public. This practice was not considered to be a lie because they were bound by an old southern tradition where they would "cross their fingers" when the information was released.

24

Dead Body Recovery

*W*orking in the Great Smoky Mountains brought a new challenge every day. For an action junkie such as myself, I found it very fulfilling to get to experience these challenges that could involve a serious law enforcement incident including rape, murder, domestic violence, and lots of disorderly conduct, and intoxication arrests, or performing a technical rescue, and of course dealing with numerous motor vehicle accidents, that occurred almost daily. There were hundreds of miles of backcountry trails where visitors became lost or experienced a major medical emergency that required an urgent response and sometimes included long hikes to get to the victims. There were a lot of emergency responses on the trails that were deteriorated from erosion and constant foot traffic of hikers. Visitors were nescient of their surroundings and unaware of hazards of falling and tripping that would result in broken bones, twisted ankles and other injuries.

Thousands of visitors hiked up and down the trails daily, without a clue of what was ahead. This usually included overweight chassis on little tiny ankles, wearing flip flops and pumps. When a visitor would go down, we would have to hike in and carry the victim back out. It would usually take about 12 to 15 people to carry the litter and victim out, depending on the terrain, and how far from an access they would be. The litter was made of plastic that the victim would lie on, strapped in, and it fastened to a frame over a large ATV wheel. It was called a TETON litter and worked much better than trying to carry someone in a litter alone. The wheel assisted in the "carry out" but would still have to be manhandled to keep it upright and not dump the victim off.

If there was an unfortunate situation where someone may have died and not near a trail or access, we would go in, and the victim was loaded in a sked. This was nothing more than a large, hard plastic sheet and the victim would be completely placed inside and the plastic folded and tied around the victim. The sked would then slide over the vegetation, downed trees and other obstacles, making it easier to get the victim out.

One such body recovery occurred on Thunderhead Mountain that is the high elevations of the Park near the Tennessee/North Carolina boundary. There had been a small plane crash and the pilot was killed in the crash. It was in a very remote area of park and the North Carolina Rangers went in and located the crash. This was not going to be a very good day for anyone. To begin with, it was at least 10 miles getting to the crash and it was all uphill. About six of us began at the Laurel Creek road going into Cades Cove and started rolling the Teton Litter up the trail to Thunderhead Mountain to meet up with the North Carolina Rangers. The weather in the beginning was good, but the higher we went, the worse it got. It was about six to eight hours getting to Thunderhead Mountain where we had met Ranger Rocky Jenkins, who had located the crashed plane that was about a mile off the trail. Rocky had already packaged the victim in the sked and was able to get the victim almost to the Thunderhead Mountain Trail. After we got the victim to the trail the weather was deteriorating fast. I quickly learned how Thunderhead Mountain got its name as it began thundering and lightning with a huge downpour of rain. This caused the trails to flood with water running down the trails and the trails turning to slick mud. We loaded the sked on the Teton and decided we would continue down the North Carolina side with the victim. The North Carolina maintenance divisions at the Smokies had a team of mules. We went to meet up with the mule team and transferred the victim onto the mules. It was at least another 10 miles before we got the victim to Fontana Lake, where we got the victim on a boat and took him another five miles to the Fontana Marina.

The trails had become almost impassable and we were unable to negotiate the litter without a lot of slipping and sliding. After a while, we met the Park Service mules and transferred the victim onto the mules. We started downhill on the rain-soaked trails with the hard rain continuing. The trails had become so slick, the mules could not get footing and the victim was thrown from the mules as the wrangler tried to keep the mules from becoming injured. It was then decided we continue with the litter down the trail without the mules' assistance. This made the trip even longer and the litter crew was small with only about 8 to 10 people trying to maneuver the litter down the steep, muddy mountain. The rain stopped and we tried again to use the mules and placed the victim back on them. They were able to carry the victim for a short distance and gave the litter crew a break, until we came to another steep, muddy area and we again had to put the victim back on the Teton.

It got dark as we rolled the litter to the waiting boats at the Fontana Lake. We hurriedly got the victim on the boat and everyone boarded the boats, headed to the Fontana Lake Marina. The litter crew quickly boarded the boat that didn't carry the victim, and I got stuck with the victim for the boat ride back. The victim was still in the sked at this point and not visible. When we got to the Marina, we transferred the victim into a soft body bag. For whatever reason, the victim had to be taken back to the Tennessee side of the park, for the coroner there. In order to do this, the victim was loaded in the back of a Suburban SUV to make the trip back. There were several vehicles there to take us back to the Tennessee side of the park, and everyone scrambled to get in a vehicle that did not carry the victim. I again got stuck riding with the victim. The back of the vehicle had some equipment along with the victim. and the victim's upper torso rested on the back of the seat between me and the back door. Of course, the victim was in a body bag, but he kept rolling against my head, making for a very uncomfortable hour and half ride, back to Tennessee on the dog leg, crooked roads. The body recovery had taken about 18 hours to complete. The recovery would have been easy but every obstacle that could have been thrown at us made for an exhausting experience I never wanted to repeat.

25

Lost

One frequent emergency that required an immediate response was visitors trapped on a trail when it got dark. Most of these calls came from visitors who made a day hike and didn't realize they couldn't make it back before dark and had no flashlights. In the Great Smoky Mountains, if you hike on a trail and it gets dark, the only recourse you have is to sit beside a tree and wait for daylight. In the latter years of my career, cell phones came into existence and visitors notified someone they were trapped by darkness, somewhere in the Smoky Mountains. Due to the lack of phone towers and depending on the location, a visitor might contact an emergency dispatcher several states away. This was a dreaded call because the call usually came in after you had worked the late shift and looked forward to getting off duty. This is when someone would call, stranded on a trail, and needed a flashlight to get back to the trailhead. It would not be an emergency at the time, but these visitors had absolutely no clue as to survival and were already in a panic from being in the dark. The environmental concerns due to weather, hazardous terrain, lack of clothing and other issues prompted these calls to be handled as emergencies. As a result, Rangers would go in after being exhausted from an already full day and night agenda and had to hike five to six miles or more and carry these visitors a flashlight and walk them off the trail. With thousands of visitors hiking the trails every day of the year, these incidents naturally occurred. This was part of the reason we were Park Rangers. As much as we would cuss these lost souls, trying to find them, the reward came in the end, when the people realized we had probably saved their life, and we were showered with praise and gratitude, that added to the legacy of being a National Park Ranger.

I recall one of my own blunders, hiking across country, in territory I had reviewed on the map but had not hiked before. As I hiked, I encountered terrain that was very steep and impassable, and altered my course, hiking up drainages to the next ridge to get around steep rock faced inclines This took hours away from my scheduled plans to be out of the woods before dark. As it got dark, I was not lost, but I didn't know where the hell I was. I had a gun to get me some meat but didn't have any matches to make a fire to cook it. I had some water and a flashlight and weather wasn't a concern, and I always carried a compass. I didn't want to sleep on the ground that night. I had the advantage of being a Ranger, which a visitor did not have. I had a radio and a Ranger to come to where I thought I was and turn on the siren of his patrol car. When he got where I thought I was, I couldn't hear the siren and he continued on the roadway with the siren on until I could hear it. It was at this time I considered I may be just a little lost. When I finally was able to get a bearing on my location, it was hours of fighting through the rhododendron and mountain laurel, and steep terrain and drainages before I was able to find my way out. A lot people have experienced being in a blackberry thicket with thorns. Rhododendron and Mountain Laurel do not have thorns, but is the same thing, trying to crawl through the tangled limbs, especially in the dark, where you would rip the hide off crawling through the thick twisting limbs.

Most of the backcountry patrols were on established trails, but occasionally, I would hike cross country to avoid the thousands of visitors who were hiking on established trails. Hiking those trails compared to hiking down the streets of Gatlinburg, observing hikers as if they had just left Wal-Mart. Being off trail gave us more solitude and quiet and the lack of other hikers was more invigorating. Being off trails also gave us an opportunity to find evidence of illegal activities, such as growing marijuana, poaching ginseng, illegal campsites and such.

On one trip I had taken, I found a wounded bear with part of an arrow stuck in it. It was too far out in the woods to retrieve the bear and it was in critical condition, so I killed it with my pistol. It was closer to the Gatlinburg side of the district where there were lots of hotels, and sometimes people would stay in the hotels and then slip across to the park and try to shoot a bear with a bow and arrow, where there would be no sounds of a gunshot. I suspect this was the case of this bear.

Growing marijuana in the park was a past time for some of the ole boys that lived around there and was a pretty good cash crop until we found it. We attempted to catch these farmers by setting up surveillance or installing cameras, but it was difficult and time consuming, and we didn't have much luck catching anyone. One of the biggest problems was concealing the cameras from the bears that would climb the trees and destroy the cameras. This happened several times. Bears have the best sense of smell of anything on earth with noses designed to detect anything that may be a food smell. A lot of plastics, fabric and other materials contained oils and other ingredients bears could detect and they could easily climb up to them or find them next to the ground where they would usually destroy them.

The farmers also got more sophisticated to protect their crops by putting out booby traps, such as using fishhooks hanging from the trees, mounting triggered shotgun shells that could be tripped as you walk into them. The booby traps were usually set to keep other farmers from stealing their crops, rather than deter law enforcement. Killing or hurting a rival dope grower carried a lesser penalty than injuring a law enforcement officer. We also fly in Army or National

Guard helicopters over the park in the early fall and identify the crops from the air before it was harvested. A small marijuana patch could be easily detected by eyesight in the thick vegetation from the air because it was different from the rest of the vegetation and showed where the terrain had been cleared or altered. Once it was spotted, ground crews would go in, secure the area and would just chop the stuff down, haul it to a burn pile where there seemed to always be certain Rangers that would volunteer to burn the stuff. Flying in the aircraft was a little unsettling for me. I could handle the old Huey choppers, but if I had to fly the little LOH (Low Observation Helicopters), I would need a barf bag as it was like being 'suped up' car sick.

The history of flying in helicopters, as Rangers in the Smokies, didn't have real good records. Two of my supervisors had been involved in and survived helicopter crashes shortly before I had come to the Smokies. Ranger Bill Acree flew with seven other people on a law enforcement mission when the helicopter developed a mechanical problem and stopped in midair and fell to the ground. The crash killed four of the people in the helicopter and seriously injured Ranger Acree and the others. Ranger Bobby Holland was seriously injured when the helicopter he flew on was taxiing on the runway and hit a pole and flipped the helicopter and seriously injured Bobby and the rest of the crew of the helicopter. Although Bobby was involved in a bad crash, his mentor, Ranger Acree was quick to point out Bobby's crash was only a traffic accident. I'm just glad I didn't end up next. Assuming I would survive a crash, it would have been easy, but having to get bragging rights and compare my wounds with these seasoned Park Rangers would have been difficult.

26

Ranger Morale

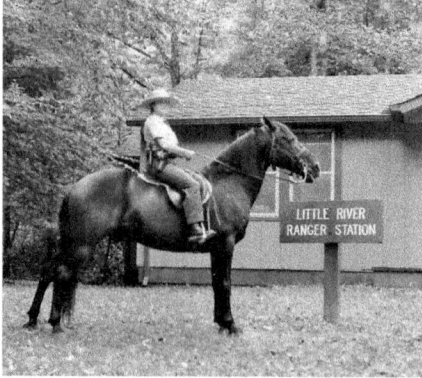

The Park Ranger image was slowly being diminished. By the time I retired, there was very little monitoring of the marijuana growth, or Ginseng poachers, or illegal hunting in the park. The Ranger staff focused more on regular law enforcement patrols that occurred on the main roads. When I first arrived at the Smokies, we had horses we would use for patrols. There were several horses throughout the districts in the park. We would use the horses instead of a patrol car or hiking patrols. The horses were a very low-key approach in providing visitor protection and did not involve any high-speed emergency responses like a patrol car. They enhanced the image of a Park Ranger patrolling on horseback, and were effective in patrolling in the back country where visitors would be surprised to encounter a mounted patrol. The horses were used for search and rescue situations and most importantly, they were used to lead the parades of the local towns. The Park Rangers, dressed in their Smoky Bear hats, rode in formation, and hailing colors was most impressive, and indicated a true profession that was quite different from other agencies as police and emergency providers.

The new management of the Park Service, as a result of the reorganization in 1994, decided the Park Ranger image was not important. They decided the horses cost too much, unlike buying a Crown Vic patrol car that cost $30,000 before it was fully equipped for service. The Park Ranger staff was drastically reduced, with the focus of the new park administration on counting hoppy toads, and providing facilities for more science and resource management operations, rather than providing protection to the visitors, and resources and the Rangers against a growing criminal element. Park Ranger duties were being more specialized, including the addition of criminal investigators. There was more intense scrutiny and supervision of everyday activities involving the visitor protection Rangers. The independent Park Ranger now faced more and more supervision to justify a supervisor's job that supported more management jobs and did nothing to assist the visitor protection.

As a result of the reorganization in 1994, it was recognized that Park Rangers involved in law enforcement would be identified by a new uniform badge that would be different than the old Buffalo badge that everyone in the Park Service wore. It is distinctive and supposed to identify the Law Enforcement Park Ranger from the rest of the Park Rangers.

I had worked for almost 20 years, and now Rangers are required to wear their gun belts and protective equipment that used to be kept under the seat and out of sight of park managers and the visiting public.

Even though the National Park Ranger had now taken on a new identity by issuing us a new, shiny badge, the law enforcement operation was still administered by a politically appointed park superintendent who still did not possess any skills in law enforcement, or visitor protection, firefighting or Emergency and Technical responses. The reorganization of 1994 created a lot of tension within the ranks of the Park Rangers. Many of the Park Service career employees, which would include me, who had enhanced supervisory leadership positions for years, lost those positions. This would allow for "diverse" employees with less experience and seniority to take over supervising the supervisors that used to supervise them. The positions weren't decided through attrition, position vacancies, retiring Rangers, or poor work performance. To qualify for the Park Ranger leadership jobs, it was all about the plumbing and color that would guarantee a position without any leadership qualities.

There was a lot of antipathy within the divisions of the park where the supervisory leaders were now working for their subordinates. The Park Ranger morale declined dramatically. There were constant internal investigations that I never heard of in my early years as a Park Ranger. Some of the Rangers in the Smokies, including me, were frustrated by the ongoing nitpicking, supervision that was deliberate and unconstructive. The new re-organizational supervisors proved to be a disaster in the operation of the Visitor Protection division. This resulted in another Ranger being shot and killed in the National Park Service.

27

Park Ranger Joseph David Kolodski
End of Watch Sunday, June 21, 1998

Joe K

It was Father's Day, in June of 1998 at the Great Smoky Mountains National Park. Park Ranger Joe Kolodski, was shot and killed after responding to a call involving an armed and intoxicated Cherokee Indian with a rifle. Several reports were called into the dispatch office, where the subject stuck the rifle inside of visitors' vehicles while they sat in their vehicles at the Big Witch over-look on the Blue Ridge Parkway. The overlook was in the Blue Ridge Parkway District and was only a few miles from the boundary of the Smoky Mountains, where it connected with the Blue Ridge Parkway. When an incident occurred and a Smoky Mountain Ranger was closer and readily available, the Blue Ridge Parkway would ask for assistance in responding and backing up the Blue Ridge Ranger. Several calls had come in and it was relayed to the Rangers working the Oconaluftee district of the Smoky Mountains. The Smoky Mountain Rangers were much closer, being only a few miles away, than the Blue Ridge Ranger who drove at breakneck speeds to get to the call. It was close to shift change, and the on-duty Rangers of the Smokies were going off duty soon, and they did not respond to the calls for assistance by the Blue Ridge Parkway, and the Great Smoky Mountains National Park dispatcher.

One of the two Rangers (getting ready to be off duty) had been in a leadership role for many years at the Great Smoky Mountains National Park. Because of the reorganization, he had been replaced by an inexperience, and less qualified individual with no people skills. It took out the highly respected and experienced Ranger who had led many law enforcement details, a fire crew boss, and many other leadership roles as a National Park Ranger for years. He was now being supervised by the same subordinates he had supervised for years. The other Ranger who heard the call also became a law enforcement supervisor. He had been put in that position because of social and political influence. He had no leadership experience and very little law enforcement experience but was now supervising this very seasoned and experienced leader. This new district supervisor of law enforcement made no decision to respond to a very serious and volatile situation that involved a public safety threat to the visitors of the National Park. There was a lot of animosity, and the morale and drive were diminished by a once great Ranger. Having known this Ranger for many years, he would never have disregarded this kind of call, regardless of any shift change or situation where a visitor or fellow Ranger needed help. Because of incompetent leadership and constant harassment, a once great Ranger's spirit and drive were destroyed. The Rangers were now reluctant to perform without direct supervision, which was none. The calls kept coming in for several minutes and a Blue Ridge Ranger was responding as fast as he could. This was never disclosed, and no one knows the background that would be the definitive moment that would cause National Park Ranger Joe Kolodski, to lose his life.

Ranger Joe Kolodski came on duty at the Smokies and met with the Rangers ending their shift. Joe said he would go and investigate the incident and proceeded to drive up the Blue Ridge Parkway, alone, to an active gun call. Joe only had his sidearm because he locked his long guns, being a shotgun and AR-15, in the Ranger Station gun locker that was further away. Instead of going to get his firearms, he decided the call was urgent and responded immediately, going to a gun call unprepared and without immediate back-up. The only reason his guns were locked away and not in his patrol car, is because he feared someone would break into his cruiser and steal them, and he would face the wrath of his supervisor for not securing his weapons. There was constant conflict between the Ranger staff and the supervisors, and more time was spent dealing with personnel issues than giving assistance to the visitors.

The Blue Ridge Parkway Ranger was on his way to the call but was many miles away and proceeded to the incident at a high rate of speed, to get there fast as he could. In the meantime, Joe arrived at the location without lights and siren and no back up. He searched for the individual. Joe parked his vehicle in the roadway and proceeded on foot. There was a tunnel under the Blue Ridge Parkway road, next to the Big Witch overlook, where the reports were made of the individual sticking the rifle in the cars of visitors. Joe observed the individual with the rifle, walking in the road, leading from the tunnel under the Blue Ridge Parkway. Joe returned to his patrol car to call for back-up, to give the location of the individual. His portable radio did not work due to the location, and he had to use his patrol car radio. Unbeknownst to Joe, the individual with the rifle had also spotted Joe, and turned and crawled up the embankment to the roadway, where he stood 27 steps from Joe in front of a pine tree. Joe did not see the individual, and stood behind the door of his patrol car, talking on his radio. The individual ambushed Joe, and opened fire with a 6.5mm rifle, hitting Joe just above his bullet proof vest, in the shoulder. It was at this very moment, the Blue Ridge Parkway Ranger arrived and pulled his patrol car behind Joe, as this unfolded, and Joe lay on the roadway.

An intense gun battle erupted as numerous gunshots were fired by the suspect and by the Blue Ridge Parkway Ranger. The other Smoky Mountain Rangers that did not initially respond with Joe, decided to back up Joe, but were far behind him, driving in a white, unmarked pick-up truck. They arrived after Joe had been shot and lay on the roadway. The gun battle continued as numerous gunshots were fired by the suspect and by the Blue Ridge Parkway Ranger. The suspect fired several rounds into Joes' patrol car. The Blue Ridge Parkway Ranger had exited his patrol car with his shotgun when he came under fire from the individual, who still stood in the same location where he had shot Joe. The suspect fired multiple rounds through the windshield of the Blue Ridge Ranger patrol car, into the driver's side, trying to kill him. He had not seen the Ranger exit his vehicle and was behind it. The Blue Ridge Ranger observed the suspect standing in front of the pine tree. The Ranger was unable to return fire because of the gunfire and bullets hitting his vehicle. The Ranger finally got a round of oo buckshot off with his shotgun just as the suspect darted from the tree. All the rounds from the buckshot hit exactly in the tree where the suspect had stood, but the suspect darted away just in time, without getting hit.

The suspect then ran into the woods and the Blue Ridge Ranger jumped in his vehicle and backed up to a safer location, as the suspect began firing multiple rounds from a hillside. Another Smokies Ranger also arrived to assist and was equipped with an AR-15 rifle. He was pinned down and could not determine where the gunshots were coming from and could not see the suspect. The suspect fired off rounds as Joe lay in the roadway. It was at this moment, the two Rangers in the pick-up decided to get Joe and drove the pick-up to Joe as shots were fired, jumped out, and loaded Joe into the back of the pick-up, and drove away. The suspect fired rounds and whooped like an Indian on the warpath. Joe had been mortally wounded and died on scene as a result of his injuries.

"Officer down" calls went out to all law enforcement agencies. The area this occurred in was remote, with the closest town being Cherokee, N.C. with a small police force. I can vividly recall where I was and what I was doing on this day. This was on Father's Day and I was off duty, nailing shingles on the roof of my house, in Gatlinburg, when the Smokies dispatch called me and told me Joe had been involved in a shooting. When I inquired if he was all right, the dispatcher replied no one knew of his status as the area was still hot, and Rangers were still sustaining gunshots. All the Smokies Rangers, Blue Ridge Rangers and other law enforcement officers were called to respond. I hurriedly got my uniform on and responded from my house that was at least 50 miles from where the shooting had occurred. A Remington 870 shotgun and Colt AR15 carbine was in my patrol vehicle that I kept at my house. The suspect was still at large, and rifles and shotguns were requested. I met Ranger Chip Nelson at the Ranger Station where he waited with an armload of long guns. He threw the guns in the backseat and we headed across the mountain on Newfound Gap road to the Blue Ridge Parkway.

There was a solemn quietness between me and Chip as we heard the engine of the Chevrolet Caprice roar, the loud siren, and radio chatter as we proceeded to the location. I cannot remember how fast I drove or how many cars I had put in the ditch as the adrenaline got more intense. I had not eaten anything, and I was weak as the adrenaline overtook me. I retrieved a Snickers candy bar I grabbed as I left my house and while driving a hundred miles per hour, somehow was able to unwrap the Snickers bar. Ranger Nelson pushed the floor out of my patrol car, and I finished off the Snickers bar. While it was not funny at the time, we look back and now laugh at what occurred while I ate the Snickers bar. When I finished with the candy, I threw the wrapper out the window. At that same moment, Ranger Nelson looked directly at me in disbelief. He then said he couldn't believe he saw me throw the candy wrapper out the window. A Park Ranger littered the National Park. I guess we both looked to establish communication of a different subject and focus on something else as we responded at breakneck speeds, hoping to hear a status report about Joe and the situation that was unfolding.

When we arrived at the Blue Ridge Parkway, both Joe's and the Blue Ridge Ranger's patrol cars had been shot up and had been moved away from the scene. Driving past the patrol cars and seeing them shot all to hell was very disturbing. Chip and I still did not know Joe's status. While we got geared up to assist in the search and apprehension of this suspect, Ranger Bobby Holland came and told us Joe had been shot and killed. I was standing behind my patrol car with the trunk open when he told us this. I can remember vividly as emotion and shock caused my knees to weaken and I became over-wrought with distress. Chip and I learned the suspect was still at large, and we continued to the area where the search parties were being staged. The area was very remote with the chances of us being ambushed. There were no major cities or back-up response close by, but when I arrived, and in less than an hour, there were over three hundred law enforcement officers present. Because of the profes-sional relationship the criminal investigator and other North Carolina Rangers had with almost all law enforcement officers in the area, an intense ground manhunt was organized within minutes of Joe being gunned down. It was steep, mountainous terrain and thou-sands of acres without roads and any other access, and the only effec-tive way to proceed was by ground search.

Park Rangers are trained in man tracking and we had some of the best in the region. Park Ranger J.R. Buchanan had pioneered the man tracking program in the Smokies in the early 60s and 70s. and was renowned for his tracking expertise. It was said J.R could track a locomotive for several hundreds of miles, but I didn't believe it. J.R.'s legacy resulted in ongoing man tracking training and it was used extensively in Search and Rescues with many of the Smokies Rangers being consulted by other agencies to assist in man tracking situations. These trained man trackers were extremely experienced and were called to assist in tracking and locating lost visitors or a criminal suspect. Rangers Pat Patton, Lamon Brown and Johnny Murphy went in knowing there could be an ambush but proceeded to try to find this guy anyway. The "officer down" call had every officer in the area searching for the suspect. A game warden with the Cherokee Indian Reservation knew the area and terrain very well and went to where a trail came out of a drainage that was adjacent across the mountains from where the shooting occurred and was several miles the way the crow flies. The suspect appeared coming off a small trail and the Cherokee officer took him into custody. The individual was brought out where the Blue Ridge Parkway Ranger identified him "eyeball to eyeball" standing 27 steps away as the subject was firing his weapon at the Blue Ridge Ranger.

The man trackers took over the scene and tracked the subject from where the Blue Ridge Ranger had shot at him, to the top of a ridge where the suspect kept shooting, pinning down the Rangers. The trackers found numerous rounds of spent and live ammunition and tracked the subject in the direction where the Cherokee game warden had apprehended the suspect. They found the weapon involved and tracked the suspect through the woods and mountainous terrain, eventually coming out to where he was apprehended, confirming the suspect was the same person who had shot Joe.

Later investigation found the suspects' vehicle stuck at a dead end road where Joe first saw him, along with some personal items including a guitar. Without a doubt, this was the individual responsible for Joe's death. The FBI assisted in the investigation and assisted the North Carolina Criminal Investigator, John Maddox. John led the investigation, and ultimately brought the complaint to the U.S. Attorney's office, where the suspect, 47-year-old Jeremiah Locust, was prosecuted for the murder of National Park Ranger Joe Kolodski. The suspect was taken to the lock-up facility in Asheville, North Carolina. I was called to transport the suspect to the lock-up facility, because I had one of the patrol vehicles equipped to secure the suspect. The news media had surrounded the police station, trying to get information about the shooting. It was getting late, and the drive to Asheville was at least an hour getting there.

When I arrived at the police station, I was informed there would be another Ranger riding with me, while transporting the suspect. I didn't know the Ranger who worked on the Blue Ridge Parkway. I was also informed there would be two FBI agents riding behind me to the lock-up. I wasn't part of the discussion on how the suspect would be transported, but later was told the reason for all the extra security was they were afraid I may try to let the suspect escape and shoot him, and extra security was added to the transport.

Because of all the news media present, the FBI planned to take the suspect out of the back door of the police station, and hurriedly load him into my cruiser, to keep the news media from getting his picture, as he was taken out of the police station. There was a lot of chaos at the police station; a large crowd was outside. The suspect's family had been in and out of the police station, visiting him, bringing him clothes and whatever. I told the FBI I was not transporting the suspect before I personally searched him for any weapons, even a handcuff key he could use before he got into my cruiser. This would mean him having to stand out in the open in public view as I conducted my search. I still don't know what the big deal was to obscure this bastard from the public, but for whatever reason, he wasn't getting in my car until I thoroughly searched him for weapons. He had just killed one Ranger and I wasn't planning on being another. The FBI was adamant I follow their orders, but I was more adamant and told them to get another transport. A police officer is trained to search an individual when he takes custody of a prisoner, and the suspect is thoroughly searched for suspected weapons or contraband. They conceded to let me search the suspect before getting in my vehicle and I made sure I searched him slowly and thoroughly, until the media was able to get a camera shot of this bastard.

I was racked with emotions as I drove the suspect quietly down I-40 to the Asheville lock-up. There was no conversation between me and the other Ranger, and I could see the suspect in my rearview mirror, in the back seat, in the headlights of the FBI following close behind me. He didn't move at all sitting in the middle of the back seat, looking forward. I had thoughts come to me that if the suspect attempted to escape, I would be able to take this bastard out for good, but the fantasy diminished in the headlights of the FBI, driving closely behind me. I reflected on my relationship with Joe, when I first met him as a classmate at the Federal Law Enforcement Training Center in Glynco, Georgia, and then working with him on a daily basis as we would meet many mornings at the Tennessee-North Carolina line as the park was gearing up for a busy day of visitation. In the quietness of the drive to the lock-up, I also reflected on another one of my Ranger friends, Bob McGhee, who had been gunned down eight years earlier. I quickly realized it was becoming a reality and a trend, and there were going to be more Rangers shot and killed. I hoped I would not be one of them because I seemed to attract a lot of criminals and I aggressively pursued any criminal who would take advantage of any citizen or visitor.

There was a long period of time, and a team of defense attorneys were appointed to defend what was clearly a drunken psychopath who had murdered Ranger Joe Kolodski. The suspect was found guilty of murder but was spared the death penalty I was hoping he would get. He was sentenced to life in prison without the possibility of parole. Although the drunken psychopath had committed the murder, one of the reasons for Joe's death clearly was a result of National Park Service mismanagement, that was compounded by ongoing management negligence. Sending a Ranger alone to an active gun assault would get no review by the park management to identify shortcomings of the supervision and direction that caused Joe to be killed. The ongoing mismanagement of the National Park Service law enforcement program was still managed by superintendents who have no law enforcement training or experience and would lead to yet another Ranger I worked with getting shot and killed before I would retire.

28

Rockslide

*J*n 1997, a huge rockslide occurred at the Tennessee/North Carolina state line, shutting down Interstate 40. As a result, traffic was routed into the Great Smoky Mountains National Park to get around the slide. When the slide occurred, a young girl from Knoxville, Tennessee, headed home from a university she attended in North Carolina. Another couple there tried to figure out where to go. The couple told the girl they were going to Knoxville and she could follow them, and they showed her the route. It was early afternoon and the traffic was heavy when they arrived at the Tennessee/North Carolina Line on U.S. 441, in the Great Smoky Mountains. The couple's car overheated, and they stopped just north of the state line to a pullover where there was a small creek. The young girl pulled in behind them and she and the female occupant of the other car walked down to the little creek and sat on a rock. The male subject carried water to his vehicle. He had two Yoo-Hoo glass bottles he carried the water in. When he returned to get more water, he walked past the young girl, turned, and hit her in the head with one of the glass bottles, leaving a large gash in her head. The girl was stunned but still conscious. She held her hand over her bleeding head, afraid to move. The male subject then told her to not get "excited" as he got more water and went back to his vehicle. He and the female subject left. The young girl sat on the rock for a while to make sure the others had left, and then returned to her car. She drove herself to her parents' house, almost 50 miles away. She was scared to stop and drove straight through, before telling anyone what happened.

Her father then contacted the park dispatch by phone. I immediately returned the call and her father told me what had happened. Her father was very angry, and when he told me what had happened, I became just as angry. I had him bring his daughter to meet with me at the Sevier County Sheriff department in Sevierville, Tennessee, so I could get the needed information as to what happened after the girl was treated for her injuries. Her father was very doubtful the suspect could be identified and told me he thought he was wasting his time coming to the Sheriff's Office. After seeing he was dealing with a Park Ranger, he was even more dubious anything would be done about the assault of his daughter. I tried to convince him we would try to get the guy, but he shrugged at me as I tried to get the information of what had happened. It was dark and getting late when they arrived. When I interviewed the girl, she identified the type of vehicle the couple drove in front of her and had memorized the tag number after following the vehicle for many miles. As a result, the vehicle owner was quickly identified, and the owner only lived a few blocks from the Sheriff's Office. I contacted the Criminal Investigator, Bill Acree, and he arrived and started the criminal investigation. Meantime, I went with a Sevierville police officer to the owner of the vehicle's residence. It turned out he was the registered owner who was divorced, and his wife had custody of the vehicle. He gave me all the information where to find her, including her phone number, but she was about 50 miles away, in Cocke county, next door to Sevier County, where the crime had occurred. I was alone with no Ranger back-up or assistance and went to Cocke County where I met a Sheriff's deputy and explained to him what had occurred. We went to a trailer park where the female subject was staying, but there was no car, and no one came to the door. I left and went back to the park and met with the criminal investigator to see if I could get some more information. It was getting late, and I contacted The Cocke County deputy and asked him to go by the trailer and see if the car was there. He checked it several times but found no vehicle or lights on at the trailer.

It had gotten very late into the night and I was scheduled to go off duty at midnight. I had the telephone number the ex-husband had given me, and I decided I would call the number to see if anyone may be at the trailer. When I called, a female subject answered the phone. I was surprised and told her I was looking for someone else and she said I had the wrong number. It was now getting around midnight and my dispatcher was getting off duty and I would have no dispatcher, except Gatlinburg Police department, who would monitor my radio. I was going into another county and my radio, as well as the Gatlinburg Police radio, would be out of range, anyway. I contacted the Cocke County deputy by telephone and told him there was someone at the trailer and asked him to watch it until I could get there.

The deputy went to the trailer where I met with him and found the trailer still dark and no vehicle there. I was sure there was someone in the trailer. We went around the trailer shining our flashlights around the windows and doors, and I could hear someone running through the trailer. The deputy and I banged on the doors and side of the trailer and the people in the trailer ran to the rear of the trailer where the deputy spotted them as they ran past the window in the back-trailer door. They conceded and let the deputy in the back door. He came and let me in the front door. I was surprised when I saw the deputy and hadn't realized he had gotten in the trailer. The couple in the trailer matched the description of the suspects given by the young girl. The female subject was very nervous, and I took her out to my patrol car and told her to give me a statement, and if she refused, she would be accessory to attempted murder and I was going to take her to jail. She stated she was with the male subject and she saw him hit the girl with the bottle, but she did not know the reason. She said she was scared he would kill her, that was the reason she was there with him in the dark trailer. The subjects had driven back to the trailer and knew the police would be looking for her car. They had hidden it behind the trailer park, in a field, and walked to the trailer, where they remained with the lights off in the trailer throughout the night.

She identified the subject as Bobby Shults. I remembered this guy for over 20 years because he was a true thug, and unbeknownst to me, I would deal with him again. The female subject gave me a written statement and identified Shults as the assailant who had hit the young girl in the head with a glass bottle. I went back into the trailer and he sat on the couch, the deputy standing over him. I entered the door and told Shults he was under arrest. He looked once left and once right and launched off the couch, trying to escape down the hallway of the trailer. As he launched off the couch, the deputy and I tackled him, and got him handcuffed. It was now almost 5:00 o'clock in the morning, and I had to transport the subject back to the Sevier County jail. I still had no dispatch, and I was apprehensive in transporting this guy this far away, alone, and without some form of communication. But there was none, so like always, I searched him good, got him secured in the back of my patrol car, and drove him back to the Sevier County jail. By 6:00 a.m. I contacted the girl's father and informed him I had arrested the suspect who had assaulted his daughter. I had a sense of pride by getting this guy, and the young girl and her father were very surprised I had gotten the suspect so quick. He told me he had little faith in law enforcement ever apprehending this guy. I really think he was impressed a National Park Ranger arrested the suspect. Little did I know at the time, I would have to deal with this bastard again. I found out early in my career, sick criminals like this can't be rehabilitated.

I took Shults before the U.S. Magistrate where he was allowed bond and released. He was later tried in Federal District Magistrates Court in the Eastern District of Tennessee for aggravated assault where he was found guilty, to serve 18 months in the Federal Penitentiary. The judge in the case allowed him to turn himself into the United States Marshals office on a certain date. Instead of turning himself in, Shults sent the federal judge a note saying he had found a woman who stood by him and he wasn't reporting to prison. A criminal should note that sending a letter of this sort, to a federal judge, is not a wise decision. The federal judge was livid and the next day after Shults did not appear, one of the U.S. Marshals contacted me and told me they had another federal arrest warrant for Shults. It was imperative we find this guy because the federal magistrate had indicated he wanted Shults as soon as possible. I began investigating him and trying to locate him along with the U.S. Marshal. It was only a couple of days and I located him again, in another trailer park, in Knox County. I got several Knox County deputies, and we surrounded the trailer, shining lights on the trailer and looking in the windows. It was like arresting him the first time. While I shined the light in the trailer, here came Shults again, running from one end of the trailer to the other, and I shined my flashlight on him. He raised his hands and exited the trailer at gunpoint and was again arrested. The woman that was going to stand behind him ended up not having a clue of Shults' background and his criminal activity and was thankful we had apprehended him. So, Mr. Shults went back before the federal magistrate where he was sentenced to serve more time on top of the original 18 months and was not released again until he served all his sentence. There are two places you would find Bobby Shults and that would be either a trailer park or a prison, and I would suspect he is still in prison, somewhere, to this day.

29

The Keeper Rock

*T*here are many environmental hazards visitors of the National Park encounter. The Sinks is an area located in the Smokies and a popular swimming hole. Little River is a shallow, unrestricted river only interrupted by a few, fast-flowing, small water troughs, where rocks and boulders cause the water to be restricted. This causes extreme hydraulic effects resembling a small waterfall. There is usually heavy visitation at the Sinks, especially in the summer. People come to the "jump off rock" that is a rock ledge about 30 feet high, making for an exciting dive.

Visitors of all ages swim and wade into the hydraulics of the water, where they can be swept into the quiet swimming hole. On a normal day, when the water is stabilized and there are no storms present, the water is about waist deep. A large thunderstorm upriver can cause the water to rise rapidly and unexpectedly, making the hydraulics extremely volatile. What no one knows is below the water, there is a rock formation, known as the Keeper Rock.

In the early 1990s, a small child became trapped when her foot became lodged in the crevice of the Keeper Rock. When the foot becomes entrapped, the force of the water will push the victim down and under the water. Luckily, the child had several people who saw her get pushed under the water. After several minutes, they were able to free her. The child suffered serious injury from near drowning but recovered.

A short time after that, several people, including a 15-year-old boy, were playing in the hydraulics of the water. The boy's foot wedged in the rock. The force of the water pushed him under, except this time, no one saw him. He drowned with his foot still caught in the rock. We worked for a long time, trying to get him free. It was now apparent there was a serious hazard that had to be addressed to keep anyone else from being killed by the Keeper Rock.

It would be a task to try to remove the rock, taking a chance of making the problem even bigger. In true government fashion, there were committee meetings held. The park service management had no expertise in dealing with this type of problem, but mulled over many suggestions, always leading back to altering the natural environment of the river. After many weeks of discussion, it was quietly forgotten about, hoping no one else would become trapped.

Signs were posted of the dangers of the area, the parking lot remained open, but the signs did not address the type of hazard that lurked beneath the water of the Little River.

A short time later, another victim was entrapped in the rock. This time, it was a Blount County paramedic. Being an adult, he was able to hold himself up, but could not free his foot. Several others in the water assisted him by holding him up as they tried in vain to free his foot.

We worked for hours trying to free him. A technical rigging system was hurriedly put in place to try to assist the victim, while others frantically tried to free his foot, but it was in vain.

To make things worse, there was a severe thunderstorm looming north of the river and the rains would cause the water to rise rapidly, overtaking the victim. Time was running out and the victim was exhausted, becoming lethargic and hypothermic. The river began rising, but rescuers continued working for many hours. A doctor was summoned with tools to amputate the victim's leg to save his life as a last resort.

Then, a miracle occurred, and the victim's foot slipped from the jaws of the rock. He survived his harrowing ordeal.

Ranger Grubb and Ranger Moses in action over the sinks

Again, more committee meetings were held by the park managers. Instead of using explosives to alter the natural flow of the river, or instead of closing off the area completely, more signs were placed with a bulletin board to alert visitors of the hazards of the area. The parking area was further improved to allow more visitors to use the area. We then trained in technical rescues by using an overhead haul system in case of another victim. Not only was this very time consuming, but usually there were only minutes to save someone's life, and this system would then be used as a tool for a body recovery.

Ranger Grubb descending a bridge

Danger below the surface

The Keeper Rock continues without any action taken to correct the serious problem that remains today. The visitation has increased, and the water is still a playground for children and adults alike, with none of them aware of what lurks beneath the surface.

30

After Hours

*B*ecause I lived in the park, I was the closest Ranger to
respond to all the afterhours emergencies. After midnight,
the park would close without a patrol or dispatcher, and if something
happened, I would get called out. Overtime logs showed I had more
overtime than all the other Rangers combined in the Smokies. The
Chief Ranger called me in and told me I was making too much overtime and I had to cut back. I told him to have the other agencies and
the dispatchers quit calling me to respond to all these emergencies
and call the other Rangers. The other Rangers lived many miles away
and it would take them longer to respond to these emergencies, and I
would always get called, because I would be able to respond quicker.
The local law enforcement agencies would always respond and
secure the scene while a Ranger, that would most always be me, were
called to come and investigate. These emergencies were mainly
vehicle accidents that occurred on the Foothills Parkway four-lane,
connecting Pigeon Forge and Gatlinburg.

There were a lot of afterhours emergencies and I worked alone
with the assistance of one of the local city police departments. The

police departments would also be my dispatcher that would monitor our radios during these emergencies. They were always reliable, but if they had an emergency, they would turn down my radio to dispatch their officers, and I may be without a dispatcher. The Park Service got this dispatch for free, emergency back-up and emergency medical service for free, and being the emergency call center for problems that would occur in the park, after hours. There were hundreds of serious incidents that I responded to that had me alone, in a remote area of the Great Smoky Mountains National Park. Cell phones were beginning to be more common, and I had put one of the old "bag" phones in my patrol car. I used the telephone regularly while I was on patrol and especially at night, when I didn't have a dispatcher. I was called on the carpet several times by the Chief Ranger that I used the phone too much, and it cost too much, and he threatened to take it away. This was basically my life support when I was called out in the middle of the night and didn't have a dispatcher.

When I transferred to the Smokies I had agreed I would live in a Park Service house next to headquarters, and I would be the main response to all the emergencies occurring in the district after the park shut down at midnight. I didn't realize there were that many emergencies after hours or I would have rethought my decision.

The Park Service house came with a lot of baggage. It was an old house, with the floors rotting out, and in need of major repairs. It was cold and had a small wood stove to supplement the electric heat. I had to pay rent of almost $400 a month in 1990 and the electric and utilities bill was as much as the rent. It was financially impossible to live with these conditions. The city of Gatlinburg was only two miles away, with lots of housing to purchase, with a mortgage cheaper than paying rent. After about a year, I decided I was going to have to move out of the Park House. The park management came unglued when they found out I was discontinuing our housing arrangement. The chief Ranger threatened me with everything to keep me paying rent in their slum. I was the only one living in the Park who was required, and everyone else had the option of owning their own homes. A battle began and I had to take my case to Washington. Washington would not be a part of the discriminating policy of the Great Smoky Mountains park management, and they reluctantly allowed me to leave the Park Service house.

In the meantime, I had found a house within three miles of where the headquarters was, and across the street from the park boundary. I told the Chief Ranger I would continue taking most of the call outs that would occur within a mile of where my house was. The other problem was, I could not have a patrol car at my house and I would have to go to the headquarters, after I was called out, and get a patrol vehicle, and return literally hundreds of feet where most of the vehicle accidents occurred, in the middle of the night. I agreed to take a patrol car to my house and keep it parked there, and it would be available to answer the emergency calls in the middle of the night. The Chief Ranger told me this would not happen because I was going to have a patrol car to drive back and forth to work, even though I was next door to work. When I would respond to these emergencies, I would have to drive by them going to get a patrol car and return. It was now getting beyond silly and becoming stupid, dealing with a bunch of morons.

The Chief Ranger called me into the office one day and I was counseled for working too much overtime. I explained to him I would be called because I was the closest Ranger to respond and all the police agencies knew how to contact me. I told him I would gladly give up being called out to be able to sleep for a full night. He offered no alternative to handle these after hour emergencies, and I decided I would just quit answering the telephone in the middle of the night, and I would make myself unavailable. The other Rangers would respond but they lived further away and when they responded, they would have to drive to headquarters and get a car and return also. Playing musical cars, in the middle of a cold, snowy night, made no sense. None of this made sense except the park management did not want to fund and provide Rangers to respond to emergencies after the park had closed for the night, and therefore relied on callouts.

I stopped answering my phone, and it rang constantly. The other Rangers would not answer their phones, and it became impossible for the police departments to find a Ranger. There was a bad accident one night, and a Gatlinburg officer came to my house and asked me to please come and work the accident so they could get the road open and get back to their city. I went and got a patrol car at headquarters and returned and cleared the crash at the request of the Gatlinburg Police. It was getting ridiculous, and it was affecting the credibility of the Park Rangers by the other agencies.

To protect the credibility of the Rangers, I went to my supervisor and told him I would reconsider and answer the calls if they would provide me with a vehicle and he again told me no. The calls continued to come in and I refused to answer my phone, and the other Rangers would not answer the phone either. The superintendent of the park was relatively new and not very effective. The Gatlinburg police went to her house one night when they could not find any Rangers to work a bad wreck that occurred within walking distance of my house. The next day, I was called in by my supervisor and he told me they were going to allow me to have a patrol vehicle. It came with conditions that it would have to be parked across the street from my house, in an unsecured location, so it would be available for other Rangers also. This was asinine and I told him he could park his car wherever he wanted, but I was not answering any calls after I was off duty. There was no policy or regulation that required employees to work overtime without their consent. I always felt it was my duty to respond to these incidents, but it had gotten completely absurd.

The stupidity continued and it was critical there was going to have to be Rangers responding after hours, due to the numbers of car crashes and other emergencies that occurred. The Chief Ranger didn't want me working overtime and I was justified by his directions. A couple of days went by and my supervisor again called me in and told me they were going to allow me to have a patrol vehicle at my house. I was disgusted with the accusations, and harassment that had occurred and I had gotten used to sleeping through the night, without getting up on snowy, cold nights, to work a vehicle crash. I told him I declined the offer and he could give the vehicle to another

Ranger who was not getting much overtime for the callouts. This would place a patrol car miles from the park and the other Rangers were not readily available either. He then told me he would direct me to take a patrol vehicle and park it at my house. I considered the cheap threat and told him if he parked a vehicle on my private property, it would be removed. We were again at a stalemate and the confusion continued. It was taking its toll on the Rangers' credibility and the local agencies were getting tired of waiting, in the middle of the night, for a Ranger.

One last time I went to my supervisor again and told him I would take the patrol vehicle and I would respond to most of the calls, but because the Chief Ranger didn't want me to work all the overtime, the other Rangers would have to also respond. I told him if I took the car, all the Rangers in the district should also get a car. This upset the cart, big time, and my request was angrily denied. This was the only real solution, as the area around the park was expanding and the numbers of visitors had risen to almost 10 million. There was a need for more Ranger assistance, back-up, and have the needed equipment to respond to many types of emergencies. This was typical law enforcement management in the National Park Service I had experienced for 20 years, that considered law enforcement, and visitor protection, an aggravation, rather than a necessity, in the operation of the Great Smoky Mountains National Park.

It was only a couple of days, and I was informed there was a policy being drafted concerning the vehicle use and each Ranger in the district would have a patrol vehicle to be kept at their residence if they agreed. The policy would also include the entire Great Smoky Mountains National park where personal patrol vehicles would be assigned to responding Rangers if they agreed. Twenty-five years later, and because of my efforts, all the Rangers now have personal, take-home vehicles, including the supervisors who have take-home vehicles, but rarely respond to any emergencies after hours, and issued as only a convenience and perk for being a supervisor. The patrol vehicles issued today come completely equipped. After about 60,000 miles they are replaced with new vehicles. These new Rangers haven't a clue when it comes to driving worn out patrol vehicles 100,000 plus miles, installing the law enforcement equipment, while performing law enforcement duties, and putting the PARK RANGER markings on the vehicles.

31

Rape

Only a short time after Bobby Shults was finally put away for a serious assault on a young female, a serious rape happened. A suspect, Jerry Helton, took a young female from a bar in Gatlinburg, into a remote area of the Roaring Fork Motor Nature trail in the park, where he sexually assaulted her. After the assault, Helton, being the stupid criminal he was, drove the young girl back to Gatlinburg, where she notified the Gatlinburg police of what happened. She described the vehicle, and Helton fled into the park to hide out and traveled on the Roaring Fork Motor Nature trail, which is a one-way road exiting the park. Gatlinburg police stopped and detained Helton for Criminal Investigator, Bill Acree, and pending the identification by the victim. When he was taken back for the young girl to identify, she was unable to identify him because of the darkness and remote location where the assault took place, and he was released. The next day, our criminal investigator, Bill Acree, called me to assist him in the investigation. Helton had agreed to come to the Gatlinburg police station for questioning. He was stupid to think we weren't going to pursue him further and I guess he thought, because the girl could not identify him, he was free. Acree and I examined the vehicle he drove. The girl had described the way the assault had occurred in the vehicle, and when we closely examined the car, we found body fluids and hair stuck in it. Scuffing and polishing had occurred where the road film and dirt was removed with fingerprints also present. Helton was there as we processed his car, finding the evidence. We could not arrest him until we were sure the fluids, stains, and hair were from the victim. It was clear he was now suspect, but there was nothing we could do but let him walk.

Helton was told not to leave town while we got the evidence analyzed. Helton was stupid, but not that stupid and he realized we were on to him. As soon as we left him, he left town. The evidence came back positive and an arrest warrant was issued for him. Acree filed to have his driver's license suspended, in case he was stopped somewhere and identified, and could be arrested for an outstanding Federal arrest warrant. It would take six months before he was located and arrested. This was after he moved to Virginia and worked for a timeshare company, stealing the money out of the safe, and then stealing the owners' Lincoln. He was finally stopped by a wildlife Ranger in a small park in Mississippi, where it was found his driver's license was suspended and the outstanding arrest warrant. Helton was brought back and charged with Forcible Rape and tried in Federal District Court in the Eastern District of Tennessee. His stupidity earned him 17 years in the Federal penitentiary.

This kind of criminal activity happens every day at every minute somewhere in the country. What makes this incident interesting was Helton's defense. It was, without a doubt, the forensic evidence we collected, identified him as the rapist. When Helton was arraigned, he was adamant that the girl could not identify him, and it could not have been him that committed the sexual assault. He gave his explanation in the Federal Court proceedings and told the courts prior to being sentenced, it could not have been him because he always wore "condominiums" and the forensic evidence could not have been his. His explanation is why these stupid criminals get caught.

32

Stolen

*T*hese serious criminal incidents are nothing extraordinary except the visitors of the National Parks don't think this happens in the parks. The management of the National Parks are oblivious to the criminal activities as well. As a result, Law Enforcement Rangers have always been handicapped by not having back-up or proper equipment and we were left to fend for ourselves in many situations. The saving grace was the fact there were several law enforcement agencies around the park that would provide us back-up and help. I maintained a network of professional friends, and if they knew I needed help, I could get the needed back-up, with the exception it may take a little longer to get to me, if they could find me.

One such incident involved several vehicle burglaries that occurred in the same location, at the same time, for about two weeks. My supervisor, whom I used to supervise, knew of this and had a responsibility to try to apprehend the suspects, but refused to plan or assign anyone to stake out the area and arrest the suspects responsible. I discussed this with him and told him I would go to the parking area where this was occurring and surveil the area. I told him when I came on duty, I would drive my personal vehicle to the parking area and told him to have a back-up available, in case I needed them. The area to be staked out was the Grotto Falls trailhead, that was in a remote area of the park, where radio communications were minimal to none and I would need a back-up close by.

I arrived at about 3 p.m. and got set up about 50 feet where I could see the cars parked in the parking area. It was hot as hell, and humid, and I wore my bullet proof vest, sitting still. The mosquitos were feasting, as if I were a buffet. Regardless, I stayed there as if I were hunting a big buck in deer season. Shortly after I arrived, a subject began walking around in the parking area with a female subject. People came and went, and the subjects would talk with them. There was no indication they did anything but wait at the trailhead, like hundreds of others during the day. I was concealed in the bushes with camouflage clothing and the male subject was no more than 50 feet away from me. He would sit on a rock in front of me looking around as if he were waiting for someone to come off the trail. The female subject had been talking with a woman and a small girl and they walked away out of sight. When they got out of sight, the male subject went to a van parked 20 feet in front of him. I saw him walk up to the side of the vehicle and a few seconds later he slid the side door open for just a short time and then closed it back. He then came back and sat on the rock. I watched him for about an hour and it appeared he was just another visitor. The heat and mosquitos were unbearable, and it is now getting close to 5 p.m. and after most of the vehicles would be broken into.

I slipped back into the woods and went around to the trail going to Grotto Falls so the male subject would not see me. I was camouflaged with a shirt covering my gun belt and wearing my Park Service cap with the emblem on it. I was not completely recognizable as a Ranger, but one could identify me. As I came out into the parking area, instead of going to my vehicle parked at the opposite end of where I watched the parking area, I decided to make one last check of the vehicles I had been watching. I saw the individual I had been watching earlier about 200 feet from me as I started walking toward him. I still did not suspect him of anything because I had watched him for the better part of the hour, sitting on the rock. As I approached, he began walking toward me, meeting me about halfway in the parking area. I paid little attention to him as he was walking past me, as I looked at the vehicles. When he got next to me, he asked me, "Where are the Falls?" I thought it odd he asked me where the Falls were because the parking area was posted, and he had been there long enough, he should have known. He was a Hispanic subject and when he asked me where the Falls were, he talked in broken English, and seemed confused as he looked around. I pointed to the trailhead and told him that was where he should go to get to Grotto Falls. He looked kind of bewildered and then stated to me, "We don't have any water." His response was odd, and his actions were odd. I asked him where he had come from and he replied, "the falls" and pointed in the direction where I had observed him. This was JDLR (just don't look right). At this point, I questioned him where his vehicle was and other questions he evaded. He was very nervous, and I backed away, giving him some room, while questioning him. I kept asking where his vehicle was, and he then replied and pointed to a red Plymouth Voyager van that was parked directly in front of where he was sitting on the rock, where I watched him. Beside the red van was parked a blue Plymouth Voyager van. This was the van I watched him open the sliding door. When he opened the door of the blue van I could not see if he manipulated the lock of the van before sliding the door open and closing it.

Now red flags are flying everywhere. I confirmed and asked him if the red van was his and he replied yes. He began to get very excited and aggressive and uncooperative. I knew he was suspect in entering the blue van. I called on my radio for my back-up, that my supervisor was supposed to provide me. I was in an area where my radio would not work at all. This was during the time cell phones were beginning to be used, but unreliable in remote areas like this. The park service did not supply us with cell phones, but I had my personal cell phone.

The cell phones were like the radios in the mountainous terrain, where there were no signals and would most likely not work.

The suspect is getting more irritated by my presence and questioning. He was a large individual and was yelling at me, telling me to leave him alone and other gibberish in Spanish I couldn't understand. I continued to stay as far away as I could but contain him in the parking area until I could get a back-up on the way. I called on the cell phone and my dispatcher answered. The dispatcher heard only one word, "backup" and my phone died. I had one of the best dispatchers ever and before I had gone to the parking area, I had told her what I would be doing. We both knew radio communications were terrible and she was listening intently while I was at the parking area. Had I had a patrol back-up, I would have been able to talk direct to them, but as I found out, there was no back-up, and no park service units anywhere near me.

My supervisor, whom I had once supervised, had left me hanging with a dangerous suspect, I would soon learn. When the dispatcher heard me say backup, she immediately contacted the Gatlinburg police department to come to me. They were about 8 to 10 miles away and had to drive a twisting, narrow mountain road to get to me, but within minutes they were there. There were no park service units nearby and the ones available were a long distance away, even though my supervisor knew of the plan to surveil the parking lot. It was not surprising, as this supervisor was totally incompetent and oblivious to law enforcement procedures.

The suspect was getting very excited and kept wanting to get to his vehicle. He finally got between his vehicle and the blue van he had entered. I had my gun drawn, but down by my side where he did not see it. After several times ordering him away from the vehicles, he complied. I holstered my gun as I could see him clearly in the parking area and I didn't want him to see the gun and possibly try to take it away from me. He calmed down at this time, and I took a chance at getting him handcuffed, knowing I would have to fight him when I contacted him. I ordered him to his knees, hands over his head and surprisingly, he had regained his composure, and he complied. I got him handcuffed and searched him for weapons. His female companion had returned to the parking area and she was ranting and causing a scene. I sat him down on his favorite rock, where I had been observing him earlier. I could hear sirens echoing throughout the mountains as several Gatlinburg police cruisers came to my aid. Within minutes, they were there. It would be about 20 minutes before a Park Ranger showed up to assist me. The Ranger who was supposed to be my back-up never showed.

I didn't know if the subject had stolen anything from the blue van, but I was certain he had entered the van and that would be trespassing. I read him his rights and advised him he was being arrested for trespassing. That would be enough to get him in jail, and I placed him in one of the Gatlinburg's police cruisers. The female subject calmed down, and I didn't have reason to arrest her at this time. At about the same time, the owners of the blue van came back from their hike. I questioned them if they had locked their vehicle and they were sure of it and found the van locked and checked to see if anything had been stolen. The only thing they had left in the van was a fanny pack lying on the rear seat and a twenty-dollar bill was missing. Surprising to me, when I searched the subject, he had one twenty-dollar bill in his pocket. Another visitor approached me with her little girl and told me the female subject had approached her in the parking area and asked her to walk down to a creek, away from the parking area. I had seen the female subject talking with the woman and little girl as they walked away from the parking area. It was obvious the female subject was a lookout and had lured the woman and little girl away from the vehicles and allowed the suspect time to enter the vehicles.

At this point, I arrested the female suspect for accessory. I got the information from the owner of the blue van and they began backing out of their parking area and I discovered an 8-inch ice pick lying on the ground under the blue van. The suspect had the ice pick concealed on him as I confronted him in the parking area. It was when he got between the two vans, he was able to throw it under the blue van, to get rid of it. This was a pretty unnerving find as a bullet proof vest will not stop an ice pick attack and I was well within the 21-foot rule of a knife or ice pick attack. Police officers are trained and justified to use deadly force if a suspect aggressively attacks you with a knife or ice pick. The 21-foot rule applied where a suspect can run at you less than 21 feet with a knife and stab you before you can draw your weapon.

On investigation, I found he used the ice pick to pick the locks on the vehicles he burglarized. The blue van had not left, and I again went and inspected the van for evidence as to how the suspect gained entry into the blue van. There were no marks or evidence of forced entry, and the owner decided they may have left the van unlocked. After closely examining the blue van, I found a tiny little hole under the rubber of the door handle. It was so small, no one would know it was there had I not discovered the ice pick. The suspect also had a Plymouth Voyager van that was red and was parked next to the identical blue Plymouth van. The suspect was familiar with the locking mechanism of the Plymouth vans and by taking the ice pick and pushing it under the rubber, it could easily manipulate the lock. This was as fast as inserting a key, and the vehicle could be unlocked without leaving any evidence of a forced entry. After we went through the files of the recent vehicle larcenies, we found most of the vehicles involved were the Plymouth Voyager vans and none of the vehicles had any visible signs of forced entry. We had conceded our unidentified suspect that burglarized vehicles, had to have a set of master keys they were using to unlock vehicles that were being burglarized.

I had the van towed to the park headquarters, where it was stored for further investigation, and to be impounded for possible seizure. I had a couple of Rangers go to the van and inventory the contents to see if there was more evidence in the vehicle. After I got the suspects booked in the jail, I went to the suspects' vehicle, where it was supposed to have been searched. The Rangers said they had searched it, but they had only looked around in it. The van was full of everything but the proverbial kitchen sink, including suitcase, clothing, and a lot of flotsam and jetsam. It was apparent the van had not been searched thoroughly. With the assistance of the maintenance foreman, Mark Schotter, I began at the back of the van and removed every article, piece by piece. I was sure there had to be other evidence that would link the suspects to other crimes. During the search I found lots of cash tucked in between the seats, hundreds of dollars in loose change in a container, and loose change and other monies strewn about the van. After emptying the van there was suspicion the money found may be stolen, but there was no way to confirm it. I then proceeded to locate any compartment, panels or otherwise where money could be hidden. I took off the rear seat hand rest where there was a small compartment and found the motherload. Here I found over ten thousand dollars in cash, folded up, assorted personal money orders, credit cards, and personal identifications, that had been stolen from visitors in the park and elsewhere.

These guys had been operating for weeks in the Great Smokies and had stolen the money from at least 26 victims in recent weeks. Twenty-six larceny cases were closed as a result of my efforts, and without the assistance of my supervisor and park management, and again working alone, and arresting a serious criminal. But this is the legacy of the National Park Ranger where no special recognition is sought and the only desire to protect the visitors in the National Parks. I was, however, commended by the Chief of Law Enforcement Specialization of the Southeast Region weeks later after he read the report. He sent a commendation note to the Chief Ranger of the Smokies who was aware of what had occurred but offered no thanks or appreciation. I still have the note where the Chief Ranger only forwarded the comments of the regional chief with a note that said, "I don't commend Rangers for doing their jobs, but in this case, you did a good job," period. I didn't need his ingratiating comment, that was delivered weeks after he received the note from the Law Enforcement specialist. He had to insure he was delivering his response to get brownie points from a higher up manager. He should have been concerned I was left hanging without a back-up by an incompetent supervisor. His dereliction was the exact reason we lost a Ranger in the Great Smoky Mountains. He and his new supervisors he hand-picked in 1994, led to divisiveness and turmoil, leading to ongoing animosity and mismanagement practices concerning the protection and wellbeing of the law enforcement Rangers in the Great Smoky Mountains National Park.

One victim of these larcenies was a small boy about nine years old. He had his wallet stolen from his parents' vehicle that was broken into. In the wallet was a five-dollar bill. I had taken the larceny report only a couple of days before, after his parents' vehicle was broken into. The young boy was very upset that someone would steal his five dollars. His parents explained to me he had mowed the yard and done other chores and had earned the money and he was going to buy something special on his vacation and he was heart-broken when his wallet was stolen. When I searched the suspects' van, I found the wallet with the five dollars still in it. The suspects had just thrown the wallet in the van and apparently didn't need the extra cash. As I processed the evidence, I kept the wallet out, with the five dollars, and sent it back to him. I don't know if any of the other victims were as impressed as this little boy. According to his parents, he was overjoyed and impressed that a Park Ranger had found his wallet and got his money back and arrested the bad guys. This is the personal satisfaction I cherish, and not the bureaucratic ass kissing response the Chief Ranger gave me.

In the end, these suspects were found to be illegal aliens from Cuba. They were touring the country, stealing from the visitors of the National Parks, State Parks, and other locations where there were masses of people enjoying their vacations, oblivious to the fact there were serious, hard-core criminals watching their every move. They were sentenced to long prison terms by the Federal District Court in the Eastern District of Tennessee and the victims' money returned to them.

Most all Park Rangers who were conscientious and dependable did not have the extensive resumes, awards, and superficial recognitions, that were given to them by their supervisors who elevated them and their qualifications, to gain career advancement. Those that hail all these achievements, were only interested in personal gain, personal career enhancements, and mostly, personal friendships. If they had worked and assisted and helped the visitors and protected the resources, they would not have the time to gain all these awards, participation trophies, and ongoing training, that would enhance their applications to maintain a higher grade or management position.

33

Lost Souls

*C*onstantly, visitors became lost for various reasons, with some of the lost souls never to be found in the Smokies. One of these visitors was a young girl, Jennifer, about 25 years old, who hiked on the Rainbow Falls trail with some friends. She did not have a flashlight and her friends were ahead of her, getting off the trail. When her friends got to the trailhead, they realized Jennifer was not with them. It was in December, with freezing temperatures in the day and night. When she didn't show up at the trailhead at dark, a search of the trail was conducted immediately throughout the night, with no luck. The next day, search crews searched the area where Jennifer was last seen, a couple of miles up from the trailhead. Rangers formulated a search area using grids at the location where the girl was last seen with an army of searchers. Nothing could be found, and the search intensified, adding more searchers and more resources. Air support was summoned, and Blackhawk helicopters, equipped with FLIR (Forward Looking Infrared), thermographic cameras that would sense infrared radiation, or in this case, body heat, hovered at treetop level. Still no sign of the young girl as the helicopters circled over every inch of the trail and trailhead. Concerns grew because of the freezing temperatures and the young girl was reported to have only light clothing that would not keep her from becoming hypothermic or freezing to death. The search continued for about five days, with freezing temperatures, and it became frustrating to everyone there was no sign that could be found, as if the young girl had disappeared into thin air. It became obvious at this point, we were looking for a body, but continued searching for Jennifer.

I had not been part of the search that was conducted by a close clique of Rangers that were sort of a fraternity, that excluded me for whatever reason. I mostly patrolled the districts while everyone else searched. On the last day of the search, I volunteered to be part of the search teams. I wanted to get into the woods and assist in the search, but instead, I was assigned to a specific detail. At the time, there was a group of about 20 AmeriCorps kids who volunteered in the park, learning the ropes of the Park Service by participating in each division, doing menial chores, and being exposed to any activities they could assist in, to enhance their personal skills. They were assigned to me, to be supervised and be part of the ongoing search and rescue. They had no training, equipment or any expertise, but their coordinator thought it was good for them to be a part of the search. Wow! We already had one young girl missing, and now we are going to turn 20 kids into the woods, in freezing temperatures, where it would be very easy for them to be injured or lost. I wanted to be on the search, but instead was assigned to be a babysitter, trying to keep up and direct 15 to 20 kids in the woods.

The plan was for these kids to search an area about the size of a football field next to the parking area, where it was flat, with no real obstacles, and defined by the trailhead and road that would keep them from getting lost. I lead them in this search exercise that I felt was absurd. The kids searched the area over and over and became bored. I watched them from the parking area. It was ridiculous and after a couple hours, I called them all to the parking area for a break. They were itching to get further up into the woods, but I told them the Incident Commander would have to okay anything further.

The kids became antsy and roamed around out of the group. I decided to take it on my own and enhance their search area. I called them in and made another plan and they became a little more excited but were still bored with the whole search and rescue assignment. I included searching an area about the same size as the area they had just searched on the opposite side of the trailhead that included a small creek. They would still be in eyesight and I figured they would be busy for another couple of hours, and by that time, I could get rid of them.

It was at this time I experienced another God's Moment. I talked with a patrol Ranger, Mike Farley, in the parking area. I had told the kids where to go and spread out and search the opposite side of the trail. As they headed up the trail, I heard someone scream, JENNIFER!! I ran over and found Jennifer, not more than 300 feet from the trailhead. It was unbelievable! After five days and nights of freezing temperatures, Jennifer was still alive. We picked her up and carried her to Ranger Farley's patrol car that was already warmed up. She was very hypothermic, and her boots were frozen solid to her feet and we could not get them off her. These kids, as well as I, were ecstatic they had found her. She was rushed to the hospital, where she survived her ordeal with some serious hypothermic issues. The kids were hailed as heroes and interviewed by all the news media, explaining their roles in the search and rescue of Jennifer. I was dumbfounded this had taken place and I firmly believe it was clearly a divine intervention. Even though I had not done anything, I was excited I was there when Jennifer was found, and watched these kids being rewarded for their roles in the rescue of Jennifer.

Jennifer was interviewed about her ordeal and how she ended up within 300 feet of the trailhead parking area, where there was ongoing activity with search parties gearing up, vehicles coming and going and other noises that should have alerted her. She explained she was hiking down Rainbow Falls trail and her phone flashlight died, as well as her phone. Once she did not have any light it was completely dark, she could not see the trail. As she tried to feel her way on the trail, she had gotten off the trail, where there was a small creek running parallel to the trail. She then slipped and fell into the creek, getting wet and climbed out the other side, crawling over the rocks in the darkness, until she was between two small trees. It was at this point she decided to sit between the two trees and wait for help.

She wore a large fleece pullover sweater and she pulled the sweater up and over her head and remained between the two trees for five days. She could not hear anything over the running water of the creek, and the sweater kept her warm enough to survive. She had no food or water for five days, and on the last day of her ordeal, she decided to crawl over the rocks to the creek and get some water. As she crawled over the rocks, the kids saw her. There had been a Black-hawk helicopter circling directly above her, within the hour, at tree top level, but they could not see her, and she was so cold there was no body heat for the FLIR to detect. She said she thought she heard the helicopter, but she was apparently semi-conscious from the hypothermia, and it may have been the helicopter that woke her up, causing her to try to get some water. It was a miracle the kids made their way up the trail and spotted Jennifer. With Jennifer's condition and state of consciousness, she could very easily fall into the water and not survive, and no one would have seen her. There were only seconds between Jennifer being spotted before she would have been out of sight behind the rocks. Very few humans would have survived Jennifer's ordeal, and this was just another miracle I witnessed while I was a National Park Ranger.

34

Bat Man

*R*angers at the Smokies trained and qualified in many diverse fields even though law enforcement was considered the main job as a Park Ranger in the Smokies. At any given moment, a Ranger at the Smokies could be called to work on a fatal motor vehicle accident, emergency medical episodes, to cave rescues. There were several caves in the Smokies but were not accessible to the public as they were sealed off. Most of these caves were in the Cades Cove District of the park.

One of these caves was not sealed and three local young adults went to the cave. This was a "hold my beer" and "watch this" moment. These subjects went into the cave by lowering themselves on a short rope, and became stranded. They were hundreds of feet down in the cave and came to a level that required a rope to be tied to an anchor before being lowered down into the cave shaft for several hundred feet to the next level. They had no equipment, flashlights, or warm clothing and only a short rope. To get into the cave you would have to use a rope and rappel under a small waterfall before getting into the first level of the cave. When you went under the fall, you would get wet. After getting to the first level you had to hike a short distance, crawling over and under the rocks and squeezing between narrow passages of rocks with your arms to your side and unable to lift them. It was cold and damp, after getting wet from the waterfall, with the cave temperature about 50 degrees.

You had to have a headlight to see, as it was pitch dark. When these guys got to the next level, they had to tie themselves off to an anchor and lower themselves into the dark shaft that went for hundreds of feet before they could get off the rope. In order to get back up the rope, you had to climb it. To climb a vertical rope, you use technical hardware called Jumars, that allowed you to slide them up the rope and grab the rope while simultaneously pulling up your feet in the lower Jumar. It's very technical and strenuous. These three guys did not have this equipment and only had rappelling harnesses attached to the short rope. The three subjects were connected to the same rope and began lowering themselves into the darkness of the cave. It was at this time; the lower subject ran out of rope and unable to find a ledge and two of the subjects were unable to climb the rope a hundred feet back to the top. The top subject was able to climb hand over hand reaching the ledge where the rope was anchored. The other subjects remained stranded on the rope unable to go up or down and remained in the dark and cold from being wet until the third subject ran and got help.

As it turned out, none of the subjects had told anyone where they were going, or what their plans were. If the third subject would not have had the strength to climb the rope, all three of the subjects would have been stranded in the cave with no way out. The cave was off the beaten trail in the woods. They had become wet from the waterfall and the cave temperature was probably 50 to 60 degrees with the small waterfall, and being wet, made it cooler. The stranded subjects had been in the cave for several hours before help could be found. It was another several hours, rigging and getting into the cave to them. There was an extreme possibility the subjects became hypothermic, due to them being wet without appropriate clothing.

The Cades Cove District Ranger, Jack Piepenbring, was the lead

Ranger and was a very experienced and knowledgeable Ranger. If there was ever a Technical Rescue of any sort, being climbing, rigging, rappelling, or whitewater, this was the go-to Ranger. When this call came in, it was an emergency and there was not a lot of time to assemble a full rescue team, and he decided to go in to evaluate and plan or execute a rescue. I had some technical rescue training and experience, but I had never experienced a cave rescue. I was immediately available, and I had trained with Ranger Piepenbring and he was comfortable with us going in.

We rappelled into the cave on a rope, and under the waterfall. The water in the falls was very cold, but we had rain gear on that deflected most of the water. As we got deeper into the cave, I guess we found were the bats hung out, as they swarmed around our headlights. There was one bat that liked me. He kept swarming, inches in front of my face, in the beam of my headlight. I couldn't get my arms up to swat him away, as I inched sideways through the narrow passage of the rocks that only accommodated skinny Rangers. The bat then lit on my face, wrapping his little claws around my face, with me not being able to knock him off. I'm pretty sure I screamed like a little girl. He only held on for a second, but it was like being mauled by a vulture, as far as I was concerned. This was very unsettling, but I survived it, and there was only the two of us Rangers that could hear my 'little girl shrieks.'

We got to the ledge where the subjects had tied their rope off. They were barely in hearing range, down in the darkened shaft, with no light. Ranger Piepenbring rigged ropes to lower himself alone into the dark shaft. He found the two subjects, hanging on their short rope, deep in the cave. Ranger Piepenbring rigged each of the subjects separately to be hauled out. I tended the ropes as he went into the darkness. We had called for the local fire department, who sent us help in hauling the subjects up from the shaft. There was very little room for any rescue personnel, except for the two of us. The ropes had to be laid out for several hundreds of feet through the cave where the fire department personnel manned the haul ropes

Ranger Piepenbring worked tirelessly in the darkness for what seemed to be an eternity before getting the two subjects safely secured to the haul ropes. One by one, they were hauled up to the anchor level. The anchor that these ropes were tied to had been embedded in the rock from previous climbers and were only secured by nothing more than bolts. We secured the ropes to several of the anchors for a safety back-up in case one of the anchors blew. There was a lot of weight on these ropes, and how they held, is unbelievable. If the anchors had blown, the Ranger and the subjects would have fallen into the cave, and most likely killed. The ropes held and when we got the subjects to the anchor level, they were assisted by the fire department getting them through the rocks and narrow passages and eventually out of the cave.

Neither of the three subjects sustained any injuries and lived to drink more beer. They walked away with citations to pay a small fine for entering the closed caves, and for us saving their lives. This was a true lifesaving experience, and it could not have been pulled off if Ranger Piepenbring had not been there. Without his presence, there was no way to describe the intense, strenuous actions that went into this rescue. It was a very profound, exhausting, and dramatic rescue, one could only experience, watching a movie. I was glad to be a part of it, and the reason I loved being a National Park Ranger.

35

Drunk Bride

*L*ike any other law enforcement officer there, you always saw crazy antics by people. This was one of the best reasons to be a law enforcement officer because you encountered situations that could only be demonstrated by Saturday Night Live. Most of the time these people were intoxicated and would add comedy to a pitiful human condition. Then there were others who lacked intelligence and were just dense and dimwitted. The addition of in-car video cameras captured many of the moments that have made law enforcement a nightly series on television.

I was called out late one night by the Gatlinburg Police department for a vehicle crash on Newfound Gap road. It was about eight miles from Gatlinburg and Gatlinburg Police would not respond into the park unless I asked them. There were no other Rangers on duty anywhere in the park, and as always, I was alone, with no back-up, and barely able to communicate with the Gatlinburg Police department. I had just installed the first in-car video camera in the park in my new Crown Vic patrol car. The crash vehicle was turned upside down, but the occupants were not injured. It was a couple who had just gotten married a few hours prior in Gatlinburg and were going to Cherokee to gamble at the Harrah's casino. The newlywed husband was the driver of the vehicle and had not been drinking, and there didn't appear to be any excessive speed. The newlywed wife was still in her long, flowing white wedding dress, and was extremely intoxicated. It was a simple accident that warranted very little investigation, and I waited for a wrecker to come and get the vehicle. The husband was very polite and cooperative, but that woman in the wedding dress turned into a real handful.

The woman began cussing me, stumbling around, refusing to calm down. She gathered up her long wedding dress, and followed me around, yelling at me. I was unable to get away from her. All of this was captured on the video that made for a good movie, and entertaining, when court proceedings began. I kept telling her to calm down, but she insisted on chastising me, and pushed me, which led to her trying to hit me. Her husband didn't want any part of this and wouldn't intervene. He stood away from her while she tried to assault me. He had apparently also been a victim, like I was now. It was apparent she was intoxicated out of her mind. I kept warning her I would arrest her if she continued. Her husband told me he couldn't do anything. I was left to take an ass kicking from her that was probably meant for the husband later in the night. I contacted Gatlinburg police for back-up, and they were on the way. I finally had enough and told the woman she was under arrest and told her to put her hands behind her back.

This set her off even more, and she tried to hit me and fell. I must have been absent the day in defensive tactics on how to handcuff a drunk woman in a wedding dress. When I tried to grab her, all I could get a hold of was a lot of wedding dress as she fought with me. It was seemingly impossible to gather up all that material to get to her hands. I remember putting her on the ground and wrapping the wedding dress around her while she kicked and screamed, before getting her handcuffed. Her husband stood still, sort of snickering at me, as I tried to get control of his newly wed wife. After I got her handcuffed, I fought her to the back of my cruiser and got her in the back seat, and got the door closed. Most of the wedding dress was still outside the door but she was contained and handcuffed.

I had just gotten my new Ford Crown Vic cruiser, and the woman kicked and screamed in the back seat, kicking the door and bending the door frame of my cruiser. I called Gatlinburg police for back-up when the fiasco started. I was apprehensive about getting the woman back out of my cruiser and fighting her again, until back-up arrived. In the meantime, she had pretty much kicked the door, bending it completely out of the door frame.

Gatlinburg arrived and we got her out of the car and got a hobble, that is a rope to tie around a suspect's feet and got her subdued. She spent the night in the jail, until she was sober, and released to appear in court. There had been no crime and no reason to write the driver any tickets, but I am sure he was re-thinking this marriage arrangement.

There was only a minimum fine of about $25.00 for being intoxicated if you were charged. This crazy new bride ended up spending her wedding night in jail, charged with intoxication, with an additional charge of disorderly conduct and vandalism. She was sentenced by the court to pay fines, and for the repair of my cruiser, which ended up being about $2,000.00. The accident also resulted in several thousands of dollars damage to their wrecked vehicle. The poor newlywed husband rode back to his hotel with a wrecker driver, and spent his wedding night alone. I often wondered if this poor guy is still married to this woman, and if I should have made a copy of the in-car camera video for him.

36

Recycling the Drunks

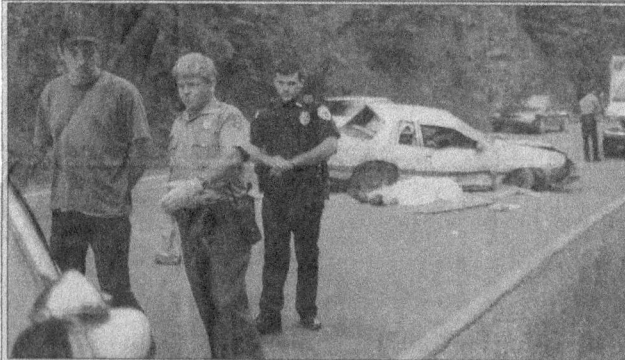

A Great Smoky Mountains National Park ranger escorts a late Tuesday evening, with three occupants in the vehicle. The handcuffed suspected driver of a wrecked Mustang to a cruis- other two occupants were not injured. Names and details were er. A man died in the one-car accident. The accident happened not available at press time. on the northbound Spur between Gatlinburg and the tunnel

here were thousands of vehicle crashes in the Smokies while I was there. The four-mile Foothills Parkway Spur between Gatlinburg and Pigeon Forge yielded more crashes than any road in the county, mainly because there were cheap hotels in Pigeon Forge and liquor in Gatlinburg. We didn't have 24-hour patrols, and if something happened after midnight, we would get called out to investigate. I lived next to the spur, and within minutes from any of the crashes or other emergencies in the park, that may happen late at night. As a result, I got called out more often than any other Ranger. There were many crashes resulting in death and serious injuries. The Rangers would do the investigations, due to the jurisdiction of the park, and I did many of them, with most of the them being alcohol related.

***

Recycling drunks was beginning to get old after I had been at the Great Smoky Mountains for many years. The foothills spur that led from Gatlinburg to Pigeon Forge was a recycling center. I had worked thousands of vehicle accidents from minor fender benders to many serious injuries and fatalities. When a fatality occurred, it would be up to me to make notification to the family. No matter how much you rehearsed, there was never an easy way to confront a family, and I choked as I made the notification. I was no stranger to witnessing tragic events. From my days in the U.S. Coast Guard Search and Rescue, I had dealt with many body recoveries and emergency situations involving death, and I continued with my many years as a National Park Ranger. It was difficult at the onset, and for many days you would reflect on the misfortune of these victims, but I was lucky, these events didn't trigger any serious emotional issues that distracted from being able to carry on day to day. The early days didn't identify Post Traumatic Stress Disorder (PTSD). You just kick a stump and carry on with your duties. Nowadays, if someone hears about a serious incident, or breaks a fingernail, one must undergo PTSD counseling. In my case, I knew what my job entailed, and I chose to be a part of a professional group of rescuers and responders that would surely lead to these events. The only other way to deal with it was to resign.

Most all the fatalities were a result of drunk driving. When these drunks performed the sobriety test it was like they were auditioning for a comedy skit. Most drunks were combative and argumentative, but still laughable. One incident involved an individual named Joel. I had stopped Joel for DUI just outside the park in the City of Gatlinburg. A Gatlinburg city police officer backed me up and had arrived just as I began to investigate Joel for DUI. Joel was a very big man, probably weighing in at about 300 plus pounds. When I talked with him, it was apparent he was under the influence of alcohol. I asked him to step out of the vehicle so I could conduct a field sobriety test.

Because of his intoxication and his size, Joel had difficulty getting out of his vehicle and standing up. I stood between the car door and the car as Joel stood up. I grabbed a hold of Joel to help him steady himself. Joel then realized this was real and he was fixing to go to jail. He had a great idea, but it was a great bad idea. Joel decided to fake a heart attack, or some other problem, that would make him collapse into unconsciousness. When he began to collapse, he fell forward and right on top of me, before I could move. This obese drunk pinned me to the ground and was lying on top of me as if he were unconscious. He crushed my legs, causing me to shout, or more like, yell as I went down. I had my portable radio in my hand and subconsciously had keyed the transmit button while I yelled. My dispatcher heard the commotion and freaked out, not knowing what was going on. I had a Gatlinburg Police officer there and I was in no real danger, except I had this 300-pound hog lying on top of me. I yelled at the Gatlinburg police officer to get this son of a bitch off me. The officer tried to pull him off, and I kicked and squirmed, finally getting my foot to his head and neck, kicking him off me.

When I finally got up, Joel was still lying on the ground, trying to pretend to be unresponsive. The Gatlinburg officer told me he thought Joel was dead. I said good for him as I tried to shake off the pain in one of my legs. I finally got composed and checked on Joel. He was lying flat on his back. When I shined my flashlight in his eyes, he flinched his eyes and when I opened his eyelids, he would forcefully close them. He was not unconscious and was obviously pretending. I got the Gatlinburg medics to come and check him as he lay on the ground for many minutes. One of the medics asked me what happened and when I told him, he laughed for a minute or so before he checked Joel. He suspected right away; Joel was faking. He gave Joel a good, hard "sternum rub," that is a painful stimulus used by the medics where the fist is closed and using the knuckles, rubbed very hard on the chest, causing a lot of pain. Joel responded immediately, trying to sit up, but saw everyone around him, so again collapsed. The medic gave him another good, hard rub and Joel repeated the same but continued to act out his unconsciousness. After the third attempt it was apparent Joel's pain level was equal to his intoxication and he was not going to react to the sternum rub. The medic went and got two small ampules of smelling salts, that is an ammonia gas used to put under the nose to trigger a response. Rather than put the salts under his nose, the medic crammed both ampules in both nostrils. Joel was rolling around and trying to get up and was flopping around, like a walrus. It was a medical miracle.

We finally got Joel rolled over and handcuffed. He was so obese, I had to use two pair of handcuffs to restrain his arms. We got him loaded into my cruiser and I carried him off to jail. At the jail, Joel continued with his act of unconsciousness and I couldn't get any information needed to book him and get him charged. I left him in the jail overnight and went the next morning to get him bonded out of jail. When I arrived at the jail, the jailers brought Joel out of the drunk tank. He was one messy drunk. His 300-pound physique was showing. He didn't have a belt, no shoes or shirt, and his trousers were barely hanging on him. He limped up to the booking desk, hanging onto the screen with his hands. Joel immediately apologized to me for the night before, as he hung onto the screen at the booking desk. I asked Joel how he felt, and he leaned over, holding his chest and told me he didn't know what he had done but his chest was so sore he couldn't touch it. I told him it was called 'getting drunk' and let it go at that. I wanted to recommend he give up alcohol and go to the gym and get on a Keto or other diet, but I just recycled him and went and got another drunk.

One of the first serious accident investigations at the Great Smoky Mountains resulted in the death of one of the passengers and serious injury to another passenger. The driver, causing the accident, didn't sustain a scratch and was intoxicated. This was one of the few drunk driver cases prosecuted in Federal Court for 2nd degree murder instead of vehicular homicide or Driving Under the Influence. Second Degree Murder carried a significant prison sentence. The suspect had been arrested several times for drunk driving. The state penalties for drunk driving were very liberal and hardly a deterrent to stop someone from drinking and driving. When the crash occurred, the suspect checked into an alcohol rehab center to try to mitigate his responsibility. In the meantime, a federal arrest warrant was issued for him, but he could not be found.

The suspect's brother-in-law contacted me and told me the suspect wanted him to come to the rehab center and get him, and he was leaving town to escape his arrest, he knew was forthcoming. When his brother-in-law called me, I went with a Blount County deputy to the rehab center that was nothing more than a small converted motel. There were several male subjects sitting around outside as we pulled our cruisers into the parking lot. These guys must have known the routine, because all of them ran into their rooms when they saw the cops arrive.

I went to the office and met with a little man in a white medical robe and explained to him I was there to arrest this individual and asked him what room he was in. The little man told me I had to leave, and I couldn't come onto the property and take anybody away because of their privacy rights. This little dweeb had given me the wrong response and I told him if the suspect escaped, he would be charged with accessory for letting the suspect escaped. The Blount County deputy wanted some of the dweeb's ass also and jumped down his throat and removed part of his voice box making him hardly able to speak. The dweeb told me he would have to make a phone call to his supervisor, who told him to let us have the suspect.

We went to the suspect's door and knocked, and the suspect met us at the door. The suspect thought we were his brother-in-law coming to get him, and had his bags packed, ready to go. He ran and jumped over the bed and curled up like a child on the floor and we handcuffed him. That was the last time he saw freedom for 15 years for 2nd degree Murder in the Federal Penitentiary.

The number of drunk drivers we encountered as Rangers was

unbelievable. It became boring, investigating crashes and arresting and recycling drunk drivers. The drunk drivers were taken to the Sevier County jail where they were offered an Intoximeter test. All the tests were entered in the Intoximeter log. One year alone, after counting the number of arrests on the Intoximeter log, it showed I had made more drunk driving arrests than all the county officers combined, and with most of them being a result of a vehicle crash on the Foothills Parkway spur.

37

Kelly Lovera Murder

*C*rimes against persons in the Great Smokies were relatively small compared with the number of visitors that entered the park annually. At last count, when I retired in 2003, was around 10 million visitors a year. When there was a crime, it would usually be horrific. There was a murder that occurred in Sevierville, Tennessee, in November 1994, and involved some of the offspring of prior influential and professional people of Gatlinburg and Sevier County who, back in the day, were involved in murder, mayhem and drugs. This murder was very heinous and was one of the few murders that had occurred in Sevier County prior to 1994 and after my arrival to the Great Smoky Mountains in July, 1990. Sevier County was still very rural on my arrival, and visitation was still seasonal with most of the tourists leaving the county after the leaves had fallen. The county quickly became a ghost town with businesses shutting down for the season and cold winter weather arriving.

The murder of Kelly Lovera on November 5th, 1994, was especially egregious, given the history of prior events in Sevier County, where a prominent banker in Gatlinburg had committed questionable "suicide." Sleepy little Sevier County, nestled in the mountains of Tennessee was inhabited by many influential people, involved in a wide range of illegal activities, that resulted in serious criminal activities and questionable deaths, described in a book written in 2000 by John Reynolds titled *Mad Notions*. The book describes some of the alleged activities by the Sevier County families and other players involved. The book also describes the murder of Kelly Lovera, who was married to Shayne Mills, whose father was the president of the First National Bank of Gatlinburg. Shayne's father, Brent Mills, had allegedly committed suicide, with questions of it being a possible murder, with ties to drug and organized crime in Sevier County. Only years later, his daughter, Shayne Mills, would soon be entwined with murder and mayhem and be the subject of the book *Mad Notions*. The book goes into detailed accounts that lead up to the murder. Lovera and her lover, Brett Rae, were guilty of murdering Kelly Lovera. After reading the book, I was compelled to add this story into this book to include the missing information. When *Mad Notions* was written, at no time was I interviewed. I was ultimately the main witness who led to the discovery of the murder. I called the criminal investigator, Bill Acree, and we began the investigation that resulted in a successful prosecution in the Kelly Lovera murder. The book had several fictional accounts of the incident and I am including this story that is factual and correct.

On November 5th, 1994, the body of Kelly Lovera was found in his black Jeep crashed into a tree over the embankment of an overlook. This was located on the bypass of U.S. 441, just past the Campbell Lead bridge, leading to the headquarters of the Great Smoky Mountains National Park. I was on my way into work in the early morning and found two Rangers with a wrecker that had the towing cable over the embankment. The Rangers explained to me a motorist was killed when his Jeep had gone over the embankment and they were in the process of towing the vehicle back onto the road. The victim had been removed from the Jeep and transported by an ambulance to the hospital and he was pronounced dead. I got out and looked at the Jeep and it was crashed into a tree and the front of the vehicle had sustained damage. The Jeep did not appear to have impacted the tree hard enough to cause any serious injury and especially a death. I checked the roadway where the vehicle had gone over the embankment, and there were no skid marks or disturbance of the gravel leading to where the victim's vehicle had gone over the embankment. I had investigated probably a thousand vehicle accidents, and this did not fit a vehicle crash that would result in a fatality or even a serious injury.

I climbed down the embankment and found a hammer lying outside the vehicle on the ground. The Jeep was positioned with the front downhill and impacted into a large tree, with the keys in the ignition. There was no blood anywhere in the driver's compartment or on the front seats. The back of the Jeep had the seats out and the deck in the back of the Jeep was covered with a large amount of dried blood. The blood was dried and appeared to have run uphill, which was impossible given the fact the Jeep was facing downhill and stopped when it hit the tree. The body of the victim had been removed but was extremely bloody with serious head injuries according to the other Rangers. On closer inspection I found tiny specks of blood on the inside of the roof of the jeep. This was not a vehicle crash, but was in fact, a murder scene and I had gotten there just in time before the crime scene was going to be compromised by removing the Jeep without collecting and photographing the evidence.

The area was secured, and I contacted our criminal investigator who came to the scene and he also confirmed the scene as a murder. The FBI does most of all the capital crimes that include murder in the park because of the Exclusive Jurisdiction of the park. The local FBI agent was contacted and came to the scene with two other FBI agents. The scene was processed by the FBI, and evidence collected, and the Jeep was removed. One of the FBI agents explained to me he didn't know why he was called to investigate a murder scene, because he worked only with stolen cars and told me he could tell me anything about a stolen car, but he knew nothing of murders. The other FBI agent was a brand-new rookie who had just graduated from the academy and had no experience with anything. When we got the Jeep back to the road, we began checking the tag and found the Jeep belonged to Kelly Lovera, and he lived in Frog Ally, which was a housing project in Sevierville about 15 miles away.

I had never worked with a team of FBI agents before at a crime scene, and these investigators dissuaded my confidence in the FBI's ability to process this crime scene. The Tremont Ranger came to the scene to assist in the investigation. The local FBI agent supervising the investigation sent us to the victim's residence in Frog Ally, in the City of Sevierville, to see if there was any evidence the crime was committed at his residence and not in the National Park. I rode with the rookie FBI agent in his unmarked vehicle and the Tremont Ranger rode with the other FBI agent. When we arrived at the apartments, Shayne Lovera, Kelly's wife, and her sister, were outside. When they saw us drive up, Shayne and her sister ran up to us and asked us if Kelly was okay. I thought it was strange they would quickly identify us as investigators or even police officers, because the FBI agent was not dressed in a uniform, and I was in my Park Service uniform. We were in an unmarked passenger vehicle which didn't look like a police type vehicle. Shayne was also familiar with the local Sevierville Police department's patrol vehicles, but we had not contacted them at this point.

It was obvious Shayne was waiting on the police to show up. Shayne had filed a missing person report with the Sevierville Police department in the early hours after Kelly was murdered, as an alibi, reporting Kelly had left in the middle of the night and had not returned. We told her what we had found, and she became emotional, but her demeanor was not quite what one expected under the circumstance. The rookie FBI agent and I went into Shayne's apartment to interview her in the aftermath of the murder. The apartment was unkept, with the lights off, curtains pulled and the inside of the apartment very dim. I sat on the left side of the sofa that was covered by a large quilt. There was a large lamp sitting on a table at the side of the sofa, but it was not turned on.

The FBI agent began questioning Shayne as I took notes on

everything that was said by the agent, and answers given by Shayne. In an interview, this was the proper way to record and question witnesses or victims at the onset of an investigation. This was an interview rather than an interrogation as we were trying to get information that would lead to the death of Kelly Lovera. Things did not feel right, and the questioning was leading to doubt that Shayne was being truthful. Shayne's emotional state was not indicative of someone who had just lost a loved one, but we treated her as a victim and not a suspect at this time. Shayne gave us consent to look around in the apartment and nothing was found indicating this may be the crime scene. The apartment was dark, with no lights and the curtains closed making it difficult to see any evidence. Since this could be a crime scene, we were careful not to disturb anything and only looked around for plain view evidence. The only interesting thing we found was several documents and papers lying on a bed that turned out later to be Kelly's life insurance policies. We didn't open doors or move things around, and only looked around, and we did not see anything that indicated any struggle or other evidence. We left the apartment and I joined up outside with the Tremont Ranger.

Brett Rae, who killed Kelly, was about three apartments down and worked on his motorcycle. Rae had not been a suspect at this time in the murder, but because he was outside and available, the Tremont Ranger and I took the opportunity to question him, if he may know anything. Rae was JDLR, (just don't look right), but we didn't have any evidence that may tie him to the murder. We asked him if we could look around in his apartment and he gave us consent to do so. Again, we did not open doors or move things around and didn't find anything that may be suspect in the murder but later, his bloody clothes were found in the washing machine of Rae's apartment, but we had no reason to search further. As we left, we both agreed this guy knew about Kelly's murder, but we did not have any evidence to investigate him further at the time.

We left the apartments and went to the Sevierville Police department, meeting with the Sevierville Police department criminal investigators. It was obvious this murder had occurred outside the park and Kelly had been rolled over the embankment of the overlook to make his murder appear to be a car crash. Federal Investigators were no longer needed, and the case was turned over to the Sevierville Police and the TBI (Tennessee Bureau of Investigation) with our Criminal Investigator, Bill Acree, assisting them.

As it turned out, Brett Rae was the murderer of Kelly Lovera. Shayne Lovera, the wife of Kelly, was an accessory of murder in the first degree. The murder of Kelly was filled with intrigue and emotional despair. The TBI had taken over the investigation and within a couple of hours, the case was solved. After Brett Rae pushed Kelly and his jeep over the embankment of the overlook, he fled the scene on foot. Rae had made his way into Gatlinburg where he had contacted a friend to pick him up and give him a ride back to Sevierville. Rae's friend arrived and picked up Rae on River Road in Gatlinburg. The friend had no idea what Rae had been doing, but when Rae got in his vehicle, his friend saw blood all over him, with Rae being very nervous. Rae, at this point, told his friend he had "finally done Kelly," indicating Rae had killed Kelly. His friend took Rae back to his apartment and left, and immediately contacted the Sevierville Police.

Everyone investigating the death of Kelly suspected at the onset the crime had occurred in Kelly's apartment. After the witness came forward, search warrants were quickly obtained, and the Tennessee Bureau of Investigations went back to Kelly's apartment and began a thorough search of the apartment. I was not part of the search and discovery of the evidence found, but when I learned what had been found, I had a very unsettling moment. When we had first gone into Kelly's apartment to interview Shayne, I sat on the sofa, on the left side, that was covered with a quilt, as we interviewed Shayne. When TBI went back to the apartment, they removed the quilt from the sofa and the sofa was saturated with the blood of Kelly Lovera. I sat where Kelly had been killed, after he was beaten to death with a small baseball bat by Brett Rae, while Shayne watched. Rae killed Kelly within feet of where Kelly's two children slept, in their bedroom. The large lamp sitting next to the sofa had been knocked over during the assault on Kelly and had been picked up and placed back on the table with a large bloody fingerprint on it, belonging to Brett Rae. TBI began spraying the apartment with Luminol, that is a chemical that reacts to the presence of blood, giving it a luminescent appearance. The apartment lit up with the luminol and showed the path of where Kelly was dragged through the apartment, into the children's bedroom and his body taken out of the window and placed into Kelly's jeep. Kelly was killed as his children slept, and after Rae killed Kelly, the children were taken out of their room and into the bedroom of Shayne, until Kelly could be taken out of the apartment.

Prior to the murder of Kelly, there had been a party on this Saturday where all the residents of the Frog Ally apartments brought potluck dinners and "pot" marijuana and alcohol. As the party waned, Brett was intoxicated, and with the marijuana and alcohol, along with Shayne's encouragement, he attacked Kelly as he slept on the sofa in his apartment. After Rae killed Kelly, he brought Kelly's Jeep around to the side of the apartments to where Kelly would be taken out of the window of the children's bedroom. Kelly was put in the Jeep and Rae left with Kelly in the back of the Jeep. There had been a water main break at the same time Kelly had been beaten in his apartment. As Rae left the apartments, the city workers working on the water main break saw the Jeep leaving. The city had shut the water off and there was no way for Shayne to clean up the blood. The apartment was quickly wiped down the best it could be, and quilts and blankets thrown around to cover the blood stains.

This was early in the morning around 2:00 a.m., and Rae drove around Sevier County in Kelly's Jeep, with Kelly lying in the back. Rae tried to figure out what to do with Kelly's body. The influence of the marijuana and alcohol wore off, leaving Rae with raw emotions, without the help of the drugs and alcohol he had consumed only hours earlier. Rae had to get rid of Kelly quickly, before it became daylight. He then drove into the Great Smoky Mountains National Park, to the overlook on the U.S. 441 by-pass, looking down on the City of Gatlinburg, where he decided to push Kelly's Jeep over the embankment, with Kelly in the back, and make it look like a vehicle accident. Rae was in desperation over-drive as the sun rose. He was alone, without any transportation to get out of the area. He was covered in blood and he quickly tried to gather clothing and other articles from the jeep as he fled the area on foot. When Kelly and the Jeep was found, it was identified as a vehicle accident and was being readied to be pulled out from over the overlook. Had it been removed, the crime scene would have been compromised, losing valuable evidence that would connect Brett Rae and Shayne Lovera to the murder of Kelly.

Once the Tennessee Bureau of Investigation began interviewing Brett Rae, he provided them with more information on how he killed Kelly and disposed of bloody clothing, and fled the scene before he arrived in Gatlinburg, early in the morning, and meeting his friend. The medical examiner had determined there were at least two different weapons used to kill Kelly. Kelly was beaten on his sofa with a small children's ball bat. What was left out would be very important, but I don't remember it being brought up in the trial, nor was there a mention of it in the book. The discovery of one piece of evidence would identify the heinous and cold-blooded killer Brett Rae was. As Brett Rae drove Kelly around in the early morning hours, Kelly was not actually deceased at that time, and was alive in the back of his Jeep. Kelly began moaning and Brett Rae stopped the vehicle somewhere in Sevier County, and beat Kelly while he was in the back of the Jeep using a weapon that we never found. Instead of trying to save Kelly's life, Rae finished off Kelly, in the middle of somewhere in Sevier County, before bringing him to the Park and pushing his vehicle over the embankment. The small blood specks I had found on the inside of the roof of the Jeep was blood being splattered as Rae beat Kelly in the back of the Jeep, when Kelly regained consciousness. It has been a very long time since the murder, but I don't recall this information being reported, even in the trial.

I was called as a witness to the trial but never testified. I tried to find my notes I had taken when the FBI agent and I first interviewed Shayne in her apartment. I had apparently placed them in the case file, and when I went to get them, they were not there. At the trial, I was not called to testify, but the rookie FBI agent was called. As he testified, he began referring to the notes I had taken during the interview and somehow, he had gotten the notes I had made and used them in his testimony. It wasn't a big deal, but if the defense knew he had not recorded the notes, it could have compromised the trial procedures.

In the book *Mad Notions*, it was hailed as a "true story," "where dialogue was drawn from personal interviews, witnessed in the courtroom court transcripts, and press accounts." I can't confirm where a lot of the information in the book was derived, but without a doubt, the investigation at the onset began as I discovered Kelly Lovera was murdered and continued the investigation with the FBI until it was relinquished to the TBI. It is at the passage in the book, where the author had referenced the criminal investigator in the park being "Stan Fielding." There had never been a criminal investigator or Park Ranger named Stan Fielding at the Great Smoky Mountains National Park, and the author apparently used it as a fictional reference. It was me and our criminal investigator, Bill Acree, that found the bloody evidence as described hereafter.

The TBI had taken over the investigation when it was found the murder had occurred outside of the park. They had contacted us about a week later to assist them in finding more evidence of the crime. Brett Rae had confessed he had committed the crime and the TBI tried to confirm Rae's information regarding him leaving the Jeep and going into Gatlinburg. Acree told me to go back to the overlook, to look for more clues and the bloody evidence Rae had described to the TBI, where he had disposed of a bag of bloody clothes. I looked for the evidence and found footprints that had trampled the vegetation along the roadway, where it appeared someone had walked. This was in an area where there would be little or no pedestrian traffic, and lead from the parking area where the Jeep was found to the Campbell Lead intersection of U.S. 441. This would have been a natural escape route walking on Campbell Lead road that would wind for miles around the mountain, leading to Graystone Heights in downtown Gatlinburg.

Rae told TBI he had walked out onto River Road by the Edgewater motel that indicated he had to have taken the Campbell Lead
road to get to Gatlinburg. I found a small, road that went off the
Campbell Lead road and into the woods that came to a dead end. At
the end of the road, I found more footprints and disturbed vegetation
as if someone had walked into the woods. Just a short distance off the
trail I found a clear, plastic bag and it contained bloody towels and a
bloody hat that was later determined to be Kelly's, that was in the
Jeep. Rae took the bloody items and threw them into the woods. The
footprints and disturbed vegetation led me back onto the Campbell
Lead road. It got late and it would be dark soon. I followed along
Campbell Lead road and found where there was a large disturbed
area where someone or something had slid off the embankment and
into the woods. It did not look like it was caused by a bear or another
animal and it appeared to be human interference. I marked the location and left the area because it was going to be dark soon and I didn't
want to disturb the area, and come back and track again.

The next day, I was scheduled to be on vacation, and instead of
going back and searching the area further, I told the criminal investigator, Bill Acree, who was not "Stan Fielding," of what I had found
and told him where I had stopped searching. I met with him and gave
him the bloody bag of evidence. The next day, he went to where I had
stopped searching, and picked up the trail, following it toward Gatlinburg, through the thick vegetation and steep mountainous terrain.

Our criminal investigator had been an old school Park Ranger for
many years and was very experienced, but now he was mostly
confined to the office, reviewing criminal complaints and dealing
with Federal court prosecutions, He had trained and worked with
Park Ranger J.R Buchanan, a renowned man tracker and a legacy in
the Great Smoky Mountains, where he taught and shared his knowledge of man tracking. J.R had successfully found many victims and
criminals during his career as a National Park Ranger. Now the Criminal Investigator was back in action as a Park Ranger. He followed the
trail just a short distance and found Rae's bloody shoes and
continued down the steep terrain coming to a log, where he found

Brett Rae's bloody clothes. This was a week or ten days after Brett Rae had murdered Kelly Lovera. Rae had tucked the bloody clothes under the log and covered them with leaves and debris. Acree recovered the clothing and continued following the track that lead him to the river in downtown Gatlinburg and the Edgewater motel, where Brett Rae had confessed to coming to, after he left the wooded area from Campbell Lead. Rae met his friend at this location and confessed to his friend he had killed Kelly and his friend took him back to Frog Ally to his apartment. After Rae had pushed Kelly and his Jeep over the embankment in the twilight hours after the murder, he walked for a couple of miles trying to escape his heinous crime. By taking the wooded route he thought no one would find any evidence to link him to the murder but didn't realize he had entered the National Park Rangers back yard.

Even though Brett Rae had confessed, and there was physical evidence he had killed Kelly, there still had to be a timeline of events to ensure the prosecution would be successful. The significance of us finding this evidence provided the timeline and framed the actions and events of Rae as he fled the area where he had left Kelly Lovera in the Jeep over the embankment to fake a vehicle accident. The TBI investigators could not believe we were able to follow the tracks of Rae in the woods a week later. They were surprised when we found the critical evidence Brett Rae had described to them. This evidence would be used in the prosecution, and eliminated any plea offered by the defense to mitigate Brett Rae and Shayne Lovera's sentences. Because of the evidence, timeline, and interviews the prosecution would not accept any pleas and the pair were prosecuted in Court. It was, without a doubt, Brett Rae and Shayne Mills Lovera had murdered Kelly Lovera. Both Brett Rae and Shayne Mills Lovera were convicted of 1st degree murder and sentenced to life imprisonment with the possibility of parole. Life imprisonment as defined by the State of Tennessee at the time meant each would have to serve at least 25 years before they would be eligible for parole.

38

Chop Shop

*B*eing a Law Enforcement Park Ranger was really no different than being any other police officer. In my career, I had thousands of law enforcement contacts from writing tickets for feeding wildlife, traffic offenses, and other misdemeanors and infractions of the law, to making numerous arrests for capital crimes including murder, rape, larcenies and wildlife violations. Any law enforcement officer could write a book detailing bizarre, tragic, and humorous stories. The difference of a Law Enforcement National Park Ranger, was transforming immediately from a law enforcement officer, to a Wildland Fire Fighter, Providing Emergency Medical treatment in remote backcountry areas, Technical high angle Rescues and Swift Water River Rescues, Wildlife management and a host of other jobs that would not be included in a police officer's job. Instead of recycling drunks, dealing with ongoing domestic violence, and other monotonous calls as a police officer, we operated in a more Natural environment, dealing with different clients and different issues. We still had to deal with a lot of criminal elements, given our jurisdiction and responsibilities. A lot of times, crimes occurred in the Park and would lead to investigations outside the park in the cities and counties and sometimes in another state due to the North Carolina area of the Great Smoky Mountains, where our jurisdiction continued. Before the 1994 Ranger Future fiasco, Park Rangers would do their own investigations, without the assistance of a criminal investigator. Prior to 1994, there were no criminal investigators and if a Ranger had a case, he would investigate and see the case through to the prosecution. Those were the days when there were competent supervisors who would only assist if a Ranger needed any assistance.

If there was a call to go outside the park for an investigation or make an arrest, the local cities and county police departments would always go out of their way to assist us with back up and resources we would not have available. One such resource would be a K-9 officer. The Great Smoky Mountains National Park had no canine officers, although I always thought one would be handy. One vehicle larceny I had investigated led to the discovery of a major automobile theft group and automobile chop shop, where stolen automobiles would be taken, stripped of the parts, and sold.

A suspect broke into vehicles and was spotted by a Ranger, driving in his very nice, expensive mustang on the steep Newfound Gap. The Ranger stopped in the road to apprehend and arrest the suspect, who fled into the woods. As the Ranger ran away from his vehicle, he stopped and looked around in time to see his nice, expensive mustang, rolling backwards and over the steep embankment, totaling his Mustang. The suspect escaped but was somehow identified. I had gotten information about the suspect and began investigating and found the suspect in another county. During my investigation and interviews, some people who knew the suspect, said he would run if confronted by law enforcement. They told me he had been running from the law since he was 15 years old. He was now about 30 years old. I had a federal arrest warrant for the subject. I contacted the county Sheriff department for assistance in apprehending the suspect. I met with a county deputy and he had a large German Shepard K-9 partner.

The suspect was in a house trailer, sitting out in the open with a large field behind it. There was a garage next to it and several vehicles parked around the outside. The county deputy, with his K-9, went to the front of the trailer and was met by the suspect's brother who claimed the suspect we were looking for was not there. The deputy tried to get into the trailer, and I was behind it, where there was a back door to the trailer but no back porch. The door was probably five feet off the ground. As I watched the door, it was thrown open and the suspect jumped out of the trailer and began running down the open field, heading for the woods. I yelled for the deputy who ran around with his canine unit.

The suspect was already a long way from us, sprinting to the woods. I had worked with some police officers and their canine units during crowd control but had never seen a K-9 attack and apprehend anyone. The K-9 was a large German Shepard, probably about my size, and just his presence was really intimidating. The K-9 spotted the suspect who was getting away fast and the deputy unleased the German Shepard. It was almost a surreal moment as the K-9 ran for the suspect and I watched the big dog's muscular body, as if it were in slow motion, going after the suspect. I had been involved with many arrests of suspects who resisted arrest by running, and for other offenses. This undoubtedly was the biggest rush I had ever experienced in apprehending a criminal. The suspect ran fast as he could, and the K-9 quickly closed the distance. The K-9 jumped on the suspect's back, knocking him down, and proceeded to eat his ass. The more the suspect would fight the K-9, the more the K-9 would eat. The suspect screamed as we ran to get to him and the dog. If the suspect would have lain still, the K-9 would have just held him, but he elected to fight and get away, and the K-9 just kept eating his ass. We got to the suspect as fast as we could and got him handcuffed.

As soon as the deputy got the dog back on leash the dog kept licking his butt. I asked the deputy why he was doing that, and the deputy said he was trying to get the bad taste out of his mouth. For some reason the suspect did not see the humor as we chuckled and laughed, walking the suspect back to the trailer. Other deputies had arrived for assistance and they checked the vehicles around the garage. It was discovered several of the vehicles were stolen. We arrested the suspect for a simple misdemeanor offense of car burglary in the park, and as a result, we uncovered a major car chop operation. Due to the number of suspects and stolen vehicles recovered by the Sheriff's office, the U.S. Attorney decided to dismiss the charges for breaking and entering cars in the park, and we remanded custody of the suspect to the County Sheriff Department for prosecution. For some reason, car burglaries subsided in the park for a while, but continued as a new crop of thugs arrived and preyed on the visitors who were oblivious and absorbed by the park atmosphere.

39

Park Ranger Kristopher William Eggle
End of Watch Friday, August 9, 2002

Kris Eggle

On August 9th, 2002, and just shortly before I retired, another National Park Ranger I had worked with was shot and killed. Kris Eggle was ambushed and gunned down by a drug smuggler. This was the third Ranger I had personally worked with who was murdered. I had known Kris when he worked in the Wildlife division at the Great Smoky Mountains as a wildlife biologist and a hog hunter. Kris wanted to become a Law Enforcement Ranger, where there were more challenges. Kris reminded me of myself when I became a Law Enforcement Officer with the National Park Service. I was 27 years old, full of piss and vinegar, and couldn't wait to get to work each day. Now Kris was 27 years old and a Law Enforcement Ranger at Organ Pipe Cactus National Monument. I had never worked with Kris on any law enforcement details, but I had trained with him in medical emergency service, technical and high angle rescue incidents, and helped him with bear immobilization and other wildlife problems. Kris had excelled at about everything he had done. He was just beginning his Park Service career.

The Organ Pipe Cactus National Monument is located on the U.S./ Mexico border, and probably the most dangerous National Park because of the drug smuggling and thousands of illegal aliens flooding the area. The law enforcement staff at the park is minimal, as most National Parks are. Kris's death, like Bob McGhee, and Joe Kolodski, was a result of mismanagement within the National Park Service that has been devoid of leadership, poorly coordinated, and failed to provide the necessary equipment and back-up to ensure a safer working environment for their Law Enforcement Park Rangers. The job of the Park Ranger has changed for the worst. Studies have shown Park Rangers are twice as likely to be assaulted more than any other Federal Law Enforcement Officer. Historically, the National Park Service has downplayed the crime in the National Parks. They continue to instill a wholesome image of "Ranger Rick" and "Yogi Bear" in a fake environment, while the reality is very different. The law enforcement program is still managed by the Superintendents of the parks who typically have no law enforcement training or background or experience at all. Kris was a National Park Ranger but thrust into another role as a military soldier dealing with the drug cartels in Mexico. Only a handful of Rangers at Organ Cactus were the front lines trying to repel the drug cartels and illegal alien invasion that had consumed the region. It was impossible to protect the resources and provide visitor protection given the vast number of people and criminals that were encountered. The park management, that included the Superintendent, knew or should have known of the consequences that occurred by allowing Rangers to be put in this kind of hostile environment, without the proper back-up and trained personnel, in dealing with guerilla tactics and not just someone picking wildflowers. Kris had flown in on a helicopter in assisting the U.S. Border patrol in apprehending drug dealers and smugglers. Kris didn't have the proper back-up and was alone as he was ambushed and killed by a drug dealer who shot Kris with an AK-47 military assault rifle. This area was basically a war zone that required the deployment of a team of trained soldiers, but instead a lone Park Ranger with no back-up, minimal equipment and training, was thrust into a law enforcement situation that I had encountered many times myself in similar circumstances.

After Kris was killed, there were congressional inquiries and investigations by the Department of the Interior where plans were made to increase the Law Enforcement Rangers in the Parks. Instead, Rangers were reduced to more seasonal and temporary employees, with minimum experience and training, and decreased the full-time, experienced Law Enforcement Rangers. Law Enforcement Rangers have been reduced by at least 20% since I have retired and replaced by more administration, and volunteers. As an example, when I worked at the Gulf Islands National Seashore there were about a dozen Law Enforcement Rangers assigned to the Seashore and now there are only two. The National Park service has reverted to the 70s and 80s where seasonal and temporary employees were used to save money, by not having to pay benefits as health insurance and 6c retirement and getting the law enforcement patrols for pennies on the dollar. Again, the superintendents manage the parks and funding. They basically operate independently with no direction or supervision. Most of them have no law enforcement training or experience in providing visitor safety, and the needed staffing and equipment is compromised.

The Ranger Future debacle in 1994, guaranteed the management staff of the Park Service, big dollars where the superintendents were promoted from the General Service Grade that was usually a GS-15, to Senior Executive Service positions that increased their pay that equaled the Vice President of the United States. Although Kris's death had enhanced the possibilities to upgrade the Law Enforcement program in the National Park Service, it fell by the way.

40

BEAR ATTACK AND THE DEATH OF MRS. GLENDA BRADLEY

J worked with the National Park Service as a National Park Ranger for over 26 years. I was 50 years old and still loved every minute of being a National Park Ranger, when a major life-changing event interrupted and ultimately ended my career. The management of the National Park Service had become unbearable. The once independent and professional Park Ranger became a bureaucratic nightmare. I never thought, at any time, there would be a finale that could make me despise being a National Park Ranger that I once was so proud to be, and a job I had envied as a small boy.

***

The next story I share with you transformed many people's lives when Mrs. Glenda Bradley was killed by a black bear in the Great Smoky Mountains National Park. The information is true that identifies a horrific event, that was compounded by lies, personal insults, and false and misleading information by the management of the Great Smoky Mountains National Park. It has been 20 years since Mrs. Glenda Bradley was killed. The story I share with you is true and the information is factual. I was there, with many witnesses, and shot and killed two bears that had killed Glenda Bradley. I meticulously conducted the on-scene investigation, collecting the evidence, and concluded exactly what happened. There will be some readers who may be apprehensive in believing the information is true and may think I am just a disgruntled employee. I whole-heartedly agree I am disgruntled, and I have the right and reason to be. The image of the National Park Ranger is far from the image of years ago, when Ranger Rick was portrayed as the friendly Park Ranger, with his side kicks, Yogi Bear and Boo Boo.

The fake cartoon portrayal of the National Park Service is why I was envious of being a National Park Ranger. The reality is, the National Park Service is nothing more than another government run organization where the fraud, waste and abuse is mitigated with false misrepresentation. Power, money and selfish egos are cultivated and are disguised to keep the public from knowing the truth about how the National Park Service operates. As an old guy now, it doesn't matter much anymore. I can't change anything about the National Park Service. It will surely become ignominious as the management continues to be reckless and careless and failing to protect the public. There will be more deaths and disaster as a result of this transgression.

What matters to me is this book has given me time to reflect on my consecrated career as a National Park Ranger. It will hopefully give me closure, and provide the absolute truth, and dispel all the rumors and innuendos that have resulted in how, and why, Glenda Bradley was attacked by a bear and killed. Although it has been almost 20 years since the afternoon Mrs. Glenda Bradley was killed, I still have cogitations how this incident could have prevented Glenda from being killed, and why and how an incident like this could be so convoluted. I have investigated numerous incidents where innocent people were tragically injured or killed. Because of the ambivalence and confliction included in this incident, it has caused me a lot of depression and ongoing anger where my professionalism and integrity were destroyed as I upheld the tradition of a National Park Ranger.

On May 21, 2000, Glenda Bradley and Ralph Hill were spending their afternoon at Great Smoky Mountains National Park. Ralph and Glenda were divorced but had remained good friends and neighbors and were schoolteachers at Jones Cove Elementary school in Sevier County. It was a quiet, warm, spring Sunday afternoon with some forecasted thunderstorms. The busy weekend for the Rangers was winding down. It was about four o'clock in the afternoon and I was at my desk finishing up a backlog of reports that had accumulated over the weekend. A call came over the radio that an individual had been attacked by a bear by the Goshen Prong bridge that is located near the Elkmont Campground. Because of the number of bears in the park it was not uncommon to get a call of a bear attack that usually resulted in a bear charging someone, trying to get to some food, or someone getting too close. When this call came in, it was different. The panic transmitted through the radio indicated this was a much different situation.

A Park Ranger, whom I will only identify as the "responding Ranger," was at the Elkmont Campground at the time the report was made by a hiker. This Ranger, by all accounts, was derelict in his response and actions after he arrived, where the bear attack had occurred. He made a horrible decision and mistake that any Ranger could have made. At the onset, I don't suspect he was in any way a part of a serious conspiracy and collusion that would occur in the aftermath of this bear attack. As the incident progressed, the Ranger was used to manipulate and cloud the investigation by narratives concocted by the management of the Great Smoky Mountains National Park. Everyone who was involved in this incident is part of the official record, media reports and official investigation. His name is not important to identify the atrocious response by the Great Smoky Mountains National Park managers. If this incident would have been handled properly, the truthful account would have palliated any wrongdoing. The reckless negligence that resulted in the aftermath is what is important, and the responding Ranger was manipulated by the actions of the park management.

The responding Ranger was closest to the trailhead that lead to the Goshen Prong Bridge. He responded immediately, up the trail by foot after he had driven to the end of the road. It was about a 1.5-mile hike from the end of the road to the Goshen Prong bridge. Meanwhile, Ranger Chip Nelson and I got the rescue van and a four-wheel drive vehicle and headed to the scene. Ranger Nelson drove the rescue van and I drove a pick-up truck, leaving our law enforcement vehicles parked at the Little River Ranger Station. It took us about 20 minutes to get to the end of the road where we would have to park and hike up the trail. In the meantime, the responding Ranger arrived on scene where the bear attack had occurred.

As we unloaded the rescue equipment, the responding Ranger called on the radio and told us to bring a long gun and get up there as quick as possible. Both Chip and I had left our law enforcement vehicles at the Ranger station that had our long guns in them. A long gun would include a weapon being a shotgun or rifle. Both of us had Remington 870 shotguns in the vehicles and .223 caliber AR-15's but the only weapon we had with us were our .40 caliber Sig Sauer semiautomatic pistols. I radioed the responding Ranger and told him we didn't have any long guns and we were coming with the rescue litter and medical supplies. He replied to drop everything and get up here. It was at this point I knew this was a serious situation.

It was a pretty muggy, humid afternoon and a mile and a half hike, had turned into a mile and a half run. Ordinarily, before I

book

hiked a trail, I lightened my load and change my shoes to hiking shoes. I always wore a class A uniform, unless I knew for certain I would be hiking on a trail, or in the woods. Because of working on the road and in the public view, I always wanted to look sharp and professional. I carried a pair of hiking boots in my cruiser that I would change from my Wellington boots I wore with my class A uniform. I would take off my gun belt and bullet-proof vest and change to a smaller shoulder holster. There was no time for the change, as Chip and I began running up the trail to the Goshen Prong bridge. While running, I tried to contact the responding Ranger by radio for any updates of what was happening, and he wouldn't answer. The park dispatch tried several times and he still would not answer. We knew things had to be bad and assumed he was occupied by a serious emergency and did not have the time to talk on the radio.

I assumed the Incident Command and called for every available Ranger in the Park to respond and to bring a long gun. Rangers were scattered from North Carolina, Cades Cove and Gatlinburg, and responded to our location. The park's wildlife division immediately responded also. It was at least a mile and a half to get to the Goshen Prong bridge, and Chip and I had run probably a half mile when the 30 pounds of gun belt, bullet proof vest, and other gear was beginning to feel like 60 pounds. The soles of my street boots were skidding in the leaves and leaf litter like bald tires on an old pick-up. I had just turned 50 years old and it was a little tougher to negotiate the trails than when I was just a young whipper snapper like Chip. The adrenaline had taken me over and I continued to run up the trail, looking back and making sure Chip was "pulling up the rear." Chip and I have been able to cultivate our private and small bit of humor out of this tragedy. I make fun of Chip because I was a little older than him and I was outrunning him on the trail, and I had to continually look back to make sure he hadn't collapsed. The fact of the matter was, if I had abruptly stopped for any reason, I would have been plowed over as Chip drafted me like a NASCAR driver, and I was fixing to lose the lead at any time. I was lucky to have Chip with me, and there was no question of his ability to take care of business (at my direction, of course).

There was still no communication from the responding Ranger, as we ran up the trail, meeting people hiking down the trail that were pointing and shouting and motioning for us to keep going. We finally arrived at the Goshen Prong bridge. The bridge is a large iron pedestrian bridge that spanned the Little River. When we arrived, there were five or six people standing along the trail looking into the woods. I was out of breath as I ran up to them and asked them where the Ranger was, and they pointed out into the woods where I could see the responding Ranger standing with his arms crossed about 30 yards away. I asked them where the bear was, and they pointed straight in front of them. There was thick vegetation along the trail, and I was unable to see out into the woods. I pulled my pistol and ran into the thick underbrush busting out into the open woods where I saw the most horrific sight I had encountered in my professional career.

Glenda Bradley was lying on her back and the larger bear was standing over her and licking and eating her face. The smaller bear was on her right side sitting on her right arm on its rear haunches and looking around. It was a surreal moment that seemed like minutes, getting from the trail to Glenda, but was only seconds as I ran, while trying to digest what was occurring with the responding Ranger standing 30 yards or more out in the open woods, with his arms crossed, and the bears were on Glenda. It had been at least 45 minutes when the responding Ranger arrived. The bears were about 30 yards from the trail, and I ran on a small animal trail trying to get to the bears. It seemed like a long time, but it was only seconds as I closed in and tried to get as close to the bears as possible. I got within 12 feet of the bears and a small tree blocked me from getting closer to the bears without crawling around and over it. I wanted to get just as close as I possibly could, without scaring the bears and causing them to run off. I intended to shoot and kill both bears. I stopped and fired off three shots at the largest bear that was licking and eating the victims' face. I had hit the bear and it stumbled and ran toward me and within just a couple of feet where I fired another round at it. It ran behind me and within a split second I turned, and I fired two rounds across Glenda's body hitting the smaller bear and causing it to run into the woods. The bears were no longer on or next to Glenda. I could hear the smaller bear only a few yards into the woods make a crying sound. I thought at the time it was the larger bears' cub and it was calling for the mama bear.

I holstered my pistol and knelt to check on the victim for any signs of life. Her face was horrifying, and the bears had scratched dirt on top of her. I guess because of the training I had as a medical responder, I automatically checked the victim's vitals for any signs of life that was only a formality. One could tell by just looking at the visible condition of the victim, there would be no vital signs. As I touched the victim, BOOM!! Chip fired off his .40 caliber pistol only feet behind me without me knowing he was there. My adrenaline was already maxed out and the startling sound of a .40 caliber cannon surprisingly going off within a few feet behind me tested my medical stability and condition that could have cause a heart attack.

The smaller bear I shot ran into the woods and had made a circle and came back to find the other bear. The smaller bear was hit center mass and bled profusely. The largest bear was lying only a few feet behind me where it fell after I shot it. I hadn't focused on where it had run. My only concern was to immediately attend to the victim. Chip stood behind me and saw the larger bear fall within just a couple of feet from us. He then saw the smaller bear coming from the woods to the larger bear. It came within a few feet of me and Chip and the other bear. Chip fired a round off and finished the smaller bear. We had successfully killed both bears that killed Mrs. Glenda Bradley. While all of this is going on, the responding Ranger never drew his pistol or even approached us as Chip and I moved in to try to kill the bears. It had been at least 45 minutes the responding Ranger was on scene and watched these bears eat the victim, and not answered his radio to give us an update of what was happening. The radio log showed it took Chip and me twenty-seven minutes to get to the Goshen Prong bridge and we immediately rushed in to engage the two bears and took only a few seconds before we got close enough to kill the bears.

This was going to be a complicated investigation to understand what had transpired and caused these bears to kill someone. My supervisor intervened immediately, from miles away at his home, by radio, and called for another Ranger to respond and begin tracking and finding the bears. He was excited and confused and probably drunk, and I couldn't get on the radio to tell him we had already shot and killed the bears. The supervisor called another Ranger who was miles away, hiking a trail at Mount Le Conte, and would be hours getting to our location. Besides, this Ranger had no expertise in any investigations, but was only a crony of my supervisor. I was finally able to get across to him by radio, I had already killed the bears and more Rangers were on the way and others were arriving at the trail head and heading to us. I had been involved in many complex investigations and was very capable of doing this investigation. I began interviewing the people at the trail and found one of the persons at the trail was Glenda's ex-husband, Ralph Hill. Ralph was in shock and shaking out of control. He was very pale and could barely talk to me. I was almost certain the tragedy Ralph had endured was going to create a medical emergency, but I had to have information of what had happened. There were about five witnesses there on the trail also. I had gotten their names for the report, but I could never find any witnesses listed on the 'official report,' but then again, I had no access to the final investigation.

I hurriedly interviewed Ralph, and he told me he and Glenda had hiked up to the Goshen Prong bridge where Glenda was going to read a book while he fished upwards of the bridge in the Little River. He had been gone for a short while and when he returned, he could not locate Glenda. It was around 5 pm and he began looking for Glenda and found her pack lying under the Goshen Prong bridge and Glenda nowhere to be found. Ralph picked up Glenda's pack and only a couple of minutes later, as Ralph walked and looked in the woods for Glenda, he saw the bears hovering over Glenda's body. Ralph yelled and threw sticks and rocks at the bears, scaring the bears away from her. Another hiker heard him calling for help and the hiker ran to the Elkmont Campground, where he made the report to the responding Ranger. While the hiker ran for help, Ralph kept the bears off Glenda by throwing sticks and rocks at them but was unable to get close to her because the bears would charge him. He continued keeping the bears off her for an hour or more before the responding Ranger arrived.

Ralph stated when the responding Ranger arrived, he made Ralph go and wait on the trail. Ralph told me, the responding Ranger would not go close to the bears and would not shoot the bears. Ralph was confused as he tried to go back and tried to get the bears off Glenda, but the responding Ranger would not let him. The bears attacked Glenda for over 45 minutes, while the responding Ranger watched this horrifying event. Ralph stood on the trail with other witnesses, and they could not see Glenda for the vegetation along the trail but could see the responding Ranger, watching the bears, and never approached them. The responding Ranger had watched the bears from a distance and never tried to get the bears away from her.

Ralph also told me the responding Ranger told him he was afraid of the bears and was waiting for a long gun to shoot the bears. Ralph's story was consistent to what I observed when I arrived, as I saw the responding Ranger standing 30 yards into the woods, away from the bears, while the bears assaulted Glenda. The responding Ranger had a .40 caliber, Sig Sauer pistol with 36 rounds of jacketed hollow point ammunition, just like Chip and I had. The responding ranger never removed his gun from his holster, even as we engaged the bears, ultimately killing them.

I had worked with many victims of death from lightning strikes, motor vehicle accidents, suicides, murders, and more. This was a horrific scene and the memory has been with me for years. Little did I know, this incident would end my career as a National Park Ranger. There were questions regarding the responding ranger's response to the bear attack, but there were far more questions to explain the attack of the bear that led to the death of Glenda Bradley. I quickly assumed the lead and began investigating where and how Glenda had been attacked. I found where Glenda had run through the river sand and where she had dropped her pack. I had trained in man tracking and I was familiar with the signs to track individuals. Glenda had run downstream in the water in attempt to get away from the bears.

Running from a black bear is the last thing to do. Black bears will chase you and they can run up to 30 miles per hour. In a panic situation, Glenda did what most people would do and ran from the bear. This engaged the bear's predator/prey instinct, and the bear chased her. The only way to fend off a black bear attack is stand your ground, make lots of noise, and slowly back away, watching the bear. Try to maintain an aggression that will stop the black bear from chasing and attacking and don't turn away from the bears. If you have food or other items, throw them away from you and slowly back away while watching the bear. If it comes to a foot race, you will certainly lose. Also, never play dead in a black bear attack. Be aggressive and shout, scream, yell, throw rocks, but don't run away. If you are with another individual, make sure you can run faster than them. Bears are wild animals and are very dangerous and unpredictable.

I waded downstream and found where Glenda had come upon a deadfall that is a tangled mass of brush and trees along the river's edge. Glenda had climbed up onto the deadfall to run through the woods. The bears chased after Glenda as she got out of the river and began running through the woods. There had been a fresh rain and the vegetation was crisp and footprints and bear tracks could be easily followed in the wet vegetation and soft ground. The grass and vegetation were also pushed and laid down where the bear's belly dragged over it as it chased Glenda. Glenda came to a rhododendron thicket, and unable to get through it. The bear had chased closely behind her, and she was now trapped between the bear and the thick Rhododendron. Footprints indicated Glenda had turned and faced the bear as it dragged her down and the bear clawed and bit her before she died.

There was no indication of how long Glenda had survived the attack before she died. There were numerous postmortem wounds that indicated she was alive as the bear attacked her. If a person is alive, and the heart beating, there will be bruising around the wound. Once the heart stops beating, the other wounds will show no signs of bruising. There were numerous teeth marks and claw marks on her body and a lot of bruising, and the bears had also consumed some of her upper torso that did not indicate any bruising. It was without a doubt to me, the bear had chased her down and killed her. I didn't find any more signs showing where the smaller bear had come from. Ranger Bobby Holland arrived as I finished the initial tracking. Ranger Holland was also a good man tracker and had also trained under Park Ranger J.R. Buchanan. Ranger Holland went and confirmed my findings, but we still did not know where the smaller bear had come from. In a few minutes, other Rangers showed up. Wildlife biologist Chuck Hester arrived, and he looked for signs as to where the smaller bear may have come from. Chuck was an expert animal tracker. He had come to work at the Smokies as a Wildlife biologist and spent much of his early career as a hog hunter, hunting and eradicating the wild hogs in the Smokies and very familiar with the mountain environment.

Almost immediately, Chuck found where the smaller bear had come from, at the opposite end of the Goshen Prong bridge, and the bear's footprints merged with the location where Glenda's body was found and the two bears. There was no indication the smaller bear had assisted in attacking Glenda, and only came to the other bear afterwards. It was obvious the larger bear had killed Glenda. The smaller teeth marks indicated no bruising, which indicated the victim was deceased. All the evidence indicated it was a confirmed bear attack, but with her estranged husband present, and being an unwitnessed death, there had to be a more in-depth investigation. As we secured the scene and prepared to get the victim and bears removed from the scene, in came a huge thunderstorm. All the natural, physical evidence that included the footprints was destroyed. Rangers Holland, Hester and I were certain of the path that Glenda and the bear had taken before she was killed, and the bear had chased her down and killed her. The evidence at the scene concluded the bears had attacked and killed Mrs. Glenda Bradley.

We were now having to focus on why the bear had attacked her. Glenda had a pack with her, and Ralph had found the pack and had carried it down the trail to where he observed the bear attacking Glenda. He told me where the pack was when he found it, and there was evidence in the sand under the bridge where the pack had been left as Glenda fled from the bear. I had the responding ranger walk Ralph out of the area and at the same time, get Glenda's pack where Ralph had left it. The pack was valuable evidence and would confirm and explain exactly what had happened at the Goshen Prong Bridge. While we walked out, the news media waited at the vehicles. This was not a good time for the media to be here and I had them leave and go to the headquarters where they would be briefed on the incident. It is now getting very late, and I arrived at headquarters to continue the investigation and get the pack to look for evidence.

When I arrived at the headquarters, I was met by my supervisor. He came to me and told me to go home. I explained to him I still had a lot of work to do and I needed to get Glenda's pack. I told him I needed to contact our criminal investigator because it was an unwitnessed death, and we had to further investigate the incident. He then told me to go home again and said there was "not going to be an investigation," and this was a "Wildlife incident" and again told me to go home. I argued with him and told him this was an unwitnessed death and the victim's estranged husband was with her when it happened. I wanted the area of the Goshen Prong bridge closed as this was a crime scene and it would have to be closed until we could go back the next morning and look for more evidence. He then told me he no longer had the pack, and never looked in it and he had given it to the family. This was unbelievable and it would later be found this pack contained the valuable evidence and information that was needed to clarify how and why the bears attacked Glenda Bradley. The reckless and careless negligence was overwhelming by an arrogant and intellectually challenged supervisor who had absolutely no clue on how to conduct an investigation. I went home very frustrated and stayed up all night without sleeping. The next morning, I arrived at the park at about 8 a.m. and the front lawn of headquarters was infested with the news media and a press conference being given by the Superintendent, Chief Ranger and my supervisor. The Park Service officials reported to the news media, "we had a bear attack occur in the park and we don't know what happened, and it is under investigation."

The Superintendent, Chief Ranger and District Supervisor were a bunch of bureaucratic clowns. They provided the news media with a narrative that was intentionally false and misleading. Rangers Nelson, Hester, Holland and I knew exactly what had happened before the sun had set and Glenda's pack would have confirmed in the early morning what had happened, had it not been sent home with the family. The management of the park attempted to mitigate the inactions of their Park Ranger who had arrived on scene and was derelict in his duty to protect a visitor from harm. His performance had nothing to do with why the bear had attacked and killed someone. The bear attack and the investigation should have focused on why the bear killed Glenda, rather than trying to thwart the attack because of a personnel issue that should have been handled separately. The suspicion of why this happened as it did, has never been disclosed. It made absolutely no sense why this investigation was so convoluted and being handled this way and the non-sense would only escalate further. Because of the Public Information system created by the National Park, all the information would be cleverly compiled in a narrative to be given to the news media. This left out the real facts, and then distributed to the news media who wouldn't have a clue of the real story. The Park Rangers were not allowed to be interviewed by the media and all the information was given after the park management cleverly crafted it to give false and misleading information to the public.

There are a lot of facts that the public is unaware of. Now, 20 years later, the false and misleading deception by the National Park Service has created a lore. There is nothing but myths that will continue in years to come and will continue to be embellished and enhanced to create more myths and false stories concerning the first bear attack in the Smokies that had killed someone. Just weeks prior, as I write this memoir, one of my friends, whom I hadn't seen for years, met me at a doctor's office. He asked me if I had killed any bears. It was bear season, and being an avid hunter, I thought he meant if I had been hunting bear. I told him I didn't bear hunt and I hadn't killed any bears. His reply was, 'You killed the two bears in the bear attack of Glenda Bradley,' and was being facetious asking me if I had killed any more bears. He then told me he had heard in the beginning that Glenda had been feeding the bears cookies and getting too close and caused the bears to attack her. He told me he had a casual conversation about the bear attack with a person who still works in the park just weeks earlier and had told him she had Twinkies in her pockets when we found her. This is the exact same type of rumors and innuendos that have been created and circulated throughout the community for the past 20 years.

When the attack occurred, there was immediate speculation by some of the public everything that occurred was being kept secret. The Park Service management maintained their narrative, "it's under investigation." Everyone knew that her ex-husband was with her when she was killed. Immediately the rumors began circulating that he had killed her and dragged her body into the woods, and she was already deceased, and the bears then found her. Animal advocates would rigorously defend the bears' behavior and place the blame on the victim and her ex-husband. To exaggerate further, people began adding to the false story and claiming her ex-husband had put honey on her body to attract the bears and her ex-husband even made a "trout necklace" and put on her. There were claims of a strained relationship where the ex-husband lured her up the trail to kill her. Now, 20 years later, she had Twinkies in her pockets. Stories were made up that accused Glenda of feeding the bears and she was the reason the bears had attacked her. All the stories and lore that have been made up to embellish a tragic incident with no facts to confirm any of it and are all false. The information I am sharing is the absolute truth as to what happened at the Goshen Prong Bridge in the Great Smoky

Mountains National Park and the misleading and false narratives that were endorsed by the management of the Great Smoky Mountains National Park were cleverly created to thwart the truth.

These are the facts that occurred in the bear attack that killed Glenda Bradley. First and foremost, her ex-husband, Ralph Hill, had absolutely nothing to do with her death. There was no honey. There was no trout, there were no cookies or Twinkies. I was the Ranger on scene, shot and killed the two bears and did the investigation that found, without any doubt, Glenda Bradley was killed by the larger bear, and the smaller bear was only an accomplice after the fact.

The reason the incident became so convoluted and palliated was nothing more than the management of the National Park Service trying to protect a minority Park Ranger who was clearly derelict in his duties. My new supervisor was a minority and had been assigned to take over my leadership role and my supervisor's leadership position as a result of the 1994 Ranger Future Park Ranger reorganization. There was animosity as a result of this where two career supervisors were replaced by an individual who had very little supervisory experience, almost no law enforcement background, including any major investigations or arrests, but qualified by being an Affirmative Action candidate. Several positions in the Great Smoky Mountains were included that placed minorities and socially connected employees in these supervisory positions and removed experienced Park Rangers who had these leadership roles for many years. Two very experienced Assistant Chief Rangers were taken out of their supervisory roles and law enforcement supervision. One of them was assigned as a V.I.P (Volunteer in the Park) coordinator. The other was reassigned and allowed to continue with law enforcement duties until he could obtain the necessary years for his law enforcement 6(c) retirement but had no more leadership roles. The new supervisors were controversial and adversaries of their subordinates. They had minimal qualifications but were placed in these roles under the guise of creating a "diverse" workforce. Employee trust and morale was destroyed, and the beatings would not stop until the morale improved. Unfortunately, this would lead to much stress, and was a direct cause in the shooting death of a Park Ranger, Joe Kolodski, at the Great Smoky Mountains National Park.

In this bear attack case, it did not really matter the color, plumbing or social connections. The responding Ranger had been derelict in his duties and now the management of the park would begin a cover up to protect the employee's image. There were many Rangers on scene who were confounded that an armed National Park Ranger would allow these bears to attack the victim for 45 minutes.

I had the responding Ranger take Ralph Hill away from the scene. He then went back to headquarters where I speculate, he briefed my supervisor before we could clear the scene. The groundwork was apparently laid at this time and it was imperative I be removed from the case as soon as possible because I would surely intervene, questioning the responding Ranger's actions at the scene. I was disgusted by what I had witnessed with an armed Ranger letting these bears continue attacking the victim. I wanted to understand the reasons this Ranger froze and failed to do his job. Hesitating and freezing up in a gun battle would have been much worse, but this was completely different. The responding Ranger was praised by the park management that he did a good job when he, in fact, did *absolutely nothing* and I was being forced out of the National Park Service because I had taken decisive and swift action when I arrived at the scene of this horrible tragedy.

My focus was strictly investigating an unwitnessed death with a possible crime scene like hundreds of others I had been involved in. I was removed from the case, the criminal investigator was not allowed to intervene, and the case was assigned to a crony that would structure the investigation to the desires of the park management. This crony was nothing but a backcountry Ranger who hiked the trails and made very few minor law enforcement contacts. He had made no major arrests, and his law enforcement contacts involved writing a few misdemeanor tickets. He had not conducted any major investigations and had no supervisory experience but had many participation trophies, keeping the backsides of his supervisors' uniforms clean.

The public had become inflamed at the onset, wanting answers concerning the bear attack. There were many people defending the bears actions and blamed Glenda and her ex-husband for her death. The park management had to craft a response to mitigate the tensions the case had created. One local newspaper had interviewed Ralph Hill and had done an in-depth story about the bears and how they had killed Glenda Bradley. Ralph condemned the responding Ranger for his inactions in the newspaper interview. The park management would only respond with the same narrative the case was "under investigation" and they would not release any information. The park management used a tactic by letting the smoke clear. This would allow for people's memories to be clouded and lose interest with the story to eventually be diminished and forgotten.

The park management quickly responded to the newspaper and media reports and attempted to place blame on Ranger Chip Nelson and me and defended the responding Ranger. The park management made a facetious statement to the newspaper that Chip and I had "charged in like John Wayne," instead of arriving and meeting with responding ranger and devise a plan to handle the bears. There was no need for any plan. This attack had to be stopped immediately and having a committee meeting was asinine. The management also remarked that we had "put people's lives in danger by firing our side arms at the bears," instead of waiting for a long gun, being a shotgun or AR-15 that the responding Ranger had asked for at the onset. The long gun would be an hour before it would arrive. An AR-15 rifle had much more range than a .40 caliber pistol, and especially if it would ricochet. A shotgun with double 00 buckshot or a slug would have been more prone to ricochet more pellets. These excuses and statements were asinine and frivolous. We were in the middle of the woods, miles from any populated area and shooting in an area that would have no visitors. By placing the required shots, the animal would stop the bullet anyways. And besides, there were no ricochets, people injured or anyone hearing the gunshots that lasted only seconds. The park management vigorously defended the responding Ranger's actions where he had done *absolutely nothing* and threw Chip and I under the bus with false and malicious remarks made to the general public by the park management. It was unknown if Glenda was still alive when the responding Ranger arrived on scene. I can only speculate from what I saw when I arrived 27 minutes later, and it would appear Glenda was deceased before anyone could respond. It didn't matter. As a law enforcement officer, we have a "duty to act" and make split second decisions to prevent injury or death. Forty-five minutes is a long time and the responding Ranger had a duty to take whatever action was needed to protect Glenda. This is what Chip and I had done, and we were condemned for it while the responding Ranger was commended for his actions, while he did *absolutely nothing* and shortly promoted to a higher paying supervisory position.

It was critically important these bears were not allowed to escape. If they ran into the woods, it would have been impossible to find these bears and it would have cost a million dollars trying to find them. This would have resulted in many bears being euthanized to determine if the right bears had been caught. During this time, it was estimated there were around 1500 bears throughout the park. Although the bears were somewhat territorial, they would roam many miles. It would have been a major undertaking to try to locate the bears later. By shooting these bears it saved a lot of bears' lives and saved a lot of money. But this wasn't considered as the management of the park shrouded the investigation with false and misleading information. To make things worse there was a report to the media there may have been a third bear involved. There was no third bear and it was only more rhetoric to further cloud a 10-month investigation that wasn't needed in the first place.

The responding Ranger had called for a long gun and stated in the official investigation he was "afraid" if he shot his pistol, he may hit someone in the middle of the woods. According to Ralph Hill, who had kept the bears off Glenda with rocks and sticks, the responding Ranger had told him he was afraid of the bears even though he carried a .40 caliber pistol and 36 rounds of hollow point ammunition. The velocity and range of an AR-15 was much greater than a .40 caliber pistol. The .40 caliber Sig Sauer pistol was more than capable of killing the bears. He could have very easily shot into the ground and scared the bears away, but he would have had to approach the bears. The fact of the matter is, the responding Ranger was scared to death of the bears and had little confidence in his ability to shoot them with a pistol. He stated he "knew" the victim was deceased and the reason he waited on a long gun. It didn't matter if the victim was deceased, he had a duty to get them bears off her and prevent them from destroying her body from recognition. His response was to do nothing. Park management arranged and created a narrative to keep the responding Ranger from appearing negligent, and a coward, instead of accepting the fact his actions were an honest mistake, that could happen to anyone under the circumstances.

This "investigation" would last for 10 months as the crony would manipulate and craft new investigative distractions designed by the park management. The autopsy of the victim was taking at least ten months and the park management was taking advantage of the extra time for the incident to be forgotten. By the end of the ten months and the autopsy was complete, the Park management issued their findings where it was confirmed in the necropsy report the bears had consumed human tissue and the bears had most likely killed Glenda Bradley. It took ten months to confirm the bears had human tissues when it was a given fact, Ranger Nelson and I had watched the bears physically attacking, licking and eating the victim. Both of us were credible and experienced Park Rangers. What we had observed could have been used to confirm by the end of the day what had happened. A follow up autopsy would confirm what we had found along with physical evidence that was inside Glenda's pack, had it been retained as evidence instead of being released to the family. During the ten-month investigation by the crony, at no time was I interviewed, and I was the initial investigating Ranger that collected and found the evidence that confirmed there was a bear attack. I had experience in managing numerous serious crimes from automobile fatalities to murder investigations and supervisory experience. The crony was only a backcountry Ranger that had little to no law enforcement and investigative experience and no experience as a supervisor. He would be instructed by the park management and intentionally disregarded any of the information I found that would confirm exactly what happened. A prolonged investigation by the crony at the direction of the park management, would give the needed time for the public to forget and would diminish the negligence by the responding Ranger.

The hunger that was prevalent at the onset for answers had waned, and the interest had subsided. It would only become small talk around the small tourist town of Gatlinburg as the rumors would be embellished by discussions brought up about the bears in the Smokies and doubt by a few of what had really happened. A couple of weeks passed when the key piece of evidence was found. The pack I have eluded to that was critical evidence had a camera inside it belonging to Glenda Bradley. Her brother had found the camera in Glenda's pack that I had adamantly sought to be maintained as evidence. He had taken the film inside the camera and got the pictures developed. The pictures showed the shocking piece of evidence I was looking for. It would confirm the bears had killed Glenda Bradley and would have concluded the case at the onset the next day without the bureaucratic interference by the park management that concocted a false narrative for whatever reason I still don't understand.

The pictures from Glenda Bradley's camera are included in the next few pages of this story. They have never been shared with the news media or the public. The pictures were taken by Glenda only minutes before the bears killed her. The pictures showed the bears standing on the outside berm of the bridge. Both bears were standing side by side and looking across the river at Glenda. It had been a light rain and a raindrop on the lens of her camera caused a dramatic affect where the picture Glenda had taken of the bears showed an eerie bright glow enhancing and framing the bears. The bear's eyes reflect in the picture, giving it a demonic look, as it stared at Glenda before walking to the end of the bridge. Glenda took the next picture as it stood on the bridge and it proceeded to come at her from about 50 feet away at the end of the bridge. Glenda was on the west side of the bridge looking east and had taken the picture of the bears in this location. Glenda had gotten her camera back in her pack as the largest bear approached Glenda on the bridge. Glenda then ran off the bridge with her pack, dropping her pack at the end of the bridge in the river sand and fleeing from the bear in the river. These pictures explained the tracks Ranger Hester had found leading from the bridge that indicated the smaller bear had remained at the east end of the bridge until the largest bear had killed Glenda, and then the smaller bear went to join the largest bear.

Water droplet on lens enhances the two bears

This was critical evidence that would have solved the case early the next day after the bear had attacked and killed Glenda. It would have prevented the enervating ordeal the family suffered and quickly given closure of the case without the ongoing lies, mismanagement, and false information the park management had cleverly crafted. It was done only to confuse the investigation while trying to cover up the inactions by a minority National Park Ranger who had been derelict in his duties. The pictures were not released and only a few sources ever knew of the pictures. The pictures were secretly placed in the investigative file without sharing them to the news media or the public. The case continued to be "under investigation" for the next 10 months. The pictures were given to the National Park Service crony investigator, by the family, but copies were retained by the family of Glenda Bradley

There is a lot of information that was never shared, and information regarding the behavior of the rogue bears. The largest of the bears was a female bear weighing anywhere between 108 pounds to 155 pounds depending on which report you read. The actual weight was 112 pounds, confirmed by a report of our Chief Wildlife biologist. If I remember correctly, the bear was about three years old and relatively small for a bear this age, and undernourished. The smaller bear was only about 70 pounds and was not the larger bear's cub as it was reported by the media. The smaller bear had just taken up with the larger bear as a partner in crime.

Just before the attack

The larger bear had been captured as a study bear for the University of Tennessee Wildlife Biology department. Permits were issued and usually to a student or student group that did essentially a science project. These studies were overseen by the University of Tennessee professors with very little oversight by the park wildlife biologist. Permits were issued regularly and over a period of 30 years. During the study, the bear would be subjected to tranquilization using the powerful drug Ketamine. It would be prodded with needles and blood taken to be analyzed, a premolar tooth extracted, and it would get a thermometer shoved up its butt, The bear would receive an ear tag it would wear like a cheap ear ring by an aspiring hippie and colored to identify the bear was a park bear. If a bear had been tagged elsewhere it could have received a different colored tag, but a specific colored tag identified a bear and its history could be quickly referenced. The bears are assigned a number and the inside of the bear's lip was tattooed with numbers. If I remember correctly, this bear was number 68. After this bear had been processed, it received a radio collar and was released back into the park to study its behavior.

Nuisance bears in the park had to be dealt with. These were mostly front country bears that had become habituated by being fed with close association by humans. There were no indications the bear that killed Glenda was a front country bear and the bear had relatively little interactions with very many people that would be using the backcountry. The process of capturing a bear can be very complicated. It looks harmless when we see a Ranger with a tranquilizer gun darting an animal and then allowing the visitors to come up and pet the bear as most of the time the capture goes well. As a Ranger, I made several tranquillizations and assisted the wildlife division with many more and never saw or knew of any complications as a result of a bear capture. The Wildlife Rangers were very experienced in handling these incidents, but they were only handled as necessary with a problem bear. I would be apprehensive with unsupervised students practicing on these Park bears that are supposed to be left in a natural state in the park as this bear was.

The dart can be very painful to the animal. There are a wide variety of drugs that are used that can cause sensitive effects that result in vomiting, seizures, inhaling its stomach contents and capture myopathy, where an animal can be injured with muscle damage from extreme exertion, struggle or stress. The animal could also receive an infection that would be a result of the capture. The sedated bears will begin salivating, sweating and have an accelerated heart rate and close monitoring is critical. The eyes begin to dry, and a lubricant must be applied to keep the eyes moist and hydrated. There would be no follow up on the bear's condition documented that would identify if the bear had any of these complications while the study was conducted on the bear that killed Glenda Bradley. The bears were destroyed soon after the coroner report was made with no further documentation released about the study of this bear.

As part of the study and while this bear was hibernating, it was located, and an orphaned bear cub was placed with the female bear. The cub was rejected by the bear and it was removed from her. It is not known how many times the bear may have been immobilized by being tranquilized during this study and if there were any complications. Once the University of Tennessee researchers finished the study, the bear was released, the radio collar would fall off and now the "wild" bear was released back into the park without any further monitoring. There was no disclosure of how long the bear had been released prior to it attacking Glenda Bradley nor how much tranquillization and drug amounts that were given to the bear. For all practical purposes, the bear had been habituated by humans when the drugs were given to it, and procedures to pull its teeth and other work-up by the students.

These study bears are subjected to habituation and acclimation. Sometimes the bear is caught in large culvert traps where it would be baited most likely by bacon or Krispy Kreme doughnuts. This is people food and being given to these bears that adds to the habituation. Usually these bears have already been habituated by human food, so it probably doesn't matter, they get a nice meal before they are trapped and sedated. If these are problem bears, they must be caught, and acorns and berries don't have the smell and lure of fresh fried bacon. Bears have the keenest smell of any of nature's creatures. A lot of everyday items from shoes, backpacks, clothing, and other gear that are made from oils attract bears. Usually wild bears don't customarily attract to these items, but once they find the smell, they can connect with it and they have attacked hikers and campers, ripping off packs and entering tents and vehicles and aggressively trying to get to the smell that is most likely a strong smell the bear has encountered before. The oil in sardines is a good example where the oils that preserves the sardines are the same oils that are used in other items. In order to count the bears in the park, Sardines are slightly opened, and the oil dripped onto the ground. In the early days, the count was made by the number of cans ripped off the trees, but now there are trail cams set up to record the bears. Sometimes the plastic and other materials in the trail cam will also attract the bears and the bears will eat them too. So essentially the bears and especially wild bears are being habituated by the National Park Service by feeding them sardines that are usually found in the oceans and not the Mountains of Tennessee. There are estimated 1500 bears in the Great Smoky Mountains, but I don't know if there were 1500 cans of sardines used to attract them.

To sedate the bears, the powerful drug Ketamine is used. Ketamine's chemical structure is like Phencyclidine or PCP. PCP was used as a hallucinogen drug and used and abused by drug addicts in the early 80s. The PCP would give a person an enormous amount of strength, putting them in a trance like state or sense of disconnection from the environment.

In the 1980s, Ketamine would also be called the "party drug" and known as a date rape drug and replicated PCP and abused by young people. This study bear was tranquilized with an anesthetic during this study, but it will not be known how much or how long or if Ketamine was used. Ketamine is approved for veterinary use in animals and a schedule 3 controlled substance, but according to studies, Ketamine replicates the symptoms in a human of schizophrenia and hallucinations. Could these symptoms be replicated also in a bear?

The bear that attacked Glenda Bradley had attacked another

camper at campsite 24, and exhibited peculiar behavior. The bear that I shot and killed that attacked Glenda Bradley was the study bear. The bear was a backcountry bear, and not subjected to a lot of human interference except for the campers in the backcountry and around campsite 24. The bear was under weight, undernourished and exhibited extremely aggressive behavior that is uncommon for these bears that are usually afraid of humans unless they have been habituated. Did this bear suffer from an infection, capture myopathy or physiological disorder from being overdosed on drugs?

A necropsy of the bears stomach was performed by the medical examiner to determine if they had human flesh inside them. There is no disclosure if there were any other tests to determine if there was a presence of Ketamine or other drugs that could affect the central nervous system of the bear. Speculation remains the drugs may contribute to the similar actions that would occur in humans where the bear could have experienced a flashback or central nervous system depression. Who will ever know? The false information and handling of this serious event were compromised by the park management of the Great Smoky Mountains National Park and the truth can never be determined.

The investigation was contaminated at the onset by an investigator/crony that was at Mount Le Conte, 10 miles away on a trail, and critical information was omitted in the investigation. The fact that there was not going to be an investigation and it would be a Wildlife incident was puzzling in the least. This was clearly an unwitnessed death that could have included other persons that were present. The Criminal Investigator was not allowed to participate in an unwitnessed death investigation by the Park Management. All evidence including the bears carcasses should have been preserved until the investigation was completed, but were quickly destroyed. At no time did the National Park Service attempt to dispel the rumors that quickly identified that Glenda Bradley had been feeding the bears and was one of the causes of the bear's attack. Rumors and innuendos abounded that Ralph Hill had killed Glenda and the bears had found her in the woods. The National Park management allowed for the rumors to run amok and the tales and disgusting lore of today remain.

Glenda Bradly did not have her day in court. A bunch of bureaucratic misfits, who gave false and misleading information caused much grief and despair for many victims of this horrific event. The cover-up of a Ranger who was grossly negligent in his duties remains, and the park management hailed his actions as heroic when he did absolutely nothing. This was a serious event that transpired, where a visitor was killed, and the park service officials intentionally manipulated the public for some unknown reason. I know for a fact if the investigation would have been conducted by competent and qualified criminal investigators, the bears would have been analyzed thoroughly, and all the evidence would have been collected and maintained in evidence and not sent home with the family. The investigation would have included the history of the bears to determine if the drugs that the bear had received, and if the habitation as a result of human interference, and the study of the bears, could have altered the bears physical and mental condition.

Wild bears attack people and wild bears have killed people and it has happened many times. It is a chance one takes when enjoying nature and in the presence of wild bears and other animals. It is the law and policy of the National Park Service that all the natural resources are to be protected and left in their natural state for the enjoyment of now and future generations. This bear was not left in a natural state and it had been acclimated by human interference. There is nowhere in the Great Smoky Mountains National Park, where you will find acorns, berries and natural foods consumed by bears to contain Ketamine. This bear could have well been a drug addict, but no one will ever know. The assignment of a crony, rather than a criminal investigator, assured the park management the information would be withheld from the public. With this bear, it had suffered all the anomalies violating the National Park Service law and policy. Basically, a bear was caught, drugged and released back into the National Park, left unsupervised with "let's see what happens next." Black bears have been studied ever since the days of Yogi and

Boo Boo and studied in the Great Smoky Mountains for over 30 years. I'm not a wildlife biologist nor an expert on the physiology of a bear. I had minimal training and experience in animal immobilization and capture. There is a lot of information readily available to understand the capture and immobilization procedures in handling wildlife tranquillization. The correlation linking these powerful sedating drugs with a bear's behavior with this horrific event, could be true.

There is more information that has not been shared, and has been kept from the public, and is the actual beginning of the bear attack that killed Glenda Bradley. I was the initial investigator of the bear attack and there was a lot of information shared with me that I was unable to disclose after being removed as a witness and investigator. Glenda Bradly was attacked on Sunday afternoon, May 21, 2000. On Saturday, May 20, 2000, the day prior to the bear attack on Glenda, a camper was at campsite #24, a backcountry campsite located about a half mile above the Goshen Prong Bridge and Little River trail junction where Glenda Bradley was attacked. The camper was attacked by presumably this same bear and fought the bear off and was able to run away from the bear. The bear ripped the camper's backpack from him while the camper was able to escape. The camper ran to the Elkmont campground office to report the bear attack. At the campground office was a fee collector who registered campers. When the camper made the report, he was told by the fee collector to write what happened on a piece of paper and they would give it to a Ranger. The camper wrote the information down, but it was never reported by the fee collector. This information was never included in the official report by the crony investigator as instructed by the park management. There was a radio and a telephone sitting on the counter, and the fee collector should have immediately called for a Ranger and reported this serious incident. Again, the devoid leadership of my supervisor who was supposed to oversee and supervise these employees was absent. Everyone is a Park Ranger, including the fee collectors, who are dressed in a Park Ranger uniform and wear the gold Buffalo badge. The authority was assumed by this person who apparently did not know or care how serious this was, and the camper assumed he had reported the information to a PARK RANGER.

If the information was reported, as it should have been, there would have been Rangers responding immediately in an attempt to locate the bear, and the bear shot and killed or trapped. The Wildlife Division would have been alerted and the area thoroughly searched, until the bear was found. People would have been removed from the area, the campsites closed, and signs posted, alerting the hikers of the bear attack. I worked on that Saturday and there was no report or mention of a bear attack. It was unfortunate and tragic that Glenda was killed by this same bear the next afternoon. None of this was reported in the investigation or to the media. No reprimands, no training, and no supervisory action was taken with all of this being hidden from the public. The crony was instructed to leave out this important information, in an investigation, that was incomplete and fabricated in order that time would mitigate the emotions of the bear attack, where Mrs. Glenda Bradley would become the first victim of a bear attack in the eastern United States and the Great Smoky Mountains National Park. The news media would focus on new news and people would soon forgot the incident that happened 10 months prior.

The next morning, after the attack of Glenda Bradley, a fake press conference was held on the front lawn of headquarters that was cleverly prepared for the local news media. After the fake press conference, I was called into my supervisor's office. I sat across the desk from him, and he began angrily criticizing me and asked, "Why do you want to go around stirring up shit?" I was completely taken aback by his question and his actions. He then told me it was all over Jones Cove School that I had been making statements, stating the responding Ranger would not shoot the bears that killed Glenda Bradley, and "I just wanted to stir up shit." It was early in the morning, and I had just arrived at the park. I had been at my house all night and had not been anywhere near Jones Cove School, that was on the other side of the county. I had not talked with anyone when I left the park the night before and went straight home. He continued to berate me and leaned back in his chair and told me "I don't have time to deal with the wrath of Jerry Grubb." I was completely perplexed, and I tried to explain to him I had not talked with anyone at the Jones Cove school. If anything, it was probably because both Glenda, and her ex-husband, were teachers at the Jones Cove School. He leaned back and again told me, he was not going to "deal with the wrath of Jerry Grubb."

Immediately after the bear attack, a CISD (Critical Incident Stress Debriefing) was held at headquarters. A lot of money was spent bringing in a trained NPS CISD counselors. Everyone that was associated with the attack or employees that had heard about the attack, were assembled and consoled in case someone felt emotional, and distraught. There were CISD counselors brought in from around the country and everyone sat around the room in headquarters sharing their feelings about the bear attack. I was the one who witnessed a tragedy I had never seen before and took immediate and decisive action. Instead of getting consoled, I was subjected to false accusation, criticism, and ongoing emotional anguish, that would lead to further stress. I had to defend myself for years to come and eventually was forced out of the National Park Service. Through my career, I had witnessed some of the worse deaths and disasters that a professional responder could encounter. I chose this kind of work and coped with some of the most horrific challenges one could encounter, without the CISD, and getting closure for everyone involved without the need for the so-called professional counselors that have never witnessed any of these tragedies. If someone breaks a fingernail now, a CISD counseling team is called in.

My so called supervisor had pushed me to the end. He was a minority and held in esteem by the park management because of his minority status. He had not only assumed my supervisory responsibilities because of the re-organization that allowed him to replace me, but now I am being belittled and accused of something that had never occurred. I was emotionally drained from dealing with the bear attack the day before. I lost it and crawled onto his desk pointing my finger in his face, telling him, "You son of a bitch, you haven't seen the wrath of Jerry Grubb!"

It was not a good situation with both of us wearing guns. This was the beginning of the end of my career as a National Park Ranger. I left the office and went straight to Headquarters of the park and consulted with the parks Equal Opportunity counselor. Equal opportunity was only designed to protect the minorities and with me being a white male, my chances would be slim to none of getting my case documented. I prevailed and filed a discrimination suit against the National Park Service. I knew this would not be easy, and I would be harassed and forced out of the National Park Service, but my credibility as a National Park Ranger was seriously compromised. I would start a long and difficult process getting my case to an EEO Administrative judge.

I had done absolutely nothing wrong, but because of cover up to protect the minorities from ridicule and wrongdoing, I was singled out to take the blame for acting and killing two bears that had killed Glenda Bradley. It made absolutely no sense why this convoluted episode was made up, with no regard for the professionalism of the National Park Service. The only explanation was this supervisor, who was black, used his position and sanction by the Park management, to cover up an action of another black Ranger who was derelict in his duties. This harassment did not end as he intimidated me further, with the help of the management of the Great Smoky Mountains National Park. Together they would continue until I would be forced out of the National Park Service. The management of the Great Smoky Mountains National Park was on a mission to destroy my credibility and career for absolutely no reason.

I had Equal Employment Opportunity (EEO training), and I was familiar with the EEO process, as I hired and supervised minority employees. I knew it would take at least three years if I could survive the harassment of the Park Service, before my case would make it to the EEO Administrative judge. I represented myself, "Pro SE," meaning I would be representing myself without an attorney. This would be tough, and the National Park Service made it difficult by constantly sending me motions and documents by numerous attorneys that would have to be answered and returned by a certain date. If the documents missed the deadline, the case would automatically be thrown out of the courts. I struggled, but persisted, and I was not going to let these bastards win. The harassment continued by being suspended several times for minor mistakes. I had worked with the National Park Service for at least 25 years. I never had a speck of misconduct and only exceptional credibility with the community and other law enforcement agencies, and the employees of the Great Smoky Mountains National Park, as a National Park Ranger.

It was shortly afterwards, I had to endure a reprimand initiated by my black supervisor, where my law enforcement commission was suspended. By getting my law enforcement commission suspended, I was forced from my job as a law enforcement officer, and no longer a National Park Ranger.

As I said in the beginning, Park Rangers transformed, doing many different jobs. The park did not have money to equip and put the markings on our patrol vehicles and I did this to our patrol vehicles, while answering law enforcement calls or emergencies. I had been working through the day putting the decals on a vehicle, and I had my gun belt off, and inside my patrol vehicle. I worked through the day, through lunch, and no breaks, to get the new patrol car ready for duty. I decided to go to the Mountain Market, two miles from headquarters, to get a snack and cold drink. I took the vehicle I was working on, but I had left my gun belt in my cruiser parked at the office. I was in uniform, but without my gun belt. While I headed to the market, a motorcycle passed me at an extreme high rate of speed probably 80-100 miles per hour and headed into the park. My vehicle did not have an emergency light bar on it because I was still equipping it. I called for other Rangers to respond and try to apprehend the motorcycle.

Ranger Bobby Holland, who had been my supervisor, had been reduced to a field Park Ranger, after he was removed from his 'enhanced supervisor position' and replaced by a black minority supervisor. Bobby responded as the motorcycle sped back out of the park, and he stopped the vehicle. Another Ranger, whom Bobby had also supervised, with many years less in experience, responded and was at the scene. Both Rangers were armed, and I came back and identified the motorcycle as the same motorcycle that had entered the park at a high rate of speed. I was out of my vehicle without my gun belt, and it was recorded on an in-car video camera. I left and went back to the office where I went back to work on the patrol car.

In the meantime, one of the Rangers came to the office and reported to my supervisor, I was on a car stop without my gun belt. This Ranger was also black. She reported she was concerned for my safety. My supervisor immediately reviewed the in-car camera and found it to be true. I hadn't really considered my presence there as a danger to me or the others, as both Rangers were armed and had the situation under control. I had worked in so many situations that put myself at risk, and I wasn't aware or even considered this to be dangerous. This supervisor was not concerned either, except it was a lame excuse to get me suspended. He wasn't concerned he had just in the recent days put me at risk by not providing me a back-up where I encountered and arrested a felon with an ice pick. The back-up that was supposed to have been there for me was the same black female Ranger who was nowhere to be found, and now reported to him I put peoples' lives in danger.

There were two ironic situations that occurred in this incident. At the beginning of my career, as a National Park Ranger, I was conditioned and ordered to keep my firearm locked away, hiding it under the seat or kept in a briefcase. Now, 25 years later, I am being suspended for not having my gun belt on me. The other ironic part was when I was supervising, I had advocated to have the in-car video cameras and had them installed in the patrol cars to record the events encountered by Law Enforcement Rangers. Now I was recorded by these cameras in what was described as an "egregious" behavior that put citizens and law enforcement officers at risk. This was completely ridiculous, and I couldn't believe I was being suspended for something this chicken shit, but it was all in the scheme to get me removed from the National Park Service, especially after I had filed a claim against the National Park. I conceded I had done exactly what the camera had recorded, but the management of the Great Smoky Mountains National Park took the opportunity to harass me and suspended my law enforcement commission.

The Chief Ranger sanctioned by the Superintendent of the Park, convened a Board of Inquiry to determine if I would be removed from law enforcement duties permanently for not wearing my gun belt. I soon found out this was a much more egregious offense than failing to protect a park visitor from a bear attack. The fraud, waste, and abuse of the Park management was in the least, condescending, and it was unbelievable this occurred.

I was not the only Park Ranger in the National Park Service, during this time, that endured investigations and questioning the credibility of certain law enforcement officers. There were numerous, ongoing internal investigations, throughout the National Park Service where millions of dollars were expended to force Rangers from their positions. This prompted Rangers to buy personal protective liability insurance. This would be to protect them from illegal proceedings by the management of the National Park Service, knowing at any moment, the National Park Service was going to try to suspend career Rangers for any reason they felt necessary. This insurance was individually paid for by each Ranger.

There was a backlog of minority employees who needed to be put in place of career, and experienced Park Rangers, as a result of the reorganization that had occurred in 1994. I had purchased the insurance knowing with my EEO complaint that I would be subjected to the harassment and false charges. An employee is supposed to free from reprisal, but it doesn't work this way unless you are a minority. I was taken out of my position for several weeks as a Park Ranger, where I waited for a "Board of Inquiry" to be convened. This removed me as an asset to protect the visitors and respond to emergencies and the park service management falsely accused of me of putting the visitors and Rangers at risk. I played their stupid game while there was a lot of money spent, patrols were eliminated, and schedules re-arranged to accommodate the coverage needed to provide less visitor and resource safety that was already compromised from an already short-handed law enforcement staff.

Murder trials and other serious crimes were not handled like this incident, where a video camera had captured the precise violation of not having a gun belt on. The Chief Ranger approved by the Park Superintendent, approved thousands of dollars spent paying over-time, paying per diem, travel expense, renting hotel rooms, and reserving a local hotel convention center for a Board of Inquiry hearing for my egregious behavior. Investigators, park service solici-tors, and crony board members, were brought in from around the U.S. This took away more Park Rangers from the job that focused on a simple and minor incident. The hearing lasted almost a full day to view an in-car video camera that clearly showed I didn't have a gun belt on. I had to call on my legal insurance representative, and the Union representative, to represent me. The U.S. Attorney's office had an assistant U.S. Attorney there to observe the proceedings. This was the paradigm of a kangaroo court. At the end of the day, all the charges were dropped, all the park service investigators and witnesses joined at the bar for a round of celebration, courtesy of the U.S. taxpayers. The National Park Service continually whines and complains they do not have any money to operate, but to those of us who know the truth, it would appall everyday people, the waste, fraud, and abuse that is prevalent in the National Park Service.

The Board of Inquiry had backfired and my black Park Service supervisor who started all of this was found to have lied in the inves-tigation and on a background check where he had given false infor-mation. This was investigated after the proceeding began against me. The U.S. Attorney's office had instructed the Park Service to remove my supervisor. As a law enforcement Ranger, he could not perform law enforcement duties because of his lying that would compromise his credibility, and he could not appear as a witness in the Federal Court. Because he was black, instead of having a suspension or Board of Inquiry, he was quietly removed from his law enforcement position and supervisory duties. His commission was suspended, and he was moved to another job in fire duties, where he remained in his same pay status and was later promoted. No investigations, no reprimands, no board of inquiry. Just like the responding Ranger who had been derelict in his duties, getting promoted. I was able to regain my law enforcement status only to endure another round of harassment a short time later.

41

End of a Career

I was already on the "do not like" list with the management of the Great Smoky Mountains. I was still a Law Enforcement Ranger and I still had a duty to enforce the law. I was given information regarding one of the Park managers who had corresponded with a female employee, sending lewd and lascivious sexual emails on his government computer. I was also given information the park service computers were being used to view pornography. I already knew this, when two Park Rangers had found the pornography on one of our office computers. There was a suspect, but it would be the end of more park service careers, if it was reported at the time I found out about it.

This was prevalent throughout the park, and I disregarded it until I received the information regarding the lewd and lascivious e-mails. I knew it was too risky for my career, what was left of it, to report it, but these rogue managers were getting by with proverbial murder. It would only be covered up further, but the ongoing fraud, waste, and abuse that was happening, had to be stopped. I was already in litiga-

tion with the National Park Service because I was being discrimi-
nated against and harassed. It was still my duty to report any
unlawful activity as a law enforcement officer. I decided to report the
information, confidentially, to the Inspector General of the Department of the Interior. This should have gotten the information investigated, while I was supposed to remain anonymous. It was trickled
back down to the National Park Service where an investigation was
conducted by a partisan compatriot and the investigation determined
none of this information was true, even though there was documentation of it.

My confidential status was breached and with it, came more
harassment. This obsessed the management even more to have me
removed from the National Park Service. These Park managers can
be very vindictive and have no direction or supervision and basically
get by with anything. They have few morals and a selfish ego to
promote their relevance.

About a year after I had been forcibly retired, the truth finally
prevailed. The Federal Bureau of Investigation (FBI) descended on
the Great Smoky Mountains headquarters and seized all the computers. They had been monitoring the web for child pornography and
found child pornography images and networks on the Great Smoky
Mountains National Park's computers, along with other pornography.
I did not realize it was this bad when I reported the information I
had. The FBI arrived with warrants and arrested the second in
command of the Great Smoky Mountains National Park for
possessing child pornography on his park service computer. There
were computer technicians who monitored the computers for
malware and suspicious cyber activity, but for some odd reason, none
of this was found by them.

Larry Hartman was a GS-14 and the Chief of Resource Management in the Great Smoky Mountains National Park. He was the
Acting Superintendent of the Great Smoky Mountains in the absence
of the Superintendent. His park service computer was full of images
of child pornography. He also had images of his own small child

whom he and his wife had adopted, on the computer. Further investigation found, in his home, hidden cameras that recorded his adopted child, with sexual reference posted on his park service computer.

The second administrative manager the FBI arrested only had regular porn on his computer. After his arrest, he disappeared and could not be found. Later that night, he was located by the local city authorities, where he was drugged and overdosed in an apparent suicide attempt. The management of the Great Smoky Mountains had been busted. The superintendent who was supposed to oversee and supervise these employees, including the cyber breaches of the computer systems, was of course, transferred and promoted to become the Superintendent of another large National Park. Hartman received a large prison sentence and was fired from his job where he made upwards of $150,000 a year. There was no disclosure that I could find regarding the other low-level manager, except he could retire. This is what the management of the National Park Service has become. No oversight and devoid leadership with superintendents having no supervision or directions and only promoted when something of this nature occurs.

The news of these arrests was kept minimal. Once again, the management of the Park created and again crafted a news release that mitigated Hartman's arrest. This news release did not detail any of what had happened, but basically, Hartman was no longer employed by the National Park service. The cleverly crafted news releases were given to the news media a couple of days after it had happened and after the smoke cleared, and once again, shrouded another serious incident by the Great Smoky Mountains National Park Service.

The Chief Ranger had begun the campaign to remove me from the National Park Service. He had also compromised the truth and investigation of the bear attack of Glenda Bradley. He suddenly died just shortly after his role in the bear attack, where he had lied and manipulated the truth and facts of the bear attack. It was supposed to have been a medical problem, but I am pretty sure it was the devil, cashing in on another sold soul. He was then replaced with another

Chief Ranger who was handpicked by the superintendent of the Great Smoky Mountains National Park, and my agony continued.

My supervisors were also replaced by crony acquaintances, who together, would enter a criminal conspiracy and attempt to finally get me removed from the National Park Service. One of my new supervisors had a notebook where he had taken notes from the management of the Smokies about me before he was transferred to his new position as my new supervisor. He was so stupid, he left it lying around where the other Rangers had found it. When they found the notes and notified me, I retrieved the notebook and kept it in my possession. I was absolutely dumbfounded this occurred and these clowns were so condescending.

The job being a National Park Ranger was no longer fun or exciting, and the stress was overwhelming. The dignity and mission to protect the visitors and the park had been diminished and destroyed. The morality of the National Park Service principles and respect were gone. The dedicated service and commitments for the visitors was replaced with Rangers having to focus, full time, on their surviving the wrath of the National Park Service management. The entire Smoky Mountains National Park and the National Park Service employee's morale was diminished with ongoing, internal investigations, and taunting, contentious supervision that demoralized the employees.

I tried to function as a National Park Ranger. I had my commission back, and I didn't have any more suspensions at this time. A new problem was thrown at me, where one of my new supervisors had a few afternoon cocktails, when he was off work. He worked from 8am to 4pm daily. One afternoon, I investigated a vehicle crash on the U.S 441 Foothills Parkway spur, just outside the City of Gatlinburg. There were several vehicles involved, with only property damage to the vehicles, and no one hurt. Gatlinburg Police and another Ranger was with me as I sorted out the crash. My supervisor arrived, driving his marked Law Enforcement vehicle, wearing his Park Service uniform, and wearing his gun belt. He was off duty, and I hadn't called him, but he decided he would come to the crash site, which was his option as a supervisor. I investigated the drivers of the crashed vehicles for sobriety and administered the alcohol test. As soon as the supervisor arrived, I was confronted by many angry bystanders, passengers, and others, at the crash scene that complained to me and the Gatlinburg officers, that my supervisor was intoxicated, and he's the one that should be investigated for drunk driving. This added a big problem in this crash investigation by having to mitigate the actions and presence of my supervisor, who was obviously drunk, and not making an arrest in the crash investigation for drunk driving.

My supervisor had a strong smell of alcohol about him that everyone could smell, and he appeared to be incoherent and unsteady on his feet. I am in a serious compromise, having to deal with a drunk supervisor, while trying to calm the other people, telling them I would take care of it.

I should have been suspended for my actions at this time. Rather than arrest my supervisor, I was able to get him away from the other people, and back into his vehicle, and let him drive off. The people there were astonished as he drove away, but there was a lot of confusion with the crash that took people's minds off the drunk supervisor. I should never have let this happen this way, but there was no way my supervisor would be arrested, and it would surely come back and haunt me either way.

If I knew this same supervisor was going to set me up, with a false and misleading investigation, to get me removed from the Park Service, he wouldn't have left that scene, and I would have put his ass in jail, where he belonged. This is the same credibility my other supervisor had and resulted in him being removed from his position. My new supervisor would be protected at all costs by the Park Management, regardless, because he was part of their conspiracy to get me removed from the Park Service.

Again, thousands of dollars were spent as I was being followed around by "crony park investigators," that were brought in from other areas, trying to find anything on me they could. I frequented some of the local stores, just outside the park, and I was informed on several occasions there had been people inquiring about my personal information and they alerted me to this. I figured It must have been someone I had arrested, and I carried on, being more cautious.

In the past, I never carried a weapon off duty. I had been involved, in my early years, where a "contract" had been taken out on a Ranger where we had made several arrests. Because of my experience, I wasn't taking any chances of getting ambushed. I began carrying my weapon and reported what was happening to my new supervisor. I had my weapon with me in my saddlebag of my motorcycle when I met him, and I was off duty. When he saw my weapon, he told me I could not carry the weapon off duty, that was a violation of Park Rules. As a result, I was again suspended, with the Chief Ranger making statements I was threatening him, and others, and I was mentally unstable. Only a few months prior, I had been suspended because I didn't have my gun and now, I am being suspended for having my gun. This crazy stuff can't be made up.

It turned out the people that were following me around and asking the personal questions were crony investigators, paid extra on special details, who were brought in to conduct an internal investigation of me. More money was spent trying to "get me." The EEO case was getting closer to being litigated and the Park Service did not want to make any settlement. I had successfully defeated the Great Smoky Mountains park management by getting my EEO case to a closure, by getting it to an Administrative Judge for review. But this would not be the end.

This final blow came, and I was called in for an internal investigation for having my gun in the park where I was authorized to carry if I was on duty. A drunk supervisor can carry a gun, when they get ready, but a Ranger concerned for his safety, with law enforcement duties, could not. Ordinarily, if an employee would have reported to his supervisor they were concerned about a threat to their life and safety, there would have been an investigation to identify the threat. In this case the threat was standing eyeball to eyeball with me, and no one was concerned about my safety because the criminals were the park management that was stalking me. They were the criminal conspirators and had me concerned for my safety. Because of the rogue and criminal management, my new supervisor and the new Chief Ranger were sanctioned and allowed to bring false and misleading charges against me in another attempt to remove me from the National Park Service. Some of my close allies and co-workers were drawn into this investigation and they had no choice but to protect their careers and participated in railroading me. It was no specific charge against me but only a list of questions about many things and I had to answer them and truthfully.

This was the setup of the century and would include trick questions and were conducted using the Garrity Rules where an employee must be truthful or face dismissal. One of the questions I was asked, if I had called a certain crony a liar. I didn't remember calling him a liar, but he was a liar. Either way, I was not going to get this question right. The investigation ended where the new Chief Ranger had prepared a letter to me that I was being terminated from the National Park Service. The letter read, I had lied to the investigators because one of the park's cronies said I had answered a question untruthfully, and I had compromised my integrity as a Law Enforcement Officer. My black supervisor had lied and was not terminated but transferred to another position. His situation was much worse than mine, but the Park Management facilitated him by giving him another position while I was being terminated. The Chief Ranger also cited my mental condition where he was afraid of me. I had to surrender my Law Enforcement Commission and I would not get it back. I had worked my entire career for my commission and now it was being taken away because of a lying, vindictive park management, that had pursued me for years, without being able to successfully remove me from the National Park Service.

I was ready to get out of this chicken shit outfit, but I was going to fight these bastards with whatever it took. This was nothing but Felony Conspiracy Under Title 18 of the United States Code. While I was getting prepared to be terminated, I had contacted the Inspector General of the Department of Interior. He related to me he knew how

I felt and knew how the government worked. He told me if I had enough time to retire, I should retire. I was ready, but these bastards had my law enforcement commission and I wanted it back and I wasn't going to allow them to terminate me. The inspector general put me in touch with the Regional Director of the Park Service who "apologized for this mess." The regional director knew nothing about what had transpired with the management of the Great Smoky Mountains, doing their own thing, without any supervision or direction.

The management of the Great Smoky Mountains had spent a lot of taxpayer money with these illegal and rogue investigations. The investigation they had fabricated was nothing more than a Felony Conspiracy that had been devised by the management of the Great Smoky Mountains National Park and had enlisted several cronies to carry out the investigation and setup as directed by them. All this misery and despair for killing two bears that had attacked a victim, while a black Ranger watched the attack for almost 45 minutes and breaking up a sex scandal that high level park service personnel were involved with. The newspaper accounts by the Park management praised the black Ranger and said he did a good job and he received a promotion. He did absolutely nothing. I got cited and condemned in the public newspapers by the Chief Ranger, where I had "charged in like John Wayne," and putting people's lives at risk, to face ridicule, ongoing harassment, and ultimately termination from the National Park Service.

I was called to the Regional Office without the Superintendent of the Smokies knowing anything about it, to settle my complaint against the National Park Service. The Director asked me who I trusted in the park to get me a travel authorization to travel to Atlanta for a meeting and settle my complaint with the Park Service. I told her I would pay for it and told her I wanted out of this chicken shit outfit. She explained to me "they" were paying for it, referring to the management of the Smoky Mountains National Park. It happened, the only one I could trust was the secretary of the superintendent. The Regional Director knew the secretary well and they arranged my travel authorization. I traveled and met with the Regional Director, where I agreed to a significant settlement, paid for out of the budget of the Great Smoky Mountains National Park, and courtesy of the U.S. taxpayers. While I was in the Regional Director's office, getting forced out of the National Park Service for doing my job as a National Park Ranger, her phone rang. On the phone was the Superintendent of the Everglades National Park. The Superintendent was crying on the phone to the Regional Director, asking for help because she had been arrested for drunk driving, after she ran into a gas pump in the middle of the day, in Homestead, Florida. Because she made about $140,000 per year, she could afford to take the day off and get drunk, delegating her responsibilities to the next level of command. There was no Board of Inquiry, no suspension and the pay continued as she was placed on administrative leave. There was very little reported about it after the smoke cleared and she would retire with a very hefty retirement.

The Department of Interior identified the mismanagement of the high-level Director of the National Park Service. One of the past Directors for seven years, Jon Jarvis, was investigated by the Office of the Inspector General for the Department of the Interior, and it found Jarvis to be leading a "culture of sexual misconduct" in the National Park Service. There were several sexual harassments complaints filed within the Park Service and Jarvis was responsible for overseeing and stopping it, but he disregarded and allowed the culture to continue.

The morale of the Park Service employees was at a new low. He was also charged and found to violate an ethics complaint while he was the Director of the National Park Service from 2009 to 2017. He suffered no penalties and was to maintain in the position until he retired with a very healthy retirement package. Jarvis had no law enforcement experience, no search and rescue experience or any other experience that was synonymous with being a Park Ranger. He was a desk jockey who went through a career doing nothing but leading tours as an Interpreter. With this kind of leadership, it's no wonder the trickle-down effect would naturally occur, with incompetent leadership throughout the management of the National Park Service.

This is the culture of the NPS, where high level political appointees have no oversight, and when something as this happens, it is mitigated and covered up. This is the way the government works. The screwballs that caused my demise as a National Park Ranger simply wrote me a taxpayer check, when it should have been paid for by the persons that created it. I also got my law enforcement commission back, that should never have been suspended in the first place, and I got my retirement I had earned. My Park Service career had ended.

I have since found out why the National Park Service hurriedly got a settlement with me. Had I known of the information I know now, things would have been handled much differently, with criminal charges being pursued against several individuals who had committed Felony Conspiracy under Title 18 of the United States Code. It was best I didn't know the information at the time, and I retired. This is the way the federal government operates, and this is the way the National Park Service operates. I was just another casualty to the waste, fraud, and abuse that occurs daily. Lucky for me I had the number of years to retire.

I slowly got over some of my misfortunes when I was a National Park Ranger. A few months after I retired, I was in Lowes, shopping for a water hose connector, and felt someone touch my shoulder, and asked me how I had been. When I turned around, it was the Chief Ranger who led the conspiracy to have me terminated from the National Park Service. The same bastard who testified he was afraid of me and I was mentally unbalanced. The rage that came over me can't be described. This son of a bitch had the nerve to touch me and laughed and berated me.

If I had a weapon, I would have ended up in prison. I lunged for him, but the coward ran out of Lowes. I had to deal with this son of a bitch one more time. I wrote a letter to the new Superintendent of the Great Smoky Mountains National Park, warning him to keep his little bastards away from me. Within a few weeks, in typical Park Service style, the son of a bitch was promoted and became a superintendent of a large park.

It's sad, these miscreants of the National Park Service exist, but they are prevalent and will continue to abuse their authority and minimize the efficiency of the National Park Service. The management of the National Park Service continues to mirror the image of Ranger Rick and Yogi bear and keep them synonymous with the National Parks. The truth of the matter is, Ranger Rick has retired, Yogi Bear has died, and Boo Boo is in counseling for drug addiction.

Selfish miscreants, longing for power and money, are the new symbol of the National Park Service. The partisan political environment overreaches the mission of the National Park Service, to protect the ongoing culture of highly paid bureaucrats, disguised as stewards of the environment.

The recent wildfires that occurred in the Great Smoky Mountains in 2016 clearly identify this. The Park Ranger has been removed from the National Park Service. He has been replaced with bureaucratic and political appointees, with an agenda to protect the sanctity of these high paying management positions. There is little regard to protect the visitors and the resources as the National Park Rangers have done. Innocent people have died at the hands of these bureaucrats, as witnessed and documented by the 2016 wildfires where 14 innocent people were killed who put their trust in the hands of these miscreants, along with the bear attack on Glenda Bradley, and the deaths of three Park Rangers.

The people responsible for my personal demise were promoted to higher paying positions. The assistant superintendent was promoted to the Senior Executive Superintendent of the Smokies. The Chief Ranger was promoted to a Senior Executive superintendent position. My new supervisor was promoted and transferred to the Smokies to participate in the conspiracy against me. My black supervisor who had lied was transferred and promoted. The crony that falsified and misled the investigation of the bear attack was promoted to the Chief Ranger of the Smokies. The Chief Ranger that was responsible for creating the false narrative of the bear attack that killed Glenda

Bradley, suddenly died. Lastly, the Park Ranger who stood and watched the bears eating Glenda Bradley for 45 minutes was promoted to a Supervisory Park Ranger within weeks after the bear attack. I was reprimanded, chastised and forced into retirement as a result of killing the bears that attacked Glenda Bradley.

42

Gatlinburg Fires

The incompetence continues. I had been forcibly retired from the Great Smoky Mountains where I worked as a National Park Ranger for about 13 years. The Great Smoky Mountains experienced a massive wildfire in November of 2016 that consumed 10,000 acres or 15 square miles of the Great Smoky Mountains National Park and 6,000 acres in nearby cities of Sevier County, Tennessee. This was one of the deadliest and largest wildland fires in the eastern United States where 14 lives were lost and countless injuries, emotional distress and 2500 structures destroyed.

Chimneys' Top Fire

The fire began on November 23, 2016, when two juveniles threw matches into the vegetation of the popular Chimneys' Top trail. Smoke was immediately detected in the afternoon on November 23. The fire was a slow, smoldering and creeping fire that could easily have been managed.

The Smoky Mountain fire specialist, the Chief Ranger, Assistant Superintendent and Superintendent of the park decided to leave the fire burning because of the steep terrain and it was too "dangerous" to attack and would not attempt to extinguish or even access the fire. The National Park Rangers had been reduced to the ranks of boy scouts, being led by a scoutmaster who worked down at the hardware store. National Park Rangers used to be synonymous with "danger" and now they can't do anything because they may break a fingernail and they must have a good night's sleep.

2016 had experienced one of the worst droughts ever and fire danger was extreme, and warnings were issued across the region. No fire crews were assigned to even watch the Chimneys' Top fire, and no plan of attack was made. On the night of the fire, the management of the park decided they would all go home and they "went to bed," as quoted by the fire management officials, leaving a fire burning in fuel that was volatile as gasoline. This was unbelievable to do this and then make a public and arrogant statement they were going home and go to bed.

The next day, they arrived and found the fire gaining intensity and came up with a bone headed plan to allow the fire to burn itself out. They drew lines on the map of the park that was 500,000 acres, showing where they would like for it to burn to and go out. Any idiot should have known the fire couldn't read a map. The fire was becoming more dangerous and had to be attacked, but they allowed the fire to burn even more and gained even more intensity. Five days later, November 28th, the winds arrived, and the fire rapidly became an inferno and spread and became out of control. By the end of the day, the fire devastated the park, and the neighboring towns, ended up with 14 fatalities, and at least 134 injuries and 2500 homes and structures destroyed.

The aftermath of the fires left chaos and confusion as the Park Management began to try to mitigate their responsibility and place the culpability and burden of the death and destruction on Sevier County and the City of Gatlinburg, surrounding the fires. News conferences were held and anger and frustrations by the citizens and visitors were intense as they listened to the bureaucratic response being delivered to them. The superintendent nervously gave misleading and false statements, regarding the response to the fire. He attempted to lay the framework that justified their initial response that was "going home and going to bed" instead of actively engaging the fire in some sort of fashion or planning through the night and get the resources needed to attack the fire at first light. A helicopter that could deliver many gallons of water to extinguish the fire could have been utilized at first light and could have been requested through the Inter Agency fire dispatch. Fire crews could have been organized throughout the night to attack the fire. Instead, the National Park Service went home and went to bed and would ultimately cause the deaths of many innocent victims.

This was an historic fire and required leadership and expertise that would be the responsibility of the Senior Executive Service expert being the Great Smoky Mountains National Park Superintendent. His leadership experience was supposed to be the reason he was hired. However, the Superintendent had little or no experience in dealing with the fires, and delegated his responsibility to the Assistant Superintendent, who delegated the fire response to the Chief Ranger, and Fire Management Officer. The incompetence reminded me of my own experience at the Colville National Forest where the ineptitude of the fire crew leader equaled the paltriness of the fire management officials at the Great Smoky Mountains National Park.

I lived next to the Great Smoky Mountains and I observed the fire burning, in the extremely dry forest with heavy fuel. When I retired, I sold and moved from my house that was jokingly called the "Little Smoky Ranger Station." I had built the house next to the park boundary so I would be close to the park and close to my duty station. It was a log house, with its rustic look, it bore a resemblance to the "Ranger Station" in Jellystone where Ranger Rick would be found having a conversation with Yogi. I had built a couple of other log cabins there also. When I was forcibly retired, I sold them. The massive fire destroyed the Little Smoky Ranger Station along with two of the cabins I had built. Even though I had sold the cabins and the Little Smoky Ranger Station, there was still an attachment to them because of the hard work and the hands-on construction of them. The Little Smoky Ranger Station also served as break area where the Rangers would come by on the weekends to catch up on a certain football game or NASCAR race. When I visited the area after the fire, I could hardly believe this occurred. I had watched the flames of the fire from my house 10 miles away and choked on the smoke that lingered in the valley for over a week. There had been very little information posted about the fires by the National Park Service, and as an experienced firefighter, I was sure the National Park Service was actively fighting the fires. When I found out they had gone home and to bed, I was dumbstruck. I couldn't believe a National Park Ranger would do this. As a Ranger at the Great Smoky Mountains, we fought many fires in the park and none of them could burn without being attacked immediately, and none of them were "too dangerous" to attack. At no time in the history of the Great Smoky Mountains National Park, did a Park Ranger go home and go to bed while a wildfire was burning.

I watched the fiasco and aftermath of the fire being played out on national television. The Superintendent of the Great Smoky Mountains was sweating and confused and attempted to create a sequence of events, with a misleading narrative that angered the community. This was an egregious attempt to mislead the public that the National Park Service had no culpability for the loss of life, serious injuries, emotional distress, and the mass destruction of the area. My experience as a National Park Ranger was documented and credible. I publicly discredited the response by the Great Smoky Mountains National Park Superintendent and identified the negligence that was in direct violation of the required Inter-Agency and NPS fire guidelines. Tensions in the communities remained extremely volatile as people tried to come to grips with this horrendous tragedy. I had dealt with the ongoing mismanagement of the National Park Service for an entire career. I watched as innocent people were killed, including National Park Rangers, as a result of the ineptitude of NPS management, and now it had escalated out of the park into the community where there were many lives lost.

Fire on the Gatlinburg Spur, 200 yds from 'Little Smoky Ranger Station'

Only sixteen years earlier, in May of 2000, a massive wildfire that was due to negligence by the NPS management occurred in the Bandelier National Monument in New Mexico. A controlled burn began at the monument to reduce the fuel content of the parks' forest. Because of unqualified and unsupervised personnel, the fire quickly became out of control and burned 150,000 acres including the Los Alamos Nuclear Laboratories. Over 400 homes had been burned with a billion dollars in damage that was paid out to the victims of the wildfire, and again, courtesy of the taxpayers. This was again the result of management personnel that lacked the technical, proper experience, and professional guidance, and identified and documented by the Fire Review conducted in the aftermath of the fires. Millions of dollars were spent on the Cerro Grande Fire Review that identified negligence and would be a model for managing wildfires by the National Park Service. The only problem is, the National Park Superintendents pick and choose their agenda with no direction of supervision. As a result, another million-dollar fire review only 16 years later at the Great Smoky Mountains National Park also identified gross negligence.

In order to mitigate the bureaucratic nightmare that quickly became out of control, the Great Smoky Mountains Superintendent was quietly sent on a "temporary detail" to an urban park. A Park Service news release was drafted and given to the news media stating the Great Smoky Mountains Superintendent was sent on this detail because his "experience in urban park management was needed." This was only a few weeks after the massive fire, where rebuilding the park and the outlying areas would require the expertise and leadership of a Senior Executive as the Superintendent and was the reason, he was hired in the first place. Slipping off with an excuse, 'his expertise was needed' was nothing but false and misleading information and they were hiding him out until the smoke cleared.

The Superintendent was given the leadership position at the Great Smoky Mountains after he had transferred from an urban park where he didn't have a potted plant or lawn to manage, much less than a 500,000-acre forest. He had little, if any, law enforcement experience and ongoing fire experience but was promoted to a Senior Executive management position in one of the largest National Parks in the country and with the most visitation of any National Park. The

Senior Executive Service superintendent who was supposed to be in charge, leading the fire emergency, delegated the fire management to a lower management official instead of assuming his responsibilities as the qualified leader.

The superintendent was absent while the Interagency Fire Management Investigators concluded the million-dollar investigation of his park. After many months of investigation, the Interagency Fire Team released a report that was cleverly crafted to confuse many people. It concluded the Great Smoky Mountain management's misconduct caused reckless negligence that allowed the fire to burn out of control. Many lawsuits would be filed against the National Park Service for failing to act to prevent the Wildfires of 2016. After the smoke cleared, the Senior Executive Superintendent quietly slipped back into his position at the Great Smoky Mountains National Park. It is now three years later, and all the same players identified by the NPS as being reckless and negligent and responsible for the Wildfires in 2016 are still in the same high-paying positions. There have been lawsuits filed by about 400 victims that will again cost the taxpayers another billion dollars for wrongful death and loss of property lawsuits. The insurance companies have also filed another 400 million-dollar lawsuit. The arrogance and impudence by the National Park Service to let these same employees continue in their positions is unconscionable, but the National Park Service reorganization in 1994 confirmed diverse and inexperienced personnel would assume 'driving the boat' even though it has run aground many times.

43

Drug Deals

*A*s I write these memoirs, a Law Enforcement Supervisor, National Park Ranger, Gregg Wozniak, whom I worked with at the Great Smoky Mountains National Park, was recently arrested. The Ranger never had any personal accomplishments, made arrests or did investigations that I personally observed, and I worked with him almost daily for years. He became the Supervisory Law Enforcement Ranger at the Pisgah District on the Blue Ridge Parkway, which is the busiest law enforcement district on the Parkway. He had apparently been given a participation trophy somewhere that qualified him to be selected to this position as a crony and not because of accomplishments. I always knew he used marijuana. Law Enforcement Rangers were supposed to randomly test for drug use, and I know for a fact he was reported for using marijuana. Even though the drug tests are mandated, I never knew of anyone being tested because it would open a management nightmare to deal with, because of the widespread use of drugs throughout the Federal Government.

In June of 2018, the Law Enforcement Supervisor had a vehicle accident about 150 miles from the Blue Ridge Parkway in Knoxville,

Tennessee. When the accident occurred, he exited his vehicle and threw a tackle box over a guardrail that contained marijuana, mushrooms and THC-laced Gummy Bears, that are popular to entice young children to become users of marijuana. He had been drinking alcohol but was not given a Blood/Alcohol test. He was arrested by the Knoxville police but for some strange reason that hasn't been disclosed, the charges were later expunged with no record of his arrest on file. The Park Service released a statement that his arrest outside the park had nothing to do with his employment as a National Park Ranger.

However, he was later suspended as a Law Enforcement Ranger because the NPS 9 Law Enforcement Directive specifically addressed the use of drugs as unbecoming of a law enforcement officer. The NPS was boxed into a corner and had to investigate the incident, keeping the investigation secret until they could attempt to mitigate and complete a narrative that would downplay the conduct of their crony National Park Ranger. Not only did the rogue Ranger use and possess the drugs, he had traveled a long distance to make a drug deal in a desolate parking lot with a friend of a friend of his. There was apparently not much investigation to find out who his friend's friend was and get a drug dealer off the street along with this drug dealer who worked for the National Park as a Law Enforcement officer. Even though he was in possession of drugs, there was still no drug test administered that anyone knows about. Privacy rules dictate what information can be released, but I am sure this is not included. After his suspension, he could continue working in a non-related law enforcement job doing absolutely nothing but retaining his title as Law Enforcement Supervisor, and continue to receive his salary of $88,000 per year. It would take a year and a half to "investigate" and terminate him from the position of Law Enforcement, all the while, being paid over $135,000. Because of privacy rights, no disclosure was made if he resigned or was fired. If he resigned, he could later still be employed by the Federal Government, and I would assume, as in the past, he would gain further employment with the Federal Government. There were no criminal charges pursued and this was a violation of the Federal Codes as drug dealing across State lines is a Federal offense.

This is what the National Park Service has come to. The once proud and dignified position of the National Park Ranger has been mitigated by rogue, politically correct cronyism, to gain career enhancement and large salaries, while Rangers like Bob McGhee, Joe Kolodski, and Kris Eggle, and many more National Park Rangers, have given the ultimate sacrifice to ensure the Legacy of the National Park Ranger.

Since Kris's death, there have been other Rangers killed, but I can only presume the circumstances surrounding their deaths. I had a personal and professional relationship with Park Rangers Bob McGhee, Joe Kolodski, and Kris Eggle. I also have firsthand knowledge of how the law enforcement program works in the National Park Service. I have reflected on my personal experiences, and I have a better understanding on how and why their deaths occurred. I could have very well been a victim as these guys, but for whatever reason and after thousands of law enforcement situations, the good Lord let me survive.

44

Looking Back

*N*ow, looking back at my career and knowing how the National Park Service was operated and mismanaged, I feel very betrayed and overwhelmed with frustration. The once-vibrant Gulf Islands National Seashore has been turned into a ruin. Visitors are now charged a large entrance fee to enter the seashore. The entrances are closed by locked gates before sunset each day. All nighttime beach activities are closed, including fishing, and just walking on the beaches. It's without a doubt the founders of the National Seashore did not have this in mind when they got the seashore created. The National Park Service had sought to get money to build a visitor center, in the Naval Live Oaks area of the seashore. After the money was received, the visitor center became the head-quarters for the National Seashore, with just a small area of it being used as restrooms and a visitor center. The visitor center is now boarded up and used exclusively for a headquarters area. Two small outdoor restrooms were built in an unsecured, wooded area for visi-tors to use, but are frequented by homosexuals, pedophiles, drug dealers and other dangerous activities. Only two Law Enforcement

Rangers are assigned to the seashore. When the seashore was established, there were about a dozen Law Enforcement Rangers throughout the park. The law enforcement program is expensive to operate, but rather than provide visitor and resource protection and allow the public to use the facilities, the money has been diverted to pay for more management positions. Typically, about 80% of a park's budget is used to pay for personnel costs, with 20% used for maintenance and repair. The addition of more management personnel takes away the National Park Rangers who have typically managed and protected the resources and visitors that enjoy the National Parks.

By the end of my career, 30 years later, the already shorthanded Park Rangers in the National Park Service had been reduced by almost 20%. They have been replaced with bureaucratic managers, getting extremely high salaries, while adding to their staff that does not represent the duties of the National Park Rangers. The existing Rangers' jobs and duties have been diminished. A lot of the Park Ranger duties have been replaced by the V.I.P. (Volunteer in Parks) program. At the Great Smoky Mountains National Park, for instance, the volunteers have assumed some of the patrol duties of a Law Enforcement Ranger. They have marked patrol VIP vehicles and patrol the roadways, parking areas and trailheads, checking on disabled vehicles, checking on people sleeping in their cars along the road, suspicious vehicles and a lot of other activities that could lead to a serious law enforcement encounter. These volunteers are in uniform, and criminals identify a uniform as authority. This scenario had been used in the Federal Law Enforcement Training center for the National Park Rangers, where they check on a disabled vehicle only to find the driver wanted for murder and a shooting scenario erupts. This is basically what happened to Ranger Bob McGhee, who was shot and killed as described in a previous chapter. These volunteers have inadvertently been sanctioned by the management in assuming an authority role while reducing the National Park Rangers.

In the early 90s, when the VIP program was started at the Great Smoky Mountains National Park, two seasoned, highly trained senior law enforcement officers were taken out of their positions in law enforcement. One of these officers was assigned as a VIP coordinator, losing his law enforcement responsibilities. The VIP program was conceived to assist the Park Rangers and other divisions, with simple tasks in the campgrounds, visitor centers, and park maintenance. Now, VIPs respond to vehicle accidents and other emergencies. They are now doing crowd control, where the bear and elk congregate along the roadways, with no Park Rangers with them. They warn people and attempt to get people to stay away from the bears and elk, and have no means of protecting anyone should a bear or elk attack someone. Because the visitors know the volunteers have no authority, they disregard the warnings given by the VIPs. The Ranger's role has also been taken over by private, volunteer groups, in search and technical rescues, again reducing the National Park Rangers' role and responsibilities. Forging a partnership with the community and volunteers is important but it should not mitigate the role of the National Park Ranger and diminish an icon that has made the National Park Service the envy of all the visitors who come to the National Parks.

These VIPs must be supervised and monitored, and permanent full time VIP coordinator positions were created. These positions were created by reducing the number of other positions in the park, and the funding coming from the park budget and donations from park groups. There are now 2500 VIPs at the Great Smoky Mountains National Park with numerous VIP coordinators. This is two battalions of soldiers that will naturally require monetary and logistical support to function. There are only about 300 employees and they require supervision and logistical support as well. There are seven times the number of volunteers.

The role of the VIP is very important but reducing the number of National Park Rangers and replacing them with VIPs or less trained law enforcement officers, will only lead to more visitors and Rangers being killed and injured in the National Parks. There have been profound changes because of social, cultural, and most of all, the political environment of the National Parks. The National Park

Management continues, as they have for the past 30 years, operating with a disregard for the protection of the visitors, resources and the National Park Rangers, while promoting their own selfish relevance.

This is my story. The stories and information are factual events that I have been involved with. Some of the names have been eliminated but at this point, the names aren't that important. It's a personal story that has happened to many other National Park Rangers. I haven't had any closure on my demise as a National Park Ranger and especially the bear attack that killed Glenda Bradley. It has been 18 years since I was forcibly retired. I still harbor a genuine disgust for the people who took my dream and made it a nightmare. Hopefully, by writing this memoir, I will gain closure, and expose the corrupt practices that I and a lot of other National Park Rangers have endured.

The job I had so much envisioned, when I was a small boy, to become a National Park Ranger, had been destroyed. I fought every step of the way, my entire career, to maintain my professionalism as a National Park Ranger. I had worked selflessly, risked my life, saved many lives and made a difference to the visitors and natural resources of the National Park Service. I was honored and proud to be called a National Park Ranger. There is no more envy, but only disgust and hatred for a bunch of bureaucratic cowards who have replaced the image of the National Park Service Rangers as a bunch of misfits.

***

There had to be a reason my destiny happened like it did, but then again, my destiny might not be over. Maybe, just maybe, I had a dream of having won the Lottery while I dreamed of becoming a Park Ranger and a taxidermist. I'm going to have to comb through my bible, where I may have stored those valuable numbers.

ACKNOWLEDGMENTS

Jerry shares some of his experiences, perspectives, views, thoughts and opinions in a menagerie of different incidents and situations. His stories are humorous, sad, traumatic, dangerous, amusing, and emotional. His analysis makes for interesting reading, and sure to raise some eyebrows. His descriptions and accounts include it all; The Good, The Bad, and some Ugly.

    William Acree, Criminal Investigator, NPS (Ret.)

An intriguing story about the real National Park Service. Ranger Grubb is not your average everyday Smokey Bear. Took me five years to get Jerry to finally write a book. These stories need to be told. You need to hear from the man that pulled the trigger.

    David Lawhorn

The author lets you know what it's REALLY like in the Park Service. He's a great storyteller and I found the book very entertaining. I am not sure that the Park Service will, though.

    Bruce Parker, Lieutenant, Orlando Police Department (Ret.)

As an Assistant U.S. Attorney in the Eastern District of Tennessee, I was responsible for the prosecution of the criminal cases in the Great Smoky Mountains National Park. The contents of this book accurately describe Ranger Grubb's role as a dedicated and professional law enforcement officer. Ranger Grubb was one of the hardest working Rangers I have known. Many incidents given in this book are unlike any other Ranger's I worked with. It is without a doubt Ranger Grubb went beyond the call of duty and acted selflessly in protecting the visitors of the National Park. It is with regret the bureaucracy overwhelmed his efforts to maintain his role as a National Park Ranger as he was removed from a job he dearly loved. The book is filled with excitement, laughter, and emotion. The book describes a long career that ended when a black bear killed Mrs. Glenda Bradley, who was a local schoolteacher. I am proud to endorse this book for a dedicated and professional Park Ranger.

Robert E. Simpson, Assistant United States Attorney, (Ret.)

ABOUT THE AUTHOR

Jerry Grubb is a retired National Park Ranger, an avid hunter and fisherman, taxidermist, backyard farmer and log cabin builder. He spends his free time in the woods, on the French Broad River or Douglas Lake when he's not working with his tractors in his garden.

f

www.ingramcontent.com/pod-product-compliance
Lightning Source LLC
Chambersburg PA
CBHW060308030426
42336CB00011B/973

9 781734 753615